WHY
WE
LOVE
BASEBALL

WHY
WE
LOVE
BASEBALL

★ A HISTORY IN **50** MOMENTS ★

JOE POSNANSKI

DUTTON

DUTTON

An imprint of Penguin Random House LLC
penguinrandomhouse.com

DUTTON and the D colophon are registered trademarks of Penguin Random House LLC.

LIBRARY OF CONGRESS CATALOGING-IN-PUBLICATION DATA
has been applied for.

ISBN: 9780593472675 (hardcover)
ISBN: 9780593472699 (ebook)

Printed in the United States of America
1st Printing

BOOK DESIGN BY LORIE PAGNOZZI

FOR PATIENCE, SUNSHINE, AND NEW ONE . . .
AND BUCK, WHO GAVE THEM THOSE NAMES

★ ★ ★ ★ ★

CONTENTS

WHY
WE
LOVE
BASEBALL

I THINK NOW OF A BASEBALL STORY.

Gaylord Perry was a Hall of Fame pitcher best known for the expansive and marvelous array of illegal pitches he threw. He threw spitballs and greaseballs, emery balls and shine balls, Vaseline balls and puffballs, hair-tonic balls and fishing-line-oil balls. Perry threw all these pitches and also pretended to throw all of them, and he fooled batters and umpires in equal measure for more than 20 years.

This, though, is a story about Gaylord Perry's hitting.

In 1962, Perry took batting practice before his second career big-league start. This was in Pittsburgh. Standing behind Perry in the cage was his San Francisco Giants' manager Alvin Dark, along with a colorful sportswriter and saloonkeeper named Harry Jupiter. Dark was looking at something else when Perry hit a long fly ball. Jupiter was impressed.

"Hey, Al," Jupiter said, "looks like this one might be a hitter!"

Dark looked up and shook his head. "Perry?" he asked loudly. "Nah. This one's got no power. We'll have a man on the moon before he hits a home run."

Sure enough, for the first seven years of his career—the first 547 times he came to the plate—Perry did not hit a single home run. Then on a warm Sunday afternoon in Los Angeles, Perry started against the Dodgers. The date was July 20, 1969. At 1:17 P.M. Pacific time— 17 minutes after the Giants–Dodgers game started and while Perry was giving up three runs to the Dodgers in the first inning—Apollo 11's Eagle lunar module landed on the moon, with Neil Armstrong and Buzz Aldrin aboard.

In the third inning, Gaylord Perry stepped to the plate against the Dodgers' Claude Osteen. On the first pitch, Perry hit a long fly ball to center field, and it sailed over the fence, his first home run. He hit it exactly 34 minutes after mankind had put a man on the moon.

INTRODUCTION

I write these words in the afterglow. The Philadelphia Phillies and San Diego Padres just finished a wild and wonderful playoff game. You can still see the goose bumps on my arms. The Padres led the game by a run in the eighth inning; they were trying to extend the National League Championship Series. The Phillies, meanwhile, were trying to end it. Philadelphia fans were soaked—it had been raining pretty much the whole game—and they were hoarse and manic and utterly desperate for a hero.

Up stepped Bryce Harper.

There was ease in Casey's manner as he stepped into his place;
There was pride in Casey's bearing and a smile lit Casey's face.

A man named Ernest Lawrence Thayer wrote those words—and the entire poem, "Casey at the Bat: A Ballad of the Republic"—in 1888. Do you know how long ago 1888 was? It was long before iPhones and television, long before movies, long before radio, yes. But it was also before air conditioning, vacuum cleaners, cardboard boxes, and ice cream cones. It was before "America the Beautiful" or "God Bless America" was written and some four decades before "The Star-Spangled Banner" became America's national anthem.

How long ago? Sherlock Holmes debuted only a year earlier. Dracula didn't exist. Harry Houdini was a factory worker named Erich Weisz. Walt Disney wasn't born. Henry Ford had not yet built his first automobile. The Wright Brothers were trying to start a newspaper. That year, 1888, was before Hershey's bars and Wrigley's gum, before Coca-Cola and credit cards and the paper clip. The zipper had not been invented.

And in sports? There was no modern Olympics. Basketball had not been conceived. There wasn't a single 18-hole golf course on American soil. Football was being played by only a handful of universities, and the forward pass did not yet exist.

But in 1888, already, there was baseball—joyful and recognizable major league baseball. A pitcher named Tim Keefe won 19 consecutive games. Cap Anson led the league by hitting .344. A slick-fielding second baseman called Sure Shot Dunlap signed for the unheard-of price of $5,000,* the biggest contract in baseball history.

In "Casey," Thayer was writing about his own time. But his words still rang true as Harper stepped to the plate 134 years later.

San Diego's pitcher was named Robert Suarez, and he was very much a modern creation, a type of pitcher Thayer could not have imagined. He stood 6-foot-2, 210 pounds, and he threw so hard that there was nothing to compare it to in 1888.

Suarez's first pitch was 100 mph, and it raced by Harper for a strike.

From the benches, black with people, there went up a muffled roar,
Like the beating of the storm-waves on a stern and distant shore;

The two men battled for a time after that. Suarez threw two kinds of pitches—a 100-mph fastball and a changeup that, coming out of his hand, looked to be going 100 mph but was actually moving 10 mph slower. This second pitch made hitters look ridiculous.

---

* Equivalent to $156,847.37 in 2023 dollars.

Bryce Harper, meanwhile, was destined for this moment. He had been a baseball prodigy. He was on the cover of *Sports Illustrated* at 15. He was the first pick in the baseball draft at 17. He was Rookie of the Year at 19. He was the National League's most valuable player at 22.

He signed with Philadelphia for the largest contract ever handed out, $330 million in all, quite a journey from Sure Shot Dunlap.

"At the end of the day," Harper said on the day he signed, "I want to be able to go to sleep and know that I gave it my all and was able to bring back a title to Philadelphia."

This was Harper's moment to make good.

And now the pitcher holds the ball, and now he lets it go,
And now the air is shattered by the force of Casey's blow.

Suarez threw a 99-mph fastball. It was close to the outside corner of the plate . . . it does not seem possible to hit such a pitch. But Harper connected, and he knew that he'd hit it well. He stopped and watched it with his mouth open. That's a wonderful time for hitters, that instant when only they know just how well they'd hit the baseball.

It took everyone else in the ballpark only a second to catch up. The ball soared to left field and Harper watched the ball fly into the stands, and all together the city of Philadelphia made a sound of incomprehensible joy.

I thought to myself—and surely I was not alone—*God, I love baseball.*

WE KNOW THE REASONS SOME DO NOT LOVE BASEBALL. IT'S A slow game with lots of meetings, lots of standing around, lots of aimless jogging on and off the field. Over the past 25 or so years, the game slowed to the point that Major League Baseball changed a series of rules just to get the players to pick things up. Baseball can feel repetitive, one ground ball to second looking just like the rest. There is no clock—other than the new pitch timer—and games sometimes drone on interminably, and there always seems to be some scandal going on.

Baseball has no slam dunks, no breakaways, and little violence. There is no goal and no goal line, no basket, and no finish line. There are no blocked shots, no blindside hits, no blocked punts, no electrifying runs, no alley-oop passes, no kick saves, and no bicycle kicks.

Baseball does have math, though. Lots of math.

"You made me love baseball," Lisa tells Bart on *The Simpsons*. "Not as a collection of numbers but as an unpredictable, passionate game beaten in excitement only by every other sport."

With all that, why do we love baseball?

I asked around.

"I love baseball," Willie Mays said, "because it's a game you can play every day."

"For me," Bryce Harper said, "I think it just began by being able to go out with my family, enjoy a game of catch. There was nothing better than going out on a Saturday and hanging out and smelling the weather and the fresh-cut grass, crack of the bat, and you're dreaming . . ."

"You have to understand," Henry Aaron said, "in Mobile, Alabama, where I grew up, we didn't have many things to do. In fact, we didn't have anything to do. You either had to play baseball or you probably taught school or did something else. So I loved baseball. I just felt like it was made for me."

"Why?" Theo Epstein asked. "I honestly don't know. My parents tell me that from the age of two on, I was just obsessed with baseball . . . They say I'd be down in Central Park, swinging the Wiffle Ball bat, and the crowds would gather because I'd be hitting homers, which I doubt is true. But if it is, that was the peak of my athletic career."

"I don't know what it was," Justin Verlander said. "I don't ever remember not loving baseball."

Those are not *exactly* answers. If someone asked why you like a TV show, you probably would talk about the plot or the characters or the acting or the writing or the setting or the costuming. Something specific. If someone asked you why you like a band, you might talk about the lyrics or the drummer's awesomeness or the singer's voice . . .

With baseball, it's not so straightforward. I've asked the question to hundreds of people while writing this book. Some came back with simple things. Crack of the bat. Triple in the gap. Smell of the freshly mown grass. A dancing knuckleball.

One fan told me about his first baseball game—not the action on the field but the feeling of climbing up the stairs from the concourse and seeing the stadium open up to him. The colors of the sky and grass and dirt and seats overwhelmed him and stayed with him. He said it was the most beautiful thing he'd ever seen.

Another told me about a Little League moment he remembered. He grabbed a bat and nervously walked toward the plate to face a pitcher roughly the size of LeBron James. He heard the other team's chatter ("Ayyy, batter, batter, batter, batter, swing!"), and heard his own team's chatter ("He's got nothing! . . . We want a pitcher, not a belly itcher!") and he looked down to the third-base coach for some advice ("Pick out a good one!") and he stepped into the batter's box and saw his pitch and closed his eyes and swung . . . and felt that incomparable sensation of making good contact.

Is that a direct answer? No.

Does it explain why we love baseball? Absolutely it does.

A woman told me about the combination of terror and elation she felt as a foul ball soared her way in the stands. A man talked about the giddy anticipation he felt holding an unopened pack of baseball cards. Several told me that the best night's sleep they ever had was when they slept on a mattress that pressed down on a freshly oiled baseball glove, breaking it in.

Why do you love baseball? People talked about the thrill of watching Roberto Clemente throw, watching Tony Gwynn hit, watching Rickey

Henderson run, watching Greg Maddux paint the outside corner with a pitch. People told me about baseball conversations with their grandfathers about players with fabulous names like Pee Wee Reese or Cool Papa Bell. People told me about the familiar joy of listening to a hometown announcer call a baseball game over the radio.

"I saw Carlton Fisk hit that home run on television in Game 6 of the World Series," one fan said, "and I was forever hooked on baseball."

"One moment hooked you forever?" I asked.

"Yeah," he said. "That moment is forever."

WHEN I WAS A KID IN CLEVELAND, 9 OR 10 OR 11 YEARS OLD, there was a library around the corner from our house. I loved the place. Two or three times a week, minimum, I would walk over to see if they had any new sports books. They rarely did. But every now and again, a new one would magically appear on the shelf, and when that happened, whatever the sport—sometimes it was a hockey book, and I didn't know anything about hockey—I would feel this boundless joy and excitement.

This is the book I always hoped would be on the shelf.

This is a book of forever moments. We are counting down the 50 most magical baseball moments, and it's no coincidence that I have used the word *magical* a couple of times already. There have been baseball moment countdowns before, countdowns of the most important moments in baseball history, the most consequential moments, the most dramatic moments, the moments that changed the game and so on.

This ranking is a bit less tidy. There are important moments in here, naturally, and also consequential and dramatic and game-changing moments. But there are also moments that are none of those things. Some are silly. Some are virtually unknown.

All are magical or, to use my favorite definition of magical, "beautiful or delightful in such a way as to seem removed from everyday life."

That's what we're going for here. These are moments that have exhilarated us, enchanted us, lifted us, and, yes, broken our hearts. These are moments that have for more than a century made people fall in love with baseball.

I said there are 50 moments, but now that you have the book, I can let you in on a little secret. There are more than 50 in here. A lot more. Yes, the countdown goes from No. 50 all the way down to No. 1, and you will undoubtedly have disagreements with the order and with what's missing. That's part of the fun.*

But every so often we're going to interrupt the countdown with five bonus baseball memories. We'll talk about five unlikely homers, five baseball trick plays, five baseball moments that melt the heart, five blunders that will never be forgotten, and so on.

In all, there are 108 moments and memories. Even that number is magical. There are 108 stitches on one side of a baseball. The Cubs' World Series drought lasted 108 years. Some physicists did a study and determined that Nolan Ryan threw the fastest pitch ever recorded at 108 mph. The Big Red Machine—the 1975 Reds—is, I believe, the greatest team of them all. They won 108 games.

Hey, you paid for 50 moments, and you get 108! What a bargain!

///

ONE FINAL THOUGHT: IN 1992, I PLAYED A STRAT-O-MATIC World Series with my friend Jim Banks. Strat-O-Matic is a tabletop baseball game that uses dice and specially designed player cards to

---

* Ever since I wrote *The Baseball 100*, I'd say 94 percent of all my conversations have begun with "How could you leave out Jim Palmer?" and "How could you have Ichiro so low?" and so on. It will be nice to have people screaming, "Why is the Bobby Thomson homer so low?" and "How could you leave out Enos Slaughter's Mad Dash?" for a change of pace.

create a lifelike baseball simulation. We were obsessed with it. Jim managed the 1988 Cincinnati Reds. I managed the 1988 Boston Red Sox.

We had played and would play many other Strat-O-Matic series, but this was the big one, the series that would, once and for all, determine which one of us was the better manager. Nothing mattered more to us. Jim won three of the first four games, and he was about to win the clinching game and bragging rights for the rest of our lives. His Reds led 2–0 with two outs in the bottom of the ninth inning. My Red Sox put two runners on.

And up came Dwight Evans, a good hitter and excellent outfielder who I believe belongs in the Baseball Hall of Fame. Jim had a critical decision to make. His starter, Tom Browning, had been incredible. But Jim also had John Franco and Rob Dibble throwing in the bullpen, and both of those guys were close to unhittable in 1988.

Jim hesitated and wavered and vacillated like he was Hamlet. It must have taken him 20 minutes to decide what to do. Then he made his choice. He stayed with Tom Browning.

And Dwight Evans hit a walk-off three-run homer, and my Red Sox came all the way back and won the Series, and I have never let Jim live it down, and nothing makes me happier than the fact that it's now in a book for people to read forever.

See, our most magical baseball moments are sometimes our most personal ones. A Little League home run. An unforgettable play at the ballpark. A visit to the Baseball Hall of Fame. A conversation with a baseball hero. I wish I could have written about every one of your most magical baseball moments. I hope some are in here.

And Dwight Evans, if you are reading this, thank you forever.

FIVE
UNLIKELY HOMERS

The Gaylord Perry Moon Shot moment that leads off this book may be my favorite unlikely homer. It's my go-to whenever someone asks for a baseball story. There are few things more thrilling in the game than the unlikely home run.

You know about Gaylord. Here are four more:

RICK CAMP (JULY 4, 1985)

"People thought Rick couldn't hit," Dale Murphy is saying. "But they didn't see Rick the way we teammates did. They didn't see him take batting practice. They didn't see him swing in the cage."

Dale, a two-time most valuable player, smiled.

"They thought he couldn't hit," he continued. "But we *knew* he couldn't hit."

Rick Camp was a multi-use pitcher for the Braves between 1976 and 1985. Sometimes he started. Sometimes he relieved. He threw a heavy sinker that could be quite effective.

But as a hitter—no.

Flash to one of the wildest games in baseball history, an Independence Day extravaganza between the Braves and the New York Mets in Atlanta. Forty-four thousand fans showed up, mostly to catch fireworks after the game. None of them knew that the fireworks would not go off until four or so the next morning.

The game was delayed by rain, and then the game jumped around like microwave popcorn. The Mets led, the Braves led, the Mets led, the Braves led; then in the top of the ninth the Mets tied the game off future Hall of Famer Bruce Sutter. Extra innings. The Mets scored two in the 13th. The Braves also scored two in the 13th. On it went.

Finally in the 18th inning—at about three the morning of July 5—the Mets scored off Rick Camp and it finally looked like the game would end. The first two Atlanta batters in the ninth inning made outs and that brought up Camp. Under any other circumstances, the Braves would have pinch-hit for him. Camp was a lifetime .059 hitter. He'd not had a hit all year.

The Mets' Tom Gorman was pitching. Catcher Gary Carter waved the outfielders in . . . and he just kept on waving even as they got closer and closer. Mets pitching coach Mel Stottlemyre jogged to the mound and Gorman expected some scouting advice or a pep talk. Instead Stottlemyre said, "You better get him out." Then he jogged back to the dugout.

Up in the Atlanta Braves' broadcasting booth, John Sterling said to his partner Ernie Johnson Sr.: "Ernie, if he hits a home run to tie this game, this game will be certified as absolutely the nuttiest in the history of baseball."

Gorman got ahead in the count 0-2. He then threw a pitch up and Camp swung as hard as he could . . . and he connected. He hit his first big-league home run in the 18th inning of a meaningless game between Atlanta and New York . . . and no one in Atlanta will ever forget it.

"That," Atlanta catcher Bruce Benedict would say, "was the greatest thing I've ever seen."

There's one more fun part to this: The Braves lost anyway in the very next inning. The last batter of the game was, yes, Rick Camp. He struck out. Then the Braves shot off fireworks for the few fans who remained at the end, sparking hundreds of complaints to the Atlanta police department.

TOM LAWLESS (OCTOBER 21, 1987)

In his career as a utility infielder and pinch runner, Tom Lawless hit three big-league home runs. He was such a mediocre hitter that once, a Phillies relief pitcher named Tom Hume walked him . . . and Hume was released two days later.

One of Lawless's three homers came in the 1987 World Series.

He hit it off Minnesota ace Frank Viola, who would later call his pitch a "brutal, brutal fastball." The improbability of the home run was trumped by Lawless's even more improbable reaction. After he hit the ball, he walked slowly up the first-base line with the bat still in his hand. He just stared at the ball as it flew, the sort of thing Barry Bonds or Reggie Jackson might have done after hitting a 500-foot blast.

Was this a 500-foot blast? No, not even close.

"I think it hit about one foot over the fence," Cardinals' manager Whitey Herzog would say.

But even the strut was not the best part. No, the best part was that after the ball barely cleared the fence, and only then, Lawless flung the bat high in the air, like a cap thrown on graduation day, one of the more demonstrative celebrations in baseball history. If we were ranking top bat flips, this one would be in the top five. It broke at least a half dozen unwritten rules of baseball etiquette. "That was something strange to do, seeing that he's hit two home runs in his career," his teammate Gary Gaetti would say. "If I was pitching, I wouldn't forget it."

Lawless pleaded insanity. "I didn't mean anything, I just kind of blanked out there for a second," he said. "This never happened to me before."

AL WEIS (OCTOBER 16, 1969)

By the time Al Weis came to the plate in the bottom of the seventh inning on a Thursday afternoon in New York—Game 5 of the 1969 World Series—he was already an unlikely hometown hero. He grew up 23 miles from Shea Stadium. He had been in the big leagues for seven years, an impressive accomplishment considering he could not hit. What he did was play excellent defense wherever needed, bunt upon request, and *never* complain.

"The best gag about Weis," Milton Gross wrote, "is that if he were hit on the elbow with a fastball, he wouldn't even say 'Ouch.'"

Weis's bat played a wildly unlikely role in the 1969 Miracle Mets run to the World Series. He hit only two home runs all season, but he hit them in back-to-back games against the league-leading Chicago Cubs. The Mets went on to catch the Cubs and win the pennant.

Then, in the World Series, Weis hit like he never had before. He singled off Baltimore's Dave McNally to drive in the winning run in Game 2. He got two more hits and drew a walk in Game 4. The Orioles couldn't get him out. Then came Game 5, and the Orioles led by a run going into the seventh inning. McNally was pitching again, and he missed his spot. Weis turned on it and hit the ball out to tie the game. The Mets completed the comeback and won one of the most surprising and wonderful World Series titles of them all.

After the game, Weis was asked how he did it. Naturally, he didn't say anything. But his teammate Bud Harrelson did:

"When Al hit that home run," Harrelson said, "I knew we had 'em."

BARTOLO COLÓN (MAY 7, 2016)

❝He drives one! Deep left field! Back goes Upton. Back near the wall! It's outta here! Bartolo has done it. The impossible has happened. . . . The team vacates the dugout as Bartolo takes the long trot. His first career home run. . . . This is one of the great moments in the history of baseball. Bartolo Colón has gone deep.❞

—METS' BROADCASTER GARY COHEN

OK, look, a big part of the joy is how four-time All-Star pitcher Bartolo Colón looked. He looked like me. He looked like you. He was 42 years old, and the media guide charitably listed him at 285 pounds. Ah, if only we all had a media guide to underestimate our true weight. Bartolo was shaped like a rectangle, and if you saw him walking around in the mall, you'd think, *That guy's probably the high school history teacher everybody at school likes.* The notion of his being a baseball player would never enter your mind.

It goes without saying he was an atrocious hitter; goes without saying he'd never hit a home run or come close. He was hitting .088 for his career and had struck out one of every two times he came to the plate. He had not gotten a hit all season.

James Shields was pitching for San Diego. He threw a fastball. Colón swung as hard as he could. The ball left the park. The moment was so intoxicating that even Shields himself got caught up in it.

"I'm happy for him," Shields said.

There are two things I love most about the home run. First is that his home run trot took him 30.5 seconds. That is longer than it took the injured Kirk Gibson to limp around the bases after his 1988 World Series home run.

"I want to say," Mets' announcer Ron Darling said, "that was one of the longest home run trots I've ever seen. But I think that's how fast he runs."

Second is the quote that Colón gave after the game when he explained his hitting approach. "Anytime I see a fastball, I swing hard," he said, "because I'm not a curveball hitter."

NO. 50:
THE REAL DUANE KUIPER

AUGUST 29, 1977, CLEVELAND

★ ★ ★ ★ ★

Baseball is the best it has been and the best it will ever be when you're 10 years old.

I was 10 years old in the summer of 1977 when Duane Kuiper hit his one home run.

Kuip was my hero. He was second baseman for my hometown Cleveland ballclub at the same time that I was second baseman for Reno, my South Euclid Youth Baseball Team. Oddly, our team did not have a nickname. We were just Reno. We were either named after the Biggest Little City in the World or Reno Browne, a 1940s B-movie actress who was married to the famous cowboy Lash LaRue.

Duane Kuiper and I shared more than just a position. I loved the way he played. He dived for every ball . . . and I do mean, *every* ball. If you hit the ball straight at him, he dived for it. If you played catch in your backyard anywhere in America in 1977, Kuip probably dived for that ball too. He played the game with verve and love, and OK, maybe he didn't hit with a lot of power and maybe he wasn't the fastest guy out there,* but he exuded joy, and my grandest dream was to be just like him.

He hit his one home run on a Monday night. Cleveland was playing the Chicago White Sox at Cleveland Municipal Stadium, a mausoleum that smelled of stale beer and and broken dreams. Cleveland Municipal was strategically constructed to place steel beams in front of every fan in the ballpark.

---

* Kuip was caught stealing more times than he was successful, a rare feat.

I was not at the game—there were 6,236 people there, a sizeable crowd for Cleveland baseball in those days—so I listened to the broadcast on WWWE, 1100 on your AM radio dial. I listened while sitting on the beige carpeting in our so-called living room—we were rarely even allowed in there—and leaning against the speaker of the enormous Zenith music console my parents had bought on payments. That console was a dark wood, and it was the size of a coffin, and it looked like a coffin. The muffled voices of Cleveland broadcasters Herb Score and Joe Tait sounded like they might be trapped inside.

Herb Score was one of the greatest young pitchers in baseball history until he got hit in the eye by a Gil McDougald line drive, but I didn't know this until much later. Herb was much too modest to ever talk about his playing days. I'd describe Herb's announcing style as cheerful and just slightly confused, sort of like your grandfather calling a game. He began every broadcast by saying, "It's a beautiful day for baseball." Then, he'd go on, doing the best he could.

"Hey, Herb," a partner said, "that hit makes Cecil Cooper 19 for 42 against Tribe pitching."

"I'm not good at math," Herb replied. "But even I know that's over .500."

South Euclid's own Steve Stone was pitching for the White Sox. Kuip was the second batter of the game. On the second pitch, Stone threw a pitch he would call "a slider that did not slide." Duane Kuiper did something entirely out of character. He turned on it.

"That's headed for the wall," Herb's broadcast partner, Joe Tait, shouted, and then with a magnificent blend of shock and awe he added: "It's gone! Duane Kuiper has just hit his first major league home run! How about that!"

"Hey," Herb said, "look at Duane running those bases!"

"Oh, is he one happy ballplayer!" Tait said.

I didn't hear that last part because I, too, was running around the bases, imaginary ones in the living room, and I shouted and howled until my mother told me to quiet down because she was watching the ABC comedy special *McNamara's Band* with John Byner.

"Did you know it was gone when you hit it?" reporters asked Kuip after the game.

"No," he said. "I don't think any ball I hit is gone."

That was it. After Duane hit the homer, he came up another 2,371 more times but he never hit another one. One home run in 3,754 plate appearances. Much later, after he had become a beloved broadcaster for the San Francisco Giants, the team held a special Duane Kuiper day. And they gave the fans a bobblehead of Kuip hitting the home run.

I HAVE TO TELL SOMETHING ELSE EVEN THOUGH IT'S NOT directly related to the homer. As mentioned, Kuip did become an adored broadcaster in San Francisco.

Along the way, Kuip found out that I was his biggest fan. I mean, it was no secret—I wrote about him all the time. So, one day he found my wife Margo's email—she was writing a parenting blog at the time—and explained that he wanted to send me something. Margo is a casual baseball fan; all she knew about Duane Kuiper was that he was my hero.

"I'm assuming that you're the real Duane Kuiper," she wrote back to him, "though in today's internet age, it's not always so easy to tell."

Kuip loved that so much. He was not expecting anyone to ever think he was *pretending* to be Duane Kuiper.

"It's hard for me to say, with a straight face, that I'm the real Duane Kuiper," he wrote. "So, I'll say it with a smile. I'm the real Duane Kuiper."

Anyway, not long after, I got a package in the mail with an authentic game-used Duane Kuiper bat, an authentic game-used Duane Kuiper cap, and various other priceless items.

"I've come to realize that my family doesn't think this stuff is as cool as I think it is," he wrote.

My friends, almost all of them, had childhood baseball heroes who were better players than my Duane Kuiper. They idolized Tom Seaver and George Brett and Reggie Jackson and Wade Boggs and Frank Thomas and players like that.

I wouldn't trade my hero for all of them put together.

Why do I love baseball? I'm going to go and swing my Duane Kuiper bat and think about it.

NO. 49:

KERRY AND THE BLEACHER BUMS

MAY 6, 1998, CHICAGO

★ ★ ★ ★ ★

In 1977, a struggling actor named Joe Mantegna did his favorite thing. He went to a Cubs game and sat in the bleachers of Wrigley Field. He looked around; it was all so wonderfully familiar. There was Len, who owned a clothes store. Before long, Joe knew, Len would take off his shirt and wrap it around his head in a turban.

There was a kid—Ronny, Robby; Joe wasn't sure of the name—and he seemed to know everything. People would challenge him with trivia questions. "Hey, Robby [or Ronny]," they'd say, "name fifteen Republican senators from west of the Mississippi." Two to one, he'd get it right.

There was the guy who would constantly spill food or beer on himself, and a woman in a bikini sunbathing, and three blind men who kept up with the action better than anybody else. One of those guys, Craig Lynch, became a Cubs radio reporter for two decades.

Mantegna looked at the Bleacher Bums, his people, and it was a gorgeous sunny day, and the Cubs were losing, like always, and he thought, *This ought to be a play.*

Together with his friends at the Organic Theater in Chicago, he did write a play called *Bleacher Bums*. It has been performed across America. It continues to be performed still.

Twenty-one years later, Mantegna—by now a Tony Award–winning actor and successful movie star—returned to Chicago along with the *Bleacher Bums* original cast. They came back to perform the play for a National Public Radio recording. The Cubs invited the whole group out to Wrigley for a game between the Cubs and Astros.

"It was a meaningless game," Joe says. "A nothing game. Early May. It was cold and it felt like it would rain any minute. Wrigley was more than half empty. The kids weren't even out of school yet. I do remember there were a few kids at the ballpark, no doubt skipping school like I did when I was their age. But beyond that, there wasn't much energy in the place.

"And I was like, 'Who's pitching anyway?'"

"And they said, 'Yeah, we have this kid, Kerry Wood.'"

WHO WAS KERRY WOOD? RIGHT: HE WAS THE LATEST CUBS phenom. This was just his fifth big-league start, but the Chicago hype machine was in motion. The Cubs always had someone like Wood, some future star everybody was kvelling about. Joe's favorite phenom was a big first baseman in the 1970s, Pete LaCock.* He was supposed to be the next big thing. Didn't happen.

But, hey, it never happened for Cubs prospects. Terry Hughes? Brian Rosinski? Dean Burk? Scot Thompson? Jackie Davidson? Herman Segelke? Ty Griffin? Earl Cunningham? Oh, Cunningham was a beaut. I saw him play at Lancaster High School. He would hit home runs that would sail over the fence, across a street, and into a strip mall. It was jawdropping. One scout told me Cunningham was the best hitting prospect he'd ever seen. But he, like the other Cubs hopefuls, didn't pan out. Why not? As one scout said, Cunningham had two weaknesses: curveballs and McDonald's.

Kerry Wood was the next in line. He threw so hard. His curveball broke hard. People were comparing him to Nolan Ryan. But, yes, he was displaying some troubling Cubs tendencies. A week earlier, he pitched

---

* Joe particularly loved that LaCock was the son of game show host and television personality Peter Marshall. He even wrote LaCock into *Bleacher Bums*: "Gee, Pete LaCock's father's named Peter Marshall. Who do you think changed his name? You *know* who changed his name!"

against the Dodgers. He walked four batters in a row, then gave up a grand slam to Mike Piazza.

"Sure, I wanted to see the kid," Joe says. "But I wasn't holding my breath."

The Astros' first batter of the game was Craig Biggio, one of the toughest outs in baseball. With the count 2-2, Wood threw a . . . well, it's hard to describe what exactly he threw. Satchel Paige used to say he never threw an illegal pitch in his life. "The trouble is," he said, "once in a while, I toss one that ain't never been seen by this generation."

It was like that. Wood threw a never-been-seen-by-this-generation pitch, a fastball, probably 100 mph, only about halfway home it appeared to hit a sheet of ice. It jumped forward. Biggio swung after the ball was already in catcher Sandy Martínez's glove.

"That's one of the worst swings you will *ever* see Craig Biggio take," said Cubs' broadcaster (and the guy who gave up the homer to Duane Kuiper) Steve Stone.

Mantegna, sitting next to his *Bleacher Bums* co-actors, thought, *What do we have here?*

//

OUT IN THE BLEACHERS, A TRUE BELIEVER NAMED TOM Bujnowski had brought with him an assortment of K cards* so that the crowd could help him count Kerry Wood's strikeouts.

"How many K cards did you bring?" someone asked Bujnowski.

"Sixteen," he said.

Sixteen. Yes, that will tell you a little something about Tom Bujnowski. He was a physical education teacher at MacArthur Middle School up in Arlington Heights, but that was only his job. His life was

---

* You probably know this, but K is the way that you mark a strikeout in the scorebook. Nobody is entirely sure why, but it might be that S begins so many other baseball things (single, sacrifice, stolen base, etc.) and K is clearly the most unique letter in the word *strikeout.*

being the rarest sort of Cubs fan: Tom was an *optimistic* Cubs fan. Only an optimist would bring *sixteen* strikeout cards to a game being pitched by a 20-year-old Cubs' rookie making his fifth big-league start. The last Cubs' pitcher to strike out sixteen batters in a game had been Jack "The Giant Killer" Pfiester back in 1906, before Wrigley Field was even built.

But Wood struck out all three batters he faced in the first inning, another two in the second, one more in the third, and two more in the fourth. He had eight strikeouts through four innings.

In the fifth, Wood started to feel in control. He struck out Moisés Alou on a fastball, then threw three mind-bending and time-bending curveballs to Dave Clark (who didn't swing at any of them), and then blew the ball by Ricky Gutierrez. After getting one strikeout in the sixth, he struck out the side in the seventh—including his third strikeout of future Hall of Famer Jeff Bagwell. That gave him fifteen strikeouts with six outs to go.

Bujnowski, impossibly, realized that he was about to run out of K cards.

AS PART OF HIS VISIT TO WRIGLEY FIELD, JOE MANTEGNA AGREED to lead the crowd in singing "Take Me Out to the Ball Game" . . . just the way legendary Cubs' announcer Harry Caray had. Caray had died three months earlier at age 83. Mantegna, like all Cubs fans, loved him.

"Well, I think Harry would approve," Joe said as the organ began to play. "I dedicate this to all the bleacher bums, past, present and future!"

He sang his heart out. And when finished, immediately after singing "at the old ball game," he added his own flourish: "All right! Go, Kerry!"

He then joined the announcers in the television booth.

"This Kerry Wood," Mantegna said, "it sure looks like he's got the real stuff."

Below, Wood threw a curveball that had Dave Clark swinging at shadows and ghosts. That was strikeout No. 16.

"That doesn't seem fair," Steve Stone said.

He threw a fastball on the outside corner that Ricky Gutierrez swung through feebly.

Next was Brad Ausmus, who was so spooked by the moment that he swung at a pitch that bounced at least two feet in front of home plate. That was strike two. He then looked at a curveball for strike three. That was strikeout No. 18.

Out in the bleachers, Tom Bujnowski had used up all 16 of his K cards, but wily Cub fan that he was, he convinced two bleacher bums to paint Ks on their chests.

JOE MANTEGNA DID NOT JUST BRING ALONG THE ORIGINAL CAST of *Bleacher Bums,* he also brought out his older brother Ron, who worked in advertising for Montgomery Ward.

"Can you believe this?" Ron asked his brother. He was in tears.

The Astros' first batter in the ninth was a pinch hitter, Bill Spiers, who fouled off a couple of pitches before swinging and missing at a curve. Nineteen strikeouts. The record for strikeouts in a game was 20, held by Roger Clemens. Kerry Wood had two chances to tie the record and one chance to break it.

Up came Craig Biggio, who this time put wood on the ball and grounded out to short. Chicago boos crashed down upon him. The rain had stopped. "Goose bumps" was all Mantegna could remember.

The last batter was Derek Bell. He looked pale. Wood threw him a curveball; Bell swung and missed it by 3 feet. Wood threw him a second curveball, and Bell tried to hold up his swing but could not.

"One more curveball," Steve Stone said up in the booth, "and that should be about it, because Derek Bell isn't even coming close."

Wood threw that one more curveball. Bell swung and missed.

That was strikeout No. 20. Kerry Wood was 20 years old. The twenti-eth person in the Wrigley Field bleachers stood up with a K painted on his chest.

"What did we do?" Mantegna says all these years later. "What do you think we did? We all went nuts. I mean, you go to Wrigley Field to see a Cubs game, and you're expecting it to be fun. But you aren't expecting to see something you'll never forget. You aren't expecting to see his-tory. That's baseball, right? I mean, you never know. Even at a Cubs game."

NO. 48:
A KNUCKLEBALL STORY

APRIL 9, 2010, PLANT CITY, FLORIDA

★ ★ ★ ★ ★

You cannot write a book called *Why We Love Baseball* without a knuckleball story in it. Here's one you might not know.

The story begins in a backyard in Martins Ferry, Ohio, in the early 1950s. The backyard belonged to Phil Niekro Jr. When he was young, he could throw very hard; he might have been a big leaguer but he needed to work to support his family, so he took a job in the coal mines. While pitching for the company team, he hurt his arm.

He still wanted to pitch, though.

One of the other coal miners taught him how to throw a knuckleball.

Ah, the knuckleball. Nothing in the whole world like it. Willie Stargell called the knuckleball a butterfly with hiccups. Bobby Murcer said hitting one is like eating Jell-O with chopsticks. Tim McCarver said catching one is like trying to seize a moth with tweezers.

"There are two theories on hitting the knuckleball," acclaimed batting coach Charley Lau said. "Unfortunately, neither of them works."

As a baseball fan, you have surely put together that Phil Niekro Jr. was the father of Phil Niekro III, who would become perhaps the greatest knuckleball pitcher in the game's history. He learned that pitch from his father in that backyard and would go on to win 300 games. His knuckleball danced so unpredictably that nobody even wanted to catch him. Bob Uecker took on the task one year and had 23 passed balls in 15 Niekro starts.

"The easiest way to catch the knuckleball," Uecker later told Johnny

Carson on *The Tonight Show*, "is to wait for it to stop rolling and then pick it up."

But this story is not about Phil. No, it begins with Phil's brother Joe, who was five years younger. Joe also learned how to throw the knuckleball in that backyard, and while he might not have been quite as good as Phil, he was plenty good. He won 221 games in a 22-year career.

Joe, though, sometimes needed a little extra help. In 1987, for example, he was pitching a game against the Angels, and the knuckleball was breaking every law of gravity, so much so that umpire Tim Tschida started to think that maybe Joe was doctoring the baseball.

Tschida approached Joe. You can watch the whole thing on YouTube. It is timelessly funny, kind of like a Marx Brothers movie. Tschida asked to check out Niekro's glove, and Niekro tossed it to him haphazardly. If this had been a silent movie, the words *You got nothin' on me, copper!* might have popped up on the screen.

Tschida looked over the glove. Meanwhile, Joe stealthily dug his hands into the back pockets of his pants. Crew chief Dave Phillips thought that suspicious and said, "Hey, whatcha hiding back there?"

Niekro acted even more hurt by these allegations. He innocently held out his hands to show that he had nothing. But Phillips was unconvinced. "I want to see what he's got back there in his pocket," he yelled at Twins' manager Tom Kelly. Niekro then pulled out a lineup card, and Phillips said something like: "No, I want to see *everything* you have back there."

Then Niekro did something so magnificent and wonderful, it makes me smile every single time I think about it. He reached into his back pockets and turned them inside out to show they were empty. But while doing that, in one motion, he clearly threw a couple of items away.

What items? Well, he threw away an emery board. And he threw away some sandpaper.

You could not get two better tools for doctoring a baseball.

When the umpires picked those up, Joe brilliantly pantomimed: "I've never seen those objects in my life!" He got tossed from the game. But it was not all bad. Joe ended up on *Late Night with David Letterman*. He brought out an electric power sander and wire brush with him.

And we're only getting started with our story here.

///

JOE AND PHIL NIEKRO HAVE THE RECORD FOR MOST WINS BY brothers,* with a total of 539.† But Joe also has an accomplishment all his own. He pitched 20 postseason innings without giving up a single run. That's an MLB record.

Joe Niekro was 43 years old when he threw his last pitch for the Minnesota Twins. After that, he settled in Plant City, Florida, the Winter Strawberry Capital of the World and home to Cincinnati Reds' spring training. He kept a low profile, showed up for some charity events, watched his son Lance play for the San Francisco Giants. He also coached some kids around the neighborhood. His younger son J.J. was playing Little League, and Joe would come out to the games, always smiling, always positive. Sometimes, when the kids asked nicely, he'd even throw them a few knuckleballs, which always made them laugh.

This was especially true for one player. Her name was Chelsea Baker.

Joe liked her right away. She was quiet but still feisty—undaunted about playing on a boys' team—and she wasn't a bad little pitcher. She asked him a few times to teach her how to throw a knuckleball. "He always told me it was a secret," she says. "But one day he finally said, 'OK, here's how you do it.'"

At first her hands were so small that she had to use three fingers to

---

* Another fun Joe Niekro piece of trivia: He hit one home run in 1,165 plate appearances. Joe hit it off his older brother, Phil.

† Phil and Joe Niekro have 10 more wins than brothers Gaylord and Jim Perry.

hold the ball rather than the normal two. Still, she could make the ball move. Joe showed her how to make the ball come out with barely any spin. That's the key to the knuckleball. The pitch looks magical the way it zigs and zags, but it's scientific; as *Smithsonian Magazine* reported, the ball dances because of an aerodynamic phenomenon called unsteady lift forces.

Well, Chelsea was only 8, but her knuckleball began to zig and zag. Joe loved it. He told her he would keep teaching her the knuckleball, and all he asked in return was a peck on the cheek before she went out to pitch in a game.

This was 2006. Joe died that year of a brain aneurysm. He was only 61. "Coach Joe taught me so much," Chelsea wrote as an obituary tribute. "Most of all, he taught me to throw his famous knuckleball. I will always remember and love you." She placed a baseball in his casket at the funeral.

And then, in Joe's honor, she worked to perfect her knuckleball. There was nobody left to teach her, so she taught herself. Chelsea's stepfather built a wall for her to throw against. "Every day after school, I would throw the knuckleball against the wall," she said. "I taught myself to use two fingers as my hands got bigger."

The next year, she began throwing it in Little League games.

And nobody could hit her.

She did not lose a single game for four years. In 2009, she played for the Plant City League 10–11 All-Stars, and late in the year she pitched the district title game against North Lakeland. She threw a perfect game. That made some local news.

Then on April 9, 2010, she made national news. She was pitching for Brandon Farms against J.R. Farms. And she threw *another* perfect game. Not only that, she struck out 16 of the 18 batters she faced. The Baseball Hall of Fame asked to display her jersey. ESPN did a feature on her with *A League of Their Own* star Geena Davis narrating.

"At age thirteen," Geena Davis said, "she may be the best Little League pitcher in the country."

Chelsea Baker was not exclusively a knuckleball pitcher—she also threw a fastball and a curve—but it was the knuckleball that got people dreaming. "It's her Golden Ticket," said Justine Siegal, who founded Baseball for All, an organization dedicated to encouraging and providing opportunities for girls in baseball.

"A lot of times, I couldn't see the movement of the ball when I'd pitch it," Chelsea says. "I could only tell it was floating. When I'd see a video of it from different perspectives, it always surprised me."

Soon the attention was overwhelming. Reporters. Cameras. Travel. Awards. Some of the kids in her school would stop and ask for her autograph. In Japan, they called her "Knuckleball Princess." In the United States, people started talking about the possibility of her becoming the first woman pitcher in the big leagues. She was only 13.

"Throwing a knuckleball," she said for the ESPN feature, "is kind of like riding on a Ferris wheel. When you're going down a Ferris wheel, the wind kind of pushes up on your face. And when you're going up a Ferris wheel, the wind pushes down on you."

She felt a little bit like her life was a Ferris wheel. At 16, she became the first female to pitch varsity high school baseball in Hillsborough County. But already she could feel things changing.

"My all-time favorite years of playing baseball were when I was youngest, ages eight to twelve," she says. "I got to travel so much thanks to my parents, who supported me endlessly. I also absolutely dominated, which helped.

"During my high school years, I came to realize that baseball might not be everything going forward. I loved music, too, being creative, taking pictures, making art. My love for baseball didn't outshine that for me."

She did have one more baseball thrill—she was invited to pitch against the hometown Tampa Bay Rays before a game. She signed a ball for manager Joe Maddon ("This young woman is the real deal," he said). She plunked star third baseman Evan Longoria ("I blamed him for hogging the plate," she said, "but it was definitely my jitters getting to me"). She struck out David Price ("That was sick!" Price shouted out). And she had so many reporters gathered around her for interviews, the main thing she remembers was how her glasses fogged up.

That was the beautiful crescendo to her baseball journey. She played some more after that, but if she's being honest about it, baseball sort of stopped after the Rays' day. Her opportunities dried up. College teams didn't call. She went to Florida Atlantic, and the coach did ask her to try out. She appreciated the offer but declined.

"I remember the idea of going to college and getting tons of publicity day in and day out while most likely not getting as much playing time just didn't sit right with me," she says. "I knew there were new and different experiences waiting out there for me."

Chelsea Baker still lives in Florida. She is now a content creator for a company; she cooks; she plays the piano. And sure, she still thinks about Joe and still thinks about baseball. Sometimes she can get a friend to play catch with her. But more often she will see her favorite yellow glove sitting on the shelf, and she will take it down, put it on, pound her fist in it.

"I know that you can hear the sound," she says.

Yes. We hear it. And the knuckleball?

Oh yes, Chelsea says, she can still make the baseball dance.

"I think," she says, "it will live in me forever."

NO. 47:

THE DOUBLE

OCTOBER 8, 1995, SEATTLE

★ ★ ★ ★ ★

As I write these words, the Seattle Mariners are the only Major League Baseball team that has never been to a World Series. You might not have guessed that. Over the last half century, the Mariners have featured as many iconic players as almost any team in baseball—Griffey! Edgar! A-Rod! Big Unit! Ichiro! King Félix!—and yet, no World Series.

In 2001, the Mariners won 116 games, more than any team in the last century.

And yet . . . no World Series.

Teams of significantly less grandeur—the Arizona Diamondbacks, the Colorado Rockies, the Tampa Bay Rays, the Miami Marlins—have been to at least one World Series. Every team in the Mariners division has been to at least two. It's all so baffling. Why does the sun never shine on the Mariners?

The greatest moment in Seattle baseball history—and it isn't close—is a double hit in the 1995 American League Division Series. Edgar Martinez hit that double, Ken Griffey Jr. came racing around to score, the Mariners beat the Yankees.

On its own merits, that play might not be among the 50 or 100 or 500 most magical moments in baseball history. Do you know how many postseason walk-off hits there have been? I imagine you don't, off the top of your head, so I'll tell you: There have been 164 of them. David Ortiz by himself had three of them in the 2004 playoffs.

A guy named Denny Walling hit a walk-off sacrifice fly in a playoff game against Philadelphia in 1980, and the very next year he hit a walk-off single with the bases loaded in a playoff game against the Dodgers.

Point is, we can't put all the postseason walk-off hits in here.

But in Seattle, the Double is sacred. I wanted someone who lived it to explain. So I asked my friend Mike Duncan, creator of *The History of Rome* and *Revolutions* history podcasts and lifelong Mariners fan, to write about the Double.

Spoiler alert: He really got into it.

//

You must understand that the Double did not simply happen. It was instead the final explosive ingredient of the sorcerer's potion fueling the Seattle Mariners in the late summer of 1995. Seattle baseball had been nowhere for 18 years. Then for six weeks, a magical cauldron bubbled with escalating intensity as it received ingredients heretofore unknown in Seattle— spectacular plays, come-from-behind victories, and late-game heroics.

Only *then* did Edgar Martinez step to the plate in the bottom of the 11th in Game 5.

The Mariners came to be in 1977; they were the less interesting of two expansion teams that year (the other was the first Canadian team to enter the American League, the Toronto Blue Jays). I grew up on Mariners baseball in the 1980s. They were a living affront to baseball purists everywhere: a West Coast expansion team playing on Astroturf in a concrete dome. The fan base was as meager as the win totals.

To me, it was all normal. Baseball was not all-stars, pennant races, and championships. No, it was empty seats in a cavernous gray arena with falling ceiling tiles and a sea of green plastic surrounding it. I did not know it could be any other way.

Ken Griffey Jr. arrived in 1989, when I was 9, and he sparked excitement with his gorgeous swing and general coolness. But he was just one man. The Mariners jealously clung fast to their identity as anonymous losers. Even in 1995, in what would become their most magical season, they played mediocre baseball most of the way. Griffey went down in May with a broken wrist. On August 20, the Mariners lost to the Red Sox and sat 12½ games out of first place. This was no great tragedy, no great surprise, and no great mystery. This was Mariners baseball.

Then, inexplicably, the team went on one of the wildest runs in baseball history. The Mariners! They did not transform into a juggernaut, mind you. They remained flawed. They continued to regularly fall behind in games. Only now they came back! Of their final 26 wins, 14 were come-from-behind victories. They scored 13 winning runs in the seventh inning or later.

And they climbed in the standings. By September 1, they were only 6½ back. The first-place Angels were falling. For the first time, people in Seattle talked about the Mariners. Baseball stories started appearing on the *front page* of newspapers. The incantation "Refuse to Lose" proliferated throughout the city. Griffey came back from injury. The city was enthralled.

I was 15 when my favorite baseball team became animated by mystical forces beyond my comprehension. Fifteen is a wonderful age for magical baseball. I was neither too young to comprehend events nor too old to reflexively guard against disappointment. I rode the emotional wave with the unreserved ardor of adolescence.

Yes, Mariner Randy Johnson won the Cy Young Award that year and made his opening argument for the title of greatest left-handed pitcher of all time. But the most explosively vital element for those Mariners was Edgar Martinez.

Edgar had been quietly excellent for several years. In 1992, for example, he won a batting title for a team that finished last.

But in 1995, Edgar Martinez ripped through the league, terrorized pitchers, and slashed .356/.479/.628. He was, I will argue with anyone, the best hitter in baseball that year, but he remained, as ever, quiet and unassuming. He gently rocked back and forth in the box, his bat looping in casual, hypnotic circles. He seemed to never swing at a bad pitch. His swing was stoic and even noble somehow.

His specialty was hitting line drives into gaps and down the line. His specialty, in other words, was doubles. He hit 52 of them that year.

And then there was the Double. You must understand, it *had* to be a double.

The Mariners required two more eighth-inning miracles in the final four days to catch the Angels, but we were coming to expect these. They forced a one-game playoff in the Kingdome. A team that went the entire 1980s without a single sellout now packed the house nightly. Magic does draw crowds. Randy Johnson pitched a three-hit complete game with 12 strikeouts. The Mariners won 9–1. The ecstasy of a 15-year-old who had never been to the playoffs remains beyond the limited capacity of human language.

This set the stage for the 1995 ALDS between the Mariners and Yankees. It remains one of the greatest playoff series of all time. The drama, tension, and heroics of that series sit comfortably alongside any of the series in this book. Fourteen times in five games the trailing team came back to tie. Four of the five games were decided after the seventh inning; two of the games went into extra innings. The Yankees took the first two games, meaning the Mariners needed to win three straight against the most storied franchise in American sports. Then, after Seattle won Game 3 (coming from behind, of course), they fell behind 5–0 in Game 4.

We turned to Edgar. Who else? In the third inning, he hit a three-run homer to close the gap. And in the bottom of the eighth, he hit a grand slam to break a tie. My family and I were at that game. My memory is of noise so loud it could not be heard, of joy so fathomless it could not be felt, of victory so sweet it could not be tasted.

Game 5 was a microcosm of the series. The Yankees built a two-run lead. The Mariners came back again—a Griffey home run was the big blow—and then Randy Johnson came in two days after pitching seven excruciating innings. The game went into extra innings. The Yankees scored a run off Johnson in the 11th.

We want our greatest heroes to deliver the greatest heroics. That is the essence of mythmaking. Achilles standing before Troy. Gilgamesh fighting the Bull of Heaven. Beowulf slaying Grendel. Edgar Martinez is the truest of the Mariner heroes. It had to be him.

In the bottom of the 11th, Joey Cora bunted a single. Ken Griffey Jr. shot a single through the hole. And Destiny stepped to the plate in the form of Edgar Martinez. He rocked gently in the box, waving those hypnotic circles with his bat. He took strike one.

Then, what happened next, I cannot explain better than broadcaster Dave Niehaus did: "The stretch and the 0-1 pitch on the way to Edgar Martinez; *swungonandlineddown theleftfieldlineforabasehit!*"

All one word, in a voice hoarse from calling so many late-season miracles.

After that, all I heard was my own voice screaming. Griffey sprinted around third and scored and was piled on by all his teammates. I still see the smile on his face.

Funny, though it is not the hit that made the moment, I have no image of Edgar after he swung the bat. It was as if he transcended this plane of existence and transformed into a being of pure celestial energy. [Joe note: It is also possible that Edgar Martinez just stayed out of the spotlight, as was his habit.]*

---

* Mike note: But more likely it was the transforming into a being of pure celestial energy thing.

That's where it ended. The Mariners lost the next series to Cleveland. As Joe told you, the Mariners have never been to a World Series. But it hardly matters. Sport is agony. We agree to suffer endlessly in exchange for the mere possibility of sublime rapture. Sometimes we even get it.

NO. 46:

PEDRO: "AS UNHITTABLE AS YOU CAN BE"

SEPTEMBER 10, 1999, BRONX

★ ★ ★ ★ ★

In his autobiography, concisely titled *Pedro*, Pedro Martínez remembered one thing about the moments leading up to the astonishing game he pitched at Yankee Stadium: He was angry. Why was he angry? Oh, it could have been any number of things. He was angry the Red Sox had not sent him to New York early to prepare. He was angry the Red Sox had made him skip a start a couple of weeks earlier because he was late to the ballpark ("I was *not* late!" Pedro would insist).

He was angry because six years earlier, he didn't make the Dodgers as a 21-year-old coming out of spring training.

He was angry because the Dodgers traded him in 1994.

He was angry because the Red Sox were playing the Yankees and he hated the Yankees . . . and he was angry because the media was tough to deal with . . . and he was angry people doubted him all his life . . . and he was angry because coach Joe Kerrigan wouldn't get off his back.

"You're not going to the pitchers meeting?" Kerrigan asked Pedro as he sat in the whirlpool. This is how Martínez recalled the exchange in his book.

"No," Pedro said. "I've faced these guys."

"Well, you better find a way to get Derek Jeter out."

"Why don't you and Jeter go %#%# yourselves," Pedro said.

Let's be realistic. Pedro Martínez was angry because, like Bruce

Banner in *The Avengers*, he was always angry. That was his secret, too. Rage fueled him. He sought it out. He luxuriated in it.

"Keep it clean," umpire Joe West once said to him before a game, a warning to remind him not to throw at batters. No great pitcher in modern baseball hit more batters per inning than Pedro Martínez. Obviously, Pedro *hated* that West said that ("I'm not a dirty player," he said) but he also *loved* that West said that because he was always on the lookout for a new reason to be angry.

"You tell them to keep it clean," Martinez told West. "Because I am not afraid."

He threw a three-hitter against Pittsburgh that day.

But back to New York. It was a Friday night and more than 55,000 people had gathered at Yankee Stadium to watch the game of the year. Pedro Martínez sat in the whirlpool, feeling a satisfying anger pulsate through him. The Yankees were defending World Series champs. Jeter had gotten two hits off him the last time they faced. The boos would be going all night. It was time to show New York City what Pedro Martínez was all about.

PEDRO NICKED YANKEES' LEADOFF HITTER CHUCK KNOBLAUCH with the second pitch of the game. That wasn't a surprise. Martínez, as mentioned, hit a lot of batters. Plus Knoblauch got hit by a lot of pitches—he led the league in 1998. Getting hit was sort of a specialty of his. Often when he got hit, Knoblauch followed it up by trying to steal second base. He took off on Martínez's second pitch to Derek Jeter. Red Sox catcher Jason Varitek threw him out.

Then Martínez struck out Derek Jeter.

&#$@% you, Joe Kerrigan, Pedro thought.

Martínez could already tell: He had his good fastball that night. And when Pedro had his good fastball, say goodnight. *If I needed a pitcher to defeat the devil's baseball team in order to save my soul, that pitcher* would be prime Pedro Martínez with his good fastball. Pedro was unlike any other great pitcher . . . but also like every other great pitcher. He had Bob Gibson's intensity, Tom Seaver's mind, Juan Marichal's relentlessness, Greg Maddux's command, Sandy Koufax's ability to rise to the moment. He had one of the best fastballs in baseball history and one of the best changeups in baseball history, and those two pitches looked exactly the same coming out of his hand. Trying to guess between them was, as Gene Menez wrote in *Sports Illustrated*, "Red Sox Roulette."

But even if the batter *did* guess right (and Martínez had a slider and curveball he'd throw now and again), it still didn't matter, because Martínez also knew exactly where the batter's weakness was in the strike zone, and he hit that spot time after time after time.

In the second inning, New York first baseman Tino Martinez hit a lazy fly ball to center, which inspired announcer Tim McCarver to pontificate about where the phrase *lazy fly ball* even came from.*

That brought up the Yankees' designated hitter, Chili Davis, who often went by the sobriquet *professional hitter*. It's an odd thing to call a Major League Baseball player; they're all technically professionals. But I think in Chili Davis's case—and in those of others called professional hitters—the phrase is meant to mirror the professional hitmen, those contract killers who go about their jobs proficiently and without excess drama. In this way, "professional hitter" was a brilliant description of

---

* The earliest reference I can find to a "lazy fly ball" is in *The Boston Daily Globe* in 1891. The headline read like so: "ROGER'S LAZY FLY May Prove Fatal to Two Bridegrooms." Fun story! The Giants were playing the Brooklyn Bridegrooms—so named because during the off-season a few of their players got married—and Roger Connor hit a short fly ball between Brooklyn's Hub Collins and Thomas Burns. The fielders collided in spectacular and violent fashion. "Both athletes seemed to merge into one man," the *Globe* wrote. Burns, the paper continued, was suffering from "concussion of the brain," and Collins was "thought to be dying." This proved a slight exaggeration. Collins returned a week later, bruised but undaunted. Burns missed no time at all.

Chili Davis. He had been quietly but forcefully hitting for 17 years. Even at age 39, he knew what to do with mistake pitches.

With the count 1-1, Pedro threw one of those mistake pitches. My friend Mike Schur—who was at the game and will never stop talking about it—has a theory about why on Pedro's greatest night he threw a mistake pitch. See, in the Navajo culture, weavers would leave imperfections in their rugs to remind themselves that only God is perfect.

Mike's theory: Pedro Martínez's fastball caught way too much of the plate, but only as a reminder to himself that God alone is perfect.

Chili Davis hit the ball squarely and pounded it over the right-field fence for a home run.

Pedro Martínez promptly and angrily struck out Ricky Ledée to end the inning.

And with his one imperfection out of the way, Pedro proceeded for the next seven innings to pitch better baseball than, I think, anyone in the history of baseball. He got 21 consecutive outs, 14 by strikeout. Only two Yankees hit the ball out of the infield. After the fourth inning, only one Yankee hit a ball in fair territory.

In all, Martínez would allow just the one hit, strike out 17, and walk nobody.

"No pitcher," Dan Shaughnessy would write in the next morning's *Boston Globe*, "ever did to the Yanks what Pedro Martínez did last night."

Yes, that was the big thing. There were pitchers who put up games that numerically may match up with or even exceed Pedro's. But he did it against the Yankees. He did it against a World Championship team. He did it at Yankee Stadium, surrounded by New York hostility times 55,000.

He was so good that night that the mighty Yankees simply surrendered to his greatness. Three years earlier, in the World Series, the brilliant Greg Maddux threw eight shutout innings against these Yankees, but they walked away unimpressed. "The ball was right there for us, we just didn't swing the bats," Bernie Williams said, speaking for many on the team.

After Pedro's game, though, the Yankees were nothing less than awed.

"If he throws like that," Paul O'Neill said, "he'll never lose."

"Probably the best performance I've seen," Derek Jeter said.

"I don't even know what to say," Andy Pettitte said.

"I'm just glad we got a hit," Tino Martinez said.

And Yankees' manager Joe Torre talked about the greatest pitchers he'd ever faced—Gibson, Seaver, Koufax—and how on this one night they all seemed to be on the mound at the same time, all of them inside one little pitcher with a huge heart and a giant chip on his shoulder.

"That," Torre said, "was about as unhittable as you can be."

FIVE
TRICK PLAYS

Baseball, alas, doesn't have as many trick plays as football. That's just the nature of the sport. Football coaches will spend countless hours designing all sorts of deceptive plays with fakes and misdirection, and it's fun. Baseball is different, I think, because it is the defense that controls the ball.

But even in baseball there are some fantastic trick plays.

JAKE TAYLOR CALLS HIS SHOT
(1989, MOVIE *MAJOR LEAGUE*)

At the end of the movie *Major League,* Cleveland is playing the Yankees for the pennant. The score is tied in the ninth, and Cleveland's speedster Willie Mays Hayes ("Hits like Mays, runs like Hayes") is on second base with two outs. Cleveland's catcher Jake Taylor is at the plate, and all you need to know about him is that he's old and has bad knees and can't run.

He points to the outfield à la Babe Ruth in the 1932 World Series.

The Yankees' relief pitcher—the Duke*—promptly throws the

---

* Played convincingly by former big-league catcher Steve Yeager.

ball at Taylor's head, which is exactly how you would expect a pitcher to react when seeing a batter try to call his shot. More on this much later.

Taylor gets up and, without dusting himself off, again points, again calls his shot. Then, on the next pitch, Hayes takes off and Taylor lays down a bunt. The third baseman is playing way back and realizes he's in trouble; he charges and barehands the ball and throws to first, but Taylor somehow beats the throw.

And while the first baseman argues the call, Hayes keeps running, and he slides across home plate for the game-winning run.

Did it mirror any actual big-league play? Not entirely. There have been numerous times through the years that a runner scored from second on a bunt; in May 1949, Jackie Robinson scored from second on a Gil Hodges bunt to help win a game for the Dodgers, just as one example. But there's no known example of someone outside of *Major League* preceding a bunt by pointing to the outfield. I hope it happens someday.

THE ICE WAGON PLAY (MAY 22, 1893)

On a Monday afternoon in Baltimore, the New York Giants pulled off a trick play that in time changed the game.

The Orioles' Tim O'Rourke was on first base, and Jocko Milligan was at the plate. "The former," *The Baltimore Sun* would write, "is a runner, the latter an ice wagon." We will assume that means that Jocko Milligan was very slow.

Milligan lifted a fly ball. The Giants' John Montgomery Ward—a future Hall of Famer—was playing shortstop, and he purposely dropped the ball and forced O'Rourke out at second so that the Orioles would be stuck with the ice wagon Milligan on first base.

This play became famous after *The Sun* wrote about it ("Ward showed excellent judgement," they wrote). Other players soon began doing similar things. This led directly to the invention of the infield fly rule.*

THE COLAVITO CAROM (JULY 27, 1958)

Rocky Colavito's full name was Rocco Domenico Colavito. He grew up in the Bronx and dropped out of school in the 10th grade to play baseball. He always regretted it. "Kids should stay in school," he used to say. "Don't be a lug like me."

Colavito was a powerful hitter (he hit 374 home runs in his big-league career) and a Cleveland folk hero. His defining quality was that he had an incredibly strong arm. Years after he retired, Rocky was a Cleveland coach, and sometimes before games, to entertain the crowd, he would stand at home plate and throw the ball over the center-field fence.

The arm was strong, yes, but not always accurate. The Rock probably airmailed as many cutoff men as anyone in baseball history.

Which leads to the moment. In Game 1 of a 1958 doubleheader between Cleveland and the Yankees, Mickey Mantle singled for New York. He moved to second on a single. Then he stole third. Norm Siebern stepped to the plate and looped a short fly ball to Colavito.

Mantle stayed at third; Colavito caught the ball just beyond the infield. But then Colavito uncorked one of his famous throws. The ball sailed six feet over the catcher's head. Mantle trotted home thinking he would easily score on the error . . . but the ball ricocheted off the grandstand behind home plate and bounced directly into the glove of pitcher

---

* No baseball book should be without an explanation of the infield fly rule: An infield fly is any fair fly ball that can be caught by an infielder with ordinary effort when there are fewer than two outs and runners are on first and second, or first, second, and third base. In order to prevent purposely dropped fly balls, the umpire automatically calls the batter out before the ball even comes down. It should be noted, though, that the infield fly rule would not have affected the Ice Wagon Play that inspired it, because there was only one runner on base.

Cal McLish, who then flipped it to catcher Russ Nixon, who put the tag on a stunned Mickey Mantle.

Afterward, Colavito was asked if he had done it on purpose. He shrugged. But his fans had no doubt.

"Members of the Colavito Chowder and Cheering Society," the *Akron Beacon Journal* reported, "will always believe Rocky threw to the stands intentionally."

JAVY BÁEZ TAG PLAY (MARCH 14, 2017)

When Javy Báez was a teenager in Puerto Rico, he got a strange tattoo on the back of his neck. It is a tattoo of the Major League Baseball logo.

Javy and his two brothers got the same tattoo in honor of their father, Angel.

It was Angel who taught them all to love baseball. He worked all day as a landscaper in Puerto Rico, but every evening, without fail, he would take the boys to a nearby field to play exuberant, carefree, exhilarating baseball.

There has never been a more exuberant, carefree, and exhilarating play than Javy's tag play in the 2017 World Baseball Classic.

For Báez, tagging is an art form. Before he came along, tagging a base runner seemed a rudimentary part of the game. Báez infused delight. There was the time when the Giants' Denard Span tried to steal. Cubs' catcher David Ross's throw bounced about 15 feet in front of second base. Báez jumped up, caught it while in midair, then slapped a no-look tag on Span.

Another time, Trevor Story tried to steal, and Ross's throw was in the dirt on the wrong side of second base. Báez scooped the ball and made a behind-the-back tag.

Báez made so many wonderful tags that it's hard to keep up. But the best of them all came in the second round of the World Baseball Classic in 2017. Puerto Rico led the Dominican Republic 3–1 with two outs in the eighth inning when D.R. right fielder Nelson Cruz tried to steal second. Catcher Yadier Molina fired a perfect throw.

And then—how do you even say it?—Báez began to celebrate before the ball even got to him. He pointed at Molina to say, "What a great throw." This was *before* the ball got there.

He then caught the ball and without ever looking down—and while still pointing congratulations at Molina—dropped the tag on Cruz while shouting, "Yeah!"

I have never seen a happier moment on a baseball diamond.

THE GREAT POTATO PLAY (AUGUST 31, 1987)

Dave Bresnahan comes from baseball royalty. His great-uncle was Hall of Famer Roger Bresnahan, a Deadball Era ballplayer who is often called the first catcher to wear shin guards.*

Dave was never a threat to make the Hall of Fame or even play in the Major Leagues—he just didn't hit well enough—but he was a pretty good fielding catcher in the minor leagues. In 1987, he was hitting just .150 for Class AA Williamsport as the last week of the season approached. Dave understood that his baseball career was probably coming to an end. He decided to end it in style.

So he went to the Weis Market in Williamsport, Pennsylvania, and spent a long time examining the potatoes. He was there so long that eventually the produce guy asked, "Hey, why are you picking up every potato?"

"I'm looking for the perfect one," Bresnahan said.

"Perfect how?" the produce guy asked, but Bresnahan had found the potatoes he wanted, and he left as quickly as he could. Back at his place, he carefully peeled the potatoes until they were smooth and white. He

---

* He actually was not. Bud Fowler, who played for Black teams in the nineteenth century, began wearing them earlier.

then put them in his equipment bag and went to bed. There was nothing left to be done except wait for the exact right moment.

The next day, Williamsport played Reading. And the moment arrived in the fifth inning. Reading's Rick Lundblade* made it to third base. At that point, Bresnahan asked the umpire for a time-out, saying that a string on his glove had torn.

Bresnahan went to the dugout and got a different catcher's mitt.

He settled in behind the plate. Bresnahan then fired to third base in an effort to pick off Lundblade, but his throw was wild and went rolling into the outfield. Lundblade trotted home to score the run . . . only to find that Bresnahan was waiting for him with the ball still in his glove.

Bresnahan, yes, had thrown a potato he had picked up from the dugout.

The scene was chaos. One umpire went to fetch the now broken-apart potato. Another called Lundblade safe. Williamsport's manager Orlando Gómez pulled Bresnahan from the game for committing "an unthinkable act for a professional," and after the game fined Bresnahan $50. Cleveland's director of player development Jeff Scott released him.

"Bresh," he said solemnly on the call, "I can't have my players throwing potatoes."

Bresnahan paid his $50 fine in potatoes, two sacks of them that he put on the manager's desk with a note that read, "This spud's for you."

---

* You might not care about this at all, but Rick Lundblade was a star at Stanford; he's in the Stanford Athletics Hall of Fame. He would go on to a prominent law career.

NO. 45:
THE GRAND ILLUSION

JUNE 7, 1982, OMAHA, NEBRASKA

★ ★ ★ ★ ★

> "The ball is thrown away, down into the . . . oh now, they've cut it off . . . and Stephenson's gonna be out."
>
> —ESPN'S CONFUSED CALL OF THE GRAND ILLUSION

The greatest trick play in baseball history was born out of boredom. The University of Miami Hurricanes were playing in the College World Series . . . and in those days the College World Series was played over nine days. That's a lot of time in Omaha, Nebraska. Miami had two full days off before its titanic matchup with top-seeded Wichita State and had to do *something* to pass the time.

Two Miami assistant coaches—Dave Scott and Skip Bertman— thought it might be fun to practice a goofy play they had seen at a Junior College Tournament game. The play involved a fake throw, a lot of acting, and a big reveal. Everybody on the team would need to be involved. Even some people not on the team needed to be involved. It was quite the production.

"We were never actually going to *use* the play," Bertman would say. "Do you know how silly it would have looked if the other team didn't fall for it? And that game was on national TV. No, that was too big a chance to take; we were never going to try it."

They practiced the play for a while, everybody had a lot of fun with it, and then everybody got down to the serious business of preparing for Wichita State. Miami came into the game as a massive underdog. Wichita State had led the nation in hits, runs, doubles, triples, total bases, and stolen bases. There was talk of them being not only the best team in the country but the best college baseball team ever.

And speaking of best ever: The Shockers' team leader was Phil Stephenson, the younger brother of the team's coach, Gene Stephenson. There's an argument to be made that Stephenson is *still* the greatest college player ever. He has held the Division I career record for runs, hits, total bases, walks, and stolen bases for more than 40 years.

Miami needed more than some zany trick play to beat Wichita State. Right?

///

MIAMI COACH RON FRASER TOLD HIS ASSISTANT COACHES THAT the only way he would even consider letting them call the trick play was if four unlikely things happened all at once.

Thing 1: Miami had to be the home team—this was key. The home team gets the first-base dugout. And for this play to work, Miami's players had to be in the first-base dugout.

Thing 2: The time had to be just right—not the timing but the actual time. It had to be at twilight so that everything looked just a little bit fuzzy and indistinct.

Thing 3: There needed to be an opposing player on first base—and that player needed to be an ultra-aggressive base runner looking to steal second.

Thing 4: A player—not a coach—had to be coaching first base for the other team.

///

OK, IT WAS THE TOP OF THE SIXTH INNING, AND MIAMI LED 4–3. Phil Stephenson led off the inning with a walk. And Ron Fraser looked out on the field and was stupefied: All four of his prerequisites to run the play were fulfilled. Miami was the home team. It was seven P.M. and the sun was pretty low. Stephenson was the ultimate aggressive base runner; he tried to steal 90 times that season. And sure enough, a Wichita State pitcher named Bryan Oelkers was coaching first.

Miami's pitcher Mike Kasprzak looked into the dugout with a pleading look that said, *OK, are we going to do this or not?*

Bertman tried to ignore him. But Kasprzak kept looking into the dugout and finally Bertman sighed and stuck a finger in his ear.

That was the signal. The Grand Illusion had begun.

In real time, it looked like this: Kazprzak tried a pickoff throw. The ball got away from first baseman Steve Lusby. Everybody on the team, including the Miami batgirls (nicknamed the SugarCanes), screamed and pointed to where the ball had gone. Stephenson looked back and then jogged to second base.

But somehow—witchcraft? sorcery?—Miami shortstop Billy Wrona was there waiting for him with the baseball in his glove. Wrona tagged a baffled Stephenson out.

It was like a David Copperfield Las Vegas magic act.

So what the heck happened? You have to replay it several times in slow motion to understand.

- Pitcher Mike Kasprzak did not actually throw the ball to first base. He stepped off the rubber (he had to step off or else it would have been called a balk) and faked the throw to first base, keeping the actual baseball in his glove the entire time. Kasprzak put everything he had into the fake, including pretending to slip as he was throwing to give the moment even more authenticity. It was a tour de force.

- First baseman Steve Lusby then dived for the phantom baseball. He leaped over a sliding Stephenson and screamed out, "#&$@!" and began frantically running toward the bullpen, where the phantom baseball would have been heading. Lusby's performance was excellent, too, but his swearing might have been a touch over the top. Stephenson would remember feeling just the tiniest bit suspicious. He had not seen any baseball go by.

- All the players in the Miami dugout—this is why it was important to be
  on the first-base side—began yelling and pointing toward the phantom
  ball. Stephenson would admit that seeing them responding convinced
  him that the ball must have gotten away. In addition, two Miami players
  were warming up in the bullpen, and they both pretended to panic and
  jump out of the way of the baseball. They too were convincing.

Now the sting was set. It had to fool two people. They had Stephenson hooked but that was the easy part. They also needed to trick Oelkers, whose entire job was to sniff out the ploy. He had the best angle of the ruse. He would remember looking all around for a baseball and not finding one.

And he would remember yelling, "Stay!"

Unfortunately, nobody else remembered him yelling "Stay!" Wichita State's coach Gene Stephenson remembered quite vividly Oelkers yelling, "Go! Go! Go!" Phil was not sure of that, but he knew for sure that Oelkers did not yell "Stay!" The most likely scenario is that Oelkers froze and left Phil Stephenson on his own. About halfway to second base, Phil realized that he'd made a terrible mistake. The pitcher was coming at him rather than backing up third base. He ran by Kasprzak ("He wanted to tag me, but he wasn't fast enough," Stephenson would say), but by the time he got to second base, Wrona had the ball.

"You know," Oelkers would say, "I'm not sure I ever coached first base again."

OK, NOW LET'S TALK ABOUT THOSE BAT GIRLS, THE SUGARCANES.
As the years went along, Phil and Gene Stephenson would say they were the key players in the Grand Illusion.

"Everybody was fooled," Gene would say, laughing. "It's nobody's fault. I mean, the bat girls were running around. It's the greatest play in the history of college baseball, I'd say."

On the day it happened, no, Gene didn't think it was funny at all. He thought it was illegal. He didn't think it was fair that the SugarCanes—sophomores Linda Porter and Kim Merritt—jumped up out of their chairs and ran away as if there was a baseball loose. It's one thing for bench players to be deceptive. But the bat girls? Surely that's not allowed.

"I'm not saying it's a bad play," Phil said that day. "But it's bush when they've got the bat girls out there. It's a pile of crock."

"I'm a little miffed at that," Gene added. "I don't think that should be allowed. . . . I don't even understand why they were out there in the first place. Our bat girls were told to stay in the dugout."

Gene was so angry that he appealed to the umpires and College World Series officials. He insisted that it was against the rules to use the bat girls as part of a play. Miami, in response, denied that they played any role at all. Skip Bertman was particularly insistent, and not in the most respectful way: "They are bat girls," he said, "and essentially are not students of the game. There's no way we would take a chance trying to explain to them beforehand what we were trying to do."

Linda Porter confirmed that day: "We had nothing to do with it. We ran because we thought the ball was coming. We're usually on edge. I wish we had known. That would have been clever. That way we could have been nominated for Academy Awards."

As it turns out . . . they were not exactly telling the truth.

The SugarCanes were in on it.

In the fun documentary *The Grand Illusion*—produced 25 years after the play happened—Linda (Porter) Cox confessed that the SugarCanes were at the Grand Illusion practice, where they practiced jumping up and moving chairs and freaking out.

"We were supposed to position ourselves," she says, "so that we would be the first thing Phil Stephenson saw as he dove back to first."

That is exactly how it played out.

"If you notice in the replay," Gene would say, "Phil jumps up and he looks back toward the bullpen, and you'll see bat girls running as if the ball's coming at them."

He smiled. This was years later, after the play had become legend.

"It was really cool," Gene admitted.

NO. 44:
HERE COMES BREAM!

OCTOBER 14, 1992, ATLANTA

★ ★ ★ ★ ★

There's an argument to be made that this play—Francisco Cabrera getting the hit and Sid Bream coming around to score and Atlanta going to the World Series—is different from every other postseason walk-off in baseball history.

Why different? Because the moment was decisive. There were two outs in Game 7 of the 1992 National League Championship Series. The Pirates were winning. The Braves loaded the bases. Pittsburgh led by a run. If Cabrera—the last guy on the Atlanta bench—made an out, the Pirates were going to the World Series.

And if Cabrera got a hit, well, you'll see.

I never realized that none of the other famous postseason endings came at the last possible moment the way this one did. There was only one out when Bobby Thomson hit the shot heard round the world and no outs when Bill Mazeroski walked off the 1960 World Series. Carlton Fisk's wave-it-fair homer happened in Game 6, not Game 7; same with Joe Carter's homer; and Kirk Gibson's limp-around-the-bases homer came in Game 1. When the ball went through Bill Buckner in 1986, the score was already tied. The same is true of Luis Gonzalez's game-winning hit off Mariano Rivera in Game 7 of the 2001 World Series.

When Cabrera came to the plate, the game was truly in the balance.

I was there that night. I was 25 and a columnist for *The Augusta Chronicle*, a newspaper about two hours from Atlanta. I can still hear the cheers.

They were cheers of bliss and surprise; people still couldn't believe the Braves were any good. They had been so awful for years. In 1989, they were the worst team in baseball. In 1990, they were again the worst team in baseball. That year, an Atlanta newspaper asked fans to come up with a slogan for the team, and the winning entry (or at least my favorite) was: "Atlanta Braves baseball: It beats getting tattooed with a jackhammer, unless it's a doubleheader."

Then in 1991, with no warning, the Braves just got good. They picked up a light-hitting third baseman named Terry Pendleton and a gimpy-kneed first baseman named Sid Bream and their young pitchers all got good at the same time and they went to the World Series.

Everybody thought it was a fluke. But after a rough start in 1992, they again played extraordinary baseball. The Braves finished with the best record in baseball. They promptly won three of the first four games against Pittsburgh in the NLCS and seemed ready to breeze back to the World Series.

But those Pirates—featuring a young Barry Bonds—had some fight left in them. They destroyed Atlanta in the next two games and took a 2–0 lead into the ninth inning of Game 7. Their ace Doug Drabek was on the mound looking to finish things off.

There was despair in Atlanta. I remember that vividly. Fans poured out of Fulton County Stadium. I left the press box and went to the concourse and watched the fans' hearts break as they trudged to their cars in the parking lot.

Back inside, Pendleton led off the inning by pulling a long fly ball down the right-field line. On replay, it seems that Pirates' right fielder Cecil Espy misjudged the ball slightly. Maybe he could have caught it. Maybe not. He didn't. The ball landed just fair for a double.

David Justice was Atlanta's next batter, and he hit a sharp ground ball to second baseman José Lind, the Gold Glove winner that year. Lind had made only six errors all season. He tried to backhand the ball, but it skipped away. Atlanta had runners on first and third with nobody out.

Drabek then walked Sid Bream on four straight pitches to load the bases. The Braves might have put in a pinch runner for Bream, but they had run out of players.

Ron Gant's sacrifice fly made the score 2–1. Damon Berryhill walked to load the bases again (ball four looked like it went right down the middle). Then Atlanta's Brian Hunter hit a soft little bloop to Lind for the second out.

And the moment was at hand: bases loaded, two outs, Stan Belinda on the mound for Pittsburgh and pinch hitter Francisco Cabrera at the plate. Cabrera had batted just 11 times that season. He was the last available hitter on Atlanta's bench.

"A most unlikely man on the spot for Atlanta," Sean McDonough said on the national television broadcast. Cabrera was this kind of hitter: When Belinda threw the first two pitches for balls, announcer Tim McCarver suggested that he take the next pitch no matter what.

"At this point," McCarver said, "I think the chances are better with a walk than a hit."

Cabrera did swing with the count 2-0, and he drilled a line drive to left. He could not have hit the ball any harder. But it hooked way foul and into the stands. Cabrera shouted out in disgust. He had gotten the perfect pitch to hit. He wasn't likely to get another one.

With the count 2-1, Belinda threw a high fastball.

And what happened next—well, even now none of it makes sense.

Cabrera ripped a line drive to left field to score the tying run. Ridiculous!

Sid Bream rounded third on a knee that had been operated on five times. Absurd!

Barry Bonds, one of the greatest left fielders in baseball history, took too long to get to the ball. Outrageous!

Bonds then made a sluggish throw. Illogical!

Sid Bream huffed and puffed and, in the words of Atlanta humor columnist Lewis Grizzard, turned into Olympic hurdles champion Edwin Moses. Impossible!

The play at the plate was close. Bream was called safe. I can still hear the cheers.

MY FRIEND—AWARD-WINNING AUTHOR TOMMY TOMLINSON— grew up a Braves fan. I asked him to write a few words about the play:

> Let's get this part out of the way: Sid was safe. Some people, and not just in Pittsburgh, believe to this day that he was out. Bless their hearts. They do not understand perfect endings. The last player on the bench knocked in the slowest player on the field, beating a throw from maybe the greatest player of all time. That is a perfect ending. You don't mess with perfect endings.
>
> In my mind I hear the play more than I see it. That's because of Skip Caray's call on Braves' radio. He had broadcast the Braves for 16 years by then, and most of those years the team was terrible. So many bobbled grounders, so many weak pop-ups to third, so many bases-loaded walks on a Tuesday night in an empty stadium. All those thousands of hours of calling games, leading up to one moment.
>
> The whole play, from swing to slide, took seven seconds.
>
> Swung, line drive left field! One run is in! Here comes Bream! Here's the throw to the plate! He is . . . safe!
>
> And then, as David Justice tackles Bream and they roll on the ground in joy, Caray repeats the same phrase five times: BRAVES WIN! BRAVES WIN! BRAVES WIN! BRAVES WIN! BRAVES WIN!
>
> The last four sound the same. BRAVES and WIN hit the same note, like trumpet blasts. But the first time he says it, there's the smallest break in his voice, and the second note goes down a half step. That's the one that kills me. There's something about it I can't describe—it would take knowing more music theory than I know—but those two notes remind me of the orchestra in a movie's big scene, or a soul singer as she takes the chorus home. That little interval fills me with tears.
>
> Anytime I hear the name Sid Bream, I smile. But anytime I

hear Skip Caray's call, there's something that reaches a whole lot deeper, something that explains why baseball matters, or at least why it matters to me. Just a few seconds or just a couple of words can make you feel the things we're put on earth to feel— those powerful feelings of joy and release. It's the music and the magic in our hearts, waiting to be let go.

Braves win.

NO. 43:
TWO CLEMENTE THROWS

OCTOBER 11 AND 16, 1971, BALTIMORE

★ ★ ★ ★ ★

The inner game—baseball in the mind—has no season," the marvelous Roger Angell wrote, and it certainly has been like that in my life. I think about baseball all the time, all year round, often for no reason at all. Sometimes, to fall asleep, I count ballparks I have visited. Sometimes, to pass the time, I'll try to name World Series opponents going back as far as I can. Baseball numbers pop into my mind—.406 or 660 or 5,714 or 44—and I'll spend way too long lost in a baseball daydream about Ted Williams . . . or Willie Mays . . . or Nolan Ryan . . . or Henry Aaron.

"What are you thinking about?" friends and family will sometimes ask when I zone out like that, and it's hard to explain because, as Nick Hornby explains in his brilliant soccer book, *Fever Pitch*: "I rarely think. I remember. I fantasize. . . . none of this is *thought* in the proper sense of the word."

That's right. I often just melt into a memory of some beautiful baseball thing I've seen. I melt into a vision of Ken Griffey Jr. swinging the bat. Oh, how would you even describe that gorgeous thing? Junior's swing was violence and music, danger and candy, rage and sunshine. He seemed to swing the bat effortlessly, and yet it tore through the strike zone like Paul Bunyan's axe. I asked him once about his swing—a mistake, as it turned out, because Junior was not one for self-analysis or dreamy sportswriter inquiries.

"I swing like I swing, man," he said, which, looking back, was all that needed to be said.

Baseball in the mind.

I melt into a vision of Rickey Henderson dancing between second and third base. Rickey stole 1,406 bases in his career: There's another wonderful baseball number (and a permanent one; no one is ever breaking that record). Most of those steals were of second base, but I always thought Rickey was at his artistic best stealing third, something he did an astonishing 322 times.* As I lose myself in the memory, he is standing in the pitcher's blind spot, moving with the spot as the pitcher nervously tries to track him, and he is mesmerizing the infielder who is supposed to be holding him close, and by the time the pitcher begins the windup, he is already in full motion, a blur, halfway to third base.

I visualize Juan Marichal's beautiful high-kick windup, and I think about the story he told me. When he first signed to play professional baseball, Marichal threw sidearm. A minor-league coach named Andy Gilbert asked him to try throwing overhand. Marichal tried and found that the only way he could throw hard was if he kicked his leg up so high that it was at the same height as his head. "OK," Gilbert said, "but can't you kick your leg a little lower?"

Marichal could not. The windup became a part of baseball history. "First he'd kick you in the face," his teammate Orlando Cepeda said, "then he'd throw the pitch by you."

My mind is always ready to dive into a baseball reverie. Right now, as I write these words, I'm looking at a bobblehead doll. It is of Trea Turner sliding. His left hand and left knee are on the ground, and leaning left, like a speed skater making a sharp turn.

So yes, of course, I see the slide again. It happened August 10, 2021, the Los Angeles Dodgers playing in Philadelphia. With Turner on second, Dodgers' catcher Will Smith lined a single to right field. Turner is

---

* Rickey stole third base 133 more times than Vince Coleman, who is second on the all-time list.

one of the fastest players in baseball. He rounded third and headed home.

Bryce Harper's throw was late. Turner slid anyway. Only . . . it wasn't exactly a slide. It was more like he transformed into a powerboat and skimmed over a clear lake. A baseball slide, by its very nature, has a limited range; eventually your body stops sliding. But Turner's slide seemed like it could have gone on forever. He touched home plate with his left hand and then just kept on going. Only then, in one motion, he popped to his feet, rotated his body 180 degrees, and began walking casually in the opposite direction, like he was James Brown at the Apollo.

"I'm not necessarily trying to be cool or anything," he told ESPN, which is *exactly* what made it so cool.

Ah, but the coolest thing in baseball, I think, is simply Roberto Clemente throwing a baseball. I am too young, alas, to have seen Clemente play live. I wish that I had, because even over grainy film, the wonder of Clemente rushes through, no matter what he is doing. Simply watching him run is thrilling.

Clemente. The name evokes so many emotions because Clemente was such a force.

"You know what my goose-bump moment of Clemente is?" his biographer David Maraniss tells me. "It was when he talked to his parents in Spanish on national TV after that 1971 World Series. It captured everything about Clemente: Puerto Rico, pride, and baseball."

Yes. And then to watch him throw a baseball? It's life-changing.

I think of two throws specifically, both from the 1971 World Series. Clemente was already 37 and, in his own mind, diminished. How magical were those throws? Let's put it this way: Neither one even recorded an out. Still, they will endure forever.

The first throw came in Game 2 of that series between Pittsburgh and Baltimore. Baltimore's Boog Powell lifted a fly ball to right field. Clemente was playing Powell deep and toward center, so he had a long run to the ball. The Orioles' Merv Rettenmund was on second base, and when he saw how far Clemente had to go, he tagged up.

Clemente ran to the ball and caught it on his left hip—"That was Clemente's version of the Willie Mays basket catch," Bob Costas says—and in one motion he whirled his body all the way around and fired to third. The throw was so unexpectedly wonderful that Pirates' third baseman Richie Hebner, who had wandered off the bag, had to rush back, and he could not quite get the tag down on Rettenmund.

"Was that your best throw ever?" reporters asked Clemente. He scoffed.

"No," he said impatiently. "Clemente of two or three years ago—he's out."

The second Clemente throw happened in Game 6. The score was tied, and Mark Belanger stood on first. Baltimore's Don Buford rifled a double into the right-field corner. Belanger looked like he would come all the way around to score.

Instead, Clemente fielded the carom and then turned and, with no momentum behind him, fired a throw that still makes the jaw drop. The website FanGraphs put some numbers on it—the ball flew 295 feet and traveled at 98.6 mph—but even those gaudy numbers do not quite capture the awesome feeling of watching it. The baseball bounced a few feet in front of the plate and jumped up to the catcher, like a child greeting a parent returning home from work.

There was no play at the plate. Belanger, who knew a little something about the man in right field for the Pirates, had stopped at third base.

NO. 42:
THE EMBRACE

MAY 13, 1947, CINCINNATI

★ ★ ★ ★ ★

EXT. INFIELD—CROSLEY FIELD—Day

Jackie Robinson moves to his position at first base and begins to throw the ball around the infield. Many in the crowd heap abuse. Pee Wee Reese jogs across the infield from his shortstop position and stands next to Robinson.

> **ROBINSON:** What's up?
>
> **REESE:** They can say what they want. We're here to play baseball.
>
> **ROBINSON:** Just a bunch of crackpots still fighting the Civil War.
>
> **REESE:** Hell, we'd have a won that son of a gun if the cornstalks had held out.

Robinson laughs.

> **ROBINSON:** Better luck next time, Pee Wee.

Reese puts his arm around Jack's shoulder.

> **REESE:** Ain't gonna be a next time. All we got is right now.
>
> **—THE CLIMACTIC SCENE OF THE MOVIE 42**

This is the story of the Embrace, one of the most famous and celebrated moments in baseball history. It has inspired speeches and church sermons and children's books. It is a centerpiece of Ken Burns's documentary *Baseball*. A statue of Pee Wee Reese with his arm around Jackie Robinson stands in Brooklyn.

Here's, perhaps, the most remarkable thing about the Embrace:

We don't even know if it happened.

ON MAY 13, 1947, JACKIE ROBINSON'S BROOKLYN DODGERS went on a road trip to Cincinnati. It was a Tuesday. There was rain that afternoon, but the weather cleared in time for the game. The game itself was unmemorable and, in baseball terms, unimportant. The Dodgers made three errors and lost 7–5. The Reds took two hits away from Robinson with nice defensive plays.

We recall this game for one reason only: It may have been the day that Reese embraced Robinson in the face of a jeering crowd.

Also, it may not have been.

We know that it was a delicate time in the early career of Robinson. This was his 21st game and his first in Cincinnati. Only a week earlier, there had been rumblings of a player strike against Robinson (it was quashed by National League president Ford Frick). *Daily News* columnist Ed Sullivan—yes, the same Ed Sullivan of television fame—reported that Robinson's teammates were treating him badly, "making it tougher on the kid."

Dodgers' president Branch Rickey had just gone public with some of the threatening letters Robinson received and made clear that he was behind Jackie no matter what. "Robinson is our first baseman," he said defiantly. "I hope this ends the matter."

According to legend—and yes, the movie *42*—the embrace happened in the bottom of the first inning. The Dodgers took the field, and the Cincinnati crowd was particularly nasty, directing its racist rage not only at Robinson but also at Reese, who grew up in nearby Louisville and often heard from neighbors and old friends and even family that he should know better than to play ball with a Black man.

That's when, as the story goes, Reese made his move. He had been raised to think of African Americans as inferior. He had grown up in a city where Black kids were not allowed in the park where he played ball or to drink from the water fountain where he drank. He would later admit: "I don't guess that I ever even shook the hand of a Black man."

And yet, in that moment . . .

"Pee Wee went over to him," Dodgers' pitcher Rex Barney told author Peter Golenbock, "and he put an arm around him as if to say: 'This is my boy.'"

"My father," Pee Wee's son Mark Reese said, "listened to his heart and not the chorus."

"His walk across the diamond," Jonathan Eig wrote in his book *Opening Day*, "his embrace of Robinson, would be described years later as one of baseball's most glorious and honorable moments.

"But I don't think it happened," Eig added.

DID IT HAPPEN? WE ARE CHASING GHOSTS NOW. YES, KEN BURNS prominently featured the embrace in his *Baseball* documentary, but as time went on, he became one of the most vehement and outspoken embrace deniers.

"There's no image or write-up anywhere," Burns says.

He's right. Not only is there no contemporary account of the embrace, but *The Cincinnati Enquirer* also took special care to write "Jackie Robinson was applauded every time he stepped to the plate."

Ken Burns concedes that it would be unsurprising for the white press to not mention—or even actively cover up—the Embrace. But there's also no mention of it in the Black press, and Burns insists that if it had happened, "The Black newspapers would have done 15 related articles."

There's more. Robinson's 1948 book about his first season, called *Jackie Robinson: My Own Story*, does not mention the incident, nor does it make any reference to Pee Wee Reese being more supportive than others.*

More: Commissioner Happy Chandler was at the game, and considering that he was both a Kentuckian and a leading champion of Jackie Robinson, you would have expected him to celebrate the Embrace. As far as anyone knows, he never mentioned it.

More still: In 1977, Reese himself wrote a remembrance of Robinson—and he talked about playing cards with him in the clubhouse ("some of the Southern boys resented it," he wrote) but never wrote a word about embracing Robinson during a game.

"We want to feel like white people had something to do with this," Jonathan Eig says, "that we were open-minded and that we saw what was right, and we wanted to make it happen. And Pee Wee Reese is our symbol for that. . . . The myth serves a really nice purpose. Unfortunately, it's a myth."

You can find dozens of similar quotes from people who are convinced it's a myth.

So maybe it didn't happen.

But maybe it did . . .

///

IN 1972–25 YEARS AFTER HE BROKE THE COLOR BARRIER— Jackie Robinson wrote a memoir with his longtime collaborator, Alfred Duckett, called *I Never Had It Made*. He did not say anything about Pee Wee Reese embracing him in Cincinnati in 1947.

But he did write about a strikingly similar moment . . . in Boston in 1948.

---

* In the book, Robinson lists nine teammates he said were "especially nice to me," and Reese is among them.

"In Boston, during a period when the heckling pressure seemed unbearable, some of the players began to heckle Reese," he wrote. "They were riding him about being a Southerner and playing ball with a black man. Pee Wee didn't answer them. Without a glance in their direction, he left his position and walked over to me. He put his hand on my shoulder and began talking to me. His words weren't important. I don't even remember what he said. It was the gesture of comradeship and support that counted. As he stood talking with me with a friendly arm around my shoulder, he was saying loud and clear, 'Yell. Heckle. Do anything you want. We came here to play baseball.' . . . The jeering stopped, and a close and lasting friendship began between Reese and me."

OK. That sounds an awful lot like the Embrace.

Then again, if it happened in 1948, it's still touching, sure, but it's not quite the same thing. By 1948, Robinson was established in the game. There were other Black players, including Dodgers' catcher Roy Campanella. The gesture meant enough to Robinson that he wrote about it many years later but it was not exactly like embracing Robinson at the height of the fight.

And our chase might end here—with the perhaps unsatisfying conclusion that something similar to the Embrace might have happened but the details are all wrong.

Except: When it comes to baseball history, fans will not stop until they know.

And so, instead, the chase ends with one passionate baseball fan named Craig Wright. He is one of the early pioneers of advanced statistics in baseball and, more recently, an author of the excellent collection *Pages from Baseball's Past*. Wright deeply believes that the Embrace did happen. So he dug and dug and, what do you know? He found something.

In 1949, Robinson cowrote a ten-part series about his life for the *Brooklyn Eagle*, a daily afternoon newspaper widely read then. The eighth part is about Robinson's early days with the Dodgers. Here is what Jackie Robinson wrote:

> I'll never forget the day when a few loud-mouthed guys on the other team began to take off on Pee Wee Reese.
>
> They were joshing him very viciously because he was playing on the team with me and was on the field nearby. Mind you, they were not yelling at me; I suppose they did not have the nerve to do that, but they were calling him some very vile names and every one bounced off of Pee Wee and hit me like a machine-gun bullet.
>
> Pee Wee kind of sensed the hopeless, dead feeling in me and came over and stood beside me for a while. He didn't say a word, but he looked over at the chaps who were yelling at me through him and just stared. He was standing by me, I could tell you that.
>
> Slowly the jibes died down like when you kill a snake an inch at a time, and then there was nothing but quiet from them. It was wonderful the way this little guy did it. I will never forget it.

Now, there's no time or place in that story. Some of the details—it was opposing players, not the crowd jeering; Reese did not so much embrace Robinson as stand close to him—are a bit different from the story. But . . . come on. This is the Embrace. Craig was right. It happened.

"I remember Jackie talking about Pee Wee's gesture the day it happened," Robinson's widow, Rachel, said in 2005. "It came as such a relief to him that a teammate and the captain of the team would go out of his way in such a public fashion to express friendship."

So, yes, let's make our stand: It happened. Of course it happened. Maybe it wasn't in Cincinnati, maybe it wasn't a full-on embrace, maybe it was just Pee Wee standing close to his friend. But it happened, something most ordinary and extraordinary, a plain kindness between teammates, a simple gesture from a man raised to be racist toward a Black man he came to admire and love.

"You know," Reese used to say to Robinson, "I didn't particularly go out of my way just to be nice to you."

"Pee Wee," Robinson replied, "maybe that's what I appreciated most—that you didn't."

NO. 41:
PONDEROUS JOE GOES DEEP

AUGUST 31, 1954, ROSWELL, NEW MEXICO

★ ★ ★ ★ ★

In the wide-eyed summer of 1954, that time of Willie Mays and Rocky Marciano and *Brown v. Board of Education* and the miracle of color television—there was a larger-than-life ballplayer in the Pecos River Valley of New Mexico named Joe Bauman. Nobody called him that. It was an era of nicknames, and they called him Boomin' Bauman and Sluggin' Joe, Jarring Joe and Joltin' Joe and Jumbo Joe, the Man Mountain, the Mammoth Man, the Southpaw Swatter, the Roswell Rocketeer, and the Economy-Sized First Sacker.

The nickname that stuck was Ponderous Joe Bauman.

Ponderous? Well, that hardly seems complimentary. Joe didn't seem to mind. He was a laid-back sort. By day, he worked at the Texaco Station he owned along Route 55, and by night he hit long home runs in the Longhorn League. They played wild baseball in the Longhorn, teams like the Sweetwater Spudders and Carlsbad Potashers and Roswell Rockets. The altitude was high, the air was light, and games routinely ended in scores like 21–17 or 18–10. It was a league for sluggers, for big men who hit long home runs while cowboys and farmers whooped and hollered and stuffed dollar bills through the chicken wire for those who hit the longest ones.

Ponderous Joe Bauman usually hit the longest home runs.

Joe Bauman grew up in Welch, Oklahoma, about 13 miles northeast of Mickey Mantle's hometown of Commerce, Oklahoma. Joe grew up with Dale Mitchell, who would play in two World Series for Cleveland. Baseball was in the Oklahoma marrow.

Bauman was a 6-foot-4, 250-pound man by the time he was in high school. He was a natural righty, but his father, Joe Sr., taught him to hit and throw left-handed. Joe signed a baseball contract with the Brooklyn Dodgers at 19, went to play for their affiliate in Newport, Arkansas, and then in 1941, he went to war.

After being discharged from the Navy, Bauman married his high school sweetheart, Dorothy, and went to Amarillo to play baseball. He was not dreamy-eyed about the game. It was a way to make a living. He hit 48 home runs. He used the fans' tip money to buy himself a used Buick.

In 1949, the Braves offered him a contract so embarrassingly low that Bauman told them: "I can make more money selling 27-inch shoelaces in Oklahoma City." He quit professional baseball, bought a gas station back home, and picked up a few extra bucks hitting long home runs in semipro leagues around town.

Then in 1952, a doctor—Bauman never even remembered his name—showed up at Joe's filling station and said he'd heard about Bauman's hitting power. He offered Joe a chance to play for a baseball team called the Drillers in Artesia, New Mexico. Bauman declined until the doctor offered the princely sum of $600 a month with the promise that he could get a lot more from people shoving money through the chain-link fence. Bauman decided to go.

And it's fair to say that Artesia, New Mexico—heck, all of New Mexico—had never seen anyone quite like Ponderous Joe Bauman. He was a seasoned baseball veteran in a league filled with local kids just hoping to get noticed. That first year, Bauman hit .375 with a league-record 50 home runs.

He liked it so much—and made so much fence money—that he stuck around Artesia and hit 53 more home runs the next year. He made enough to buy himself a new car.

Then Bauman bought out his contract and moved forty miles west to Roswell to play for the Roswell Rockets. He was 32 years old. Bauman bought a Texaco station in Roswell and prepared to take dead aim at Roswell's inviting right-field fence, painted white, which stood a mere 324 feet from home plate.

///

PONDEROUS JOE BAUMAN BEGAN HITTING HOME RUNS RIGHT away. On April 22, he crushed two homers against Carlsbad. Three days later he mashed two more against Odessa. In all, he hit 10 home runs in Roswell's first 11 games.

Teams used extreme measures to stop him. The Big Springs' manager, Pepper Martin,* put all eight defenders he had on the right side of the field, five of them in the outfield. For one day, that seemed to put Bauman on pause.

The next day, though, Bauman hit two more home runs.

He had twenty home runs barely a month into the season, a ridiculous pace. And each of the home runs had an epic quality. On May 23, in Odessa, Texas, there was a rodeo in progress on the grounds outside the stadium. Bauman hit the ball 500 feet into that rodeo. His teammate Tom Brookshier—who was a pro football star and would later become the announcing voice of pro football for CBS—would later say that the rodeo was halted, and all the cowboys took off their hats and waved them around and hollered for Joe.

He cracked seven homers in eight games in early June. On Independence Day he hit his 36th homer, and people began talking about the impossible: Joe Bauman might hit 70 home runs in a single season! As far as anybody knew, that had never happened before, not in the major leagues and not in the minors, either.† The minor league record of 69

---

* This is not the Pepper Martin who was an All-Star for the Gas House Gang Cardinals in the 1930s.

† In truth, it surely *had* happened before—in the Negro Leagues. It is believed that Josh Gibson hit 84 home runs in a single season.

was set by a guy named Joe Hauser in 1933 and tied by Bob Crues in Amarillo in '48.

Bauman did not want to talk about hitting 70 home runs.

"Good God!" he yelped when a reporter asked him about it. But then he hit four more in a series against Big Spring, another one against Sweetwater, a couple more against Carlsbad, and he was up to 45 home runs with almost half the season left.

"I'm not hitting for the fences any more than usual," Bauman insisted. "In fact, I'm playing just about as I usually do. No changes in swing. No changes in stance. Just no change."

"So why are you hitting so many homers?" he was asked.

"I've been pretty lucky," he said.

Teams tried everything. Bauman did not like hitting against left-handed pitchers, so teams tried to pitch left-handers. Unfortunately, there was not that much left-handed pitching in the Longhorn, so managers would bring in lefty outfielders and lefty first basemen to pitch. In Sweetwater, the story goes, the manager Albert McCarty called out to the crowd to ask if anyone in the stands threw left-handed.

Also, Ponderous Joe almost never saw a fastball. Instead, he saw curveballs and changeups and knuckleballs and spitballs and mud balls and slop balls and a wide variety of unidentifiable pitches. Those pitches were rarely over the plate. Bauman walked 110 times in his first 110 games.

"I haven't seen anything but junk," he complained in early August after four straight games without a homer.

As the season went on, it did seem that the anti-Bauman strategies were beginning to wear him down. He did hit his 54th homer on August 10th—breaking the league home run record for the third year in a row—but now there were only twenty-seven games left. And the pressure, the attention, the constant cameras pointing at him, the unrealistic expectations from fans that he would hit a home run every time up—all of it was weighing on him.

What could he do? He kept swinging. By the end of August, he had 64 home runs.

He needed to hit six home runs in seven games to break the record.

Joe Bauman told his friends that the chase was over.

NOW WE COME TO THE DAY, AUGUST 31, 1954. ROSWELL WAS playing Sweetwater, far and away the worst team in the Longhorn. In front of a huge Roswell crowd, he led off the second inning with a home run. That was No. 65. He hit another one in the fifth. Two home runs! People were shoving dollars bills through the fence so fast he could hardly grab them all.

In the sixth inning, he came up with two runners on. He homered again.

And in the seventh inning, one more time, he came up with two runners on. And yes, he homered for the fourth time. By best estimates, he collected more than $500 in fence money that game. And he had 68 home runs with six games left to play. The record suddenly seemed assured.

Bauman wasn't so sure. For the first time since he was young, he felt nervous playing baseball. The next day, he hit a ferocious line drive off the top of the fence; it missed being a home run by inches. He uncharacteristically cursed his bad fortune even as the crowd pushed more than $600 through the fence.

The next night, the last home game of the season, he hit his 69th home run, tying the minor league record. "It felt good," he told the swarm of reporters that closed in on him after the game. When they asked him if he might try, once again, to climb his way up to the big leagues, he said: "Nah. I've got my filling station here. I'll probably play the rest of my ball right here in Roswell."

Roswell traveled to Big Spring, Texas, where Bauman's old nemesis Pepper Martin ordered his pitchers to not throw any strikes. They obliged, and the Big Spring crowd—"a mess of pants and big arms,"

Tom Brookshier would call them—cheered lustily as Bauman swung at terrible pitches in the hopes of connecting with just one of them. He left Big Spring stuck on 69 homers.

That left two games for Bauman—a doubleheader in Artesia. Bauman was sick with worry, but before the game, he got the best news he could imagine. Artesia's manager Jimmy Adair walked over and put an arm on Bauman's shoulder.

"Joe," he said, "we're going to try to get you out today. We're not going to walk you."

That was all Joe ever wanted. The Artesia starter was a 22-year-old kid named José Gallardo—barely 5-foot-9, skinny as a rail. Best anyone can tell, that was the only year Gallardo played professional baseball.

Joe Bauman was the first batter of the game. Gallardo—as promised—did not walk him. Instead, he threw a fastball right down the middle of the plate. It was the sort of pitch Joe Bauman saw in his happiest dreams.

Some papers called it a 365-foot home run. Others insisted it went more than 400 feet. Either way, it went far enough. That was home run No. 70, the all-time minor league record. Ponderous Joe Bauman ran happily around the bases, feeling light and alive.

In the second game of the doubleheader, with all the pressure gone, Joe Bauman hit two more home runs—one of them off José Gallardo's uncle Frank. That gave him 72 for the season. A fan chased down the last baseball and proudly displayed it on his mantel. Years later, the fan would donate the ball to the Roswell Museum, which built a Joe Bauman exhibition. When someone asked Bauman if he ever went to the museum to see the ball he hit, he shrugged and said, "Naw, what would I do that for?"

PONDEROUS JOE BAUMAN WAS MILDLY FAMOUS FOR A TIME. HIS feat was recorded across the country in hundreds of papers. Some offers came in for him to change teams. But he was true to his word: He and Dorothy stayed in Roswell for the rest of his life. He played ball for a couple more years—hitting 63 more home runs—then sold his Texaco station and worked for a Budweiser beer distributorship.

In 2001, Barry Bonds broke Mark McGwire's single-season home run record when he hit his 71st home run. Two days later, he hit his 73rd home run to break Bauman's overall record. A few people called Joe Bauman to ask what he thought.

"It didn't bother me or anything," Bauman said. "I just thought, *There goes my record.*"

FIVE
MELTDOWNS

Meltdowns are a wonderful part of baseball. Hey, it's an emotional game. I've seen a couple of them up close, one in particular when I wrote something in a Kansas City newspaper column that a fine relief pitcher (and generally good fellow) named Jeff Montgomery did not particularly like. The next day, he pulled me aside into a hallway, his hand wrapped with a towel, as if he was going to club me senseless, and for the next 15 minutes (or six hours, it was hard to tell), he proceeded to air me out like no one ever had before or since. It was the maddest I've ever seen a human being.

And while, no, it wasn't my happiest moment, I will say that after the first unsettling couple of minutes, I did manage to sort of take in the full glory of the moment. *Wow,* I remember thinking at some point as if I were an observer watching from above, *this guy is SUPER angry.*

Jeff and I have laughed about it since. Hey, it happens. Baseball is an emotional game.

"THERE'S NO CRYING IN BASEBALL" (1992, MOVIE *A LEAGUE OF THEIR OWN*)

In *A League of Their Own*, Tom Hanks's Jimmy Dugan—loosely based on the slugger Jimmie Foxx—did not want to manage a women's baseball team. He needed the money. But slowly the women won him over with their baseball skill and enthusiasm and he started to get into the games and into his managerial role.

Then Evelyn, the team's right fielder, overthrew the cutoff person. You probably know what comes next.

> **JIMMY:** Hey, Evelyn, can I ask you a question? You got a moment?
>
> **EVELYN:** Mmm-hmm.
>
> **JIMMY:** Which team do you play for?
>
> **EVELYN:** Well, I'm a [Rockford] Peach.
>
> **JIMMY:** Well, I was just wondering 'cause I couldn't figure out why you would throw home when we've got a two-run lead! You let the tying run get on second and we lost the lead because of you! Now you start using your head! That's that lump that's three feet above your ass!
>
> *Evelyn starts crying.*
>
> **JIMMY:** Are you crying?
>
> **EVELYN:** No.
>
> **JIMMY:** Are you crying?
>
> **EVELYN:** No.
>
> **JIMMY:** Are you crying? There's no crying! There's no crying in baseball!
>
> **DORIS:** Why don't you leave her alone, Jimmy?
>
> **JIMMY:** Oh, you zip it, Doris. [To Evelyn]: Rogers Hornsby was my manager. And he called me a talking pile of pig shit!

And that was when my parents drove all the way down from Michigan just to see me play the game! And did I cry?

EVELYN: No. No.

JIMMY: No. And you know why?

EVELYN: No.

JIMMY: Because there's no crying in baseball! There's no crying in baseball! No crying!

ROGER CLEMENS THROWS BAT AT MIKE PIAZZA (OCTOBER 22, 2000)

Sometimes I will still find myself in awe of this simple fact: Roger Clemens really did throw a sharp shard of broken baseball bat at Mike Piazza during a World Series game. That has to be one of the weirdest things that has ever happened in sports history.

And nothing happened. Nothing. Sure, the benches tentatively cleared, but there was no fight. Clemens stayed in the game. Piazza stayed in the game. After, like, two minutes, the game just went on like nothing happened.

The guy threw a baseball bat at an opponent!

And nothing happened. It still boggles the mind.

It went down like this: Game 2, and it was the very first inning. Clemens—who, oh, by the way, had hit Piazza in the head with a pitch just two months earlier—threw an inside fastball and Piazza swung and his bat shattered, sending the fat part of the bat toward Clemens.

Clemens picked it up and instantly fired it exactly where Piazza was running up the first-base line.

And here's what Clemens shouted: "I thought it was the ball."

Nobody knew what this was supposed to mean. He thought it was the ball? How does that make any sense at all? Who thinks a bat is a ball? And even if it were a ball, why did he throw it at Piazza? Nobody knew.

But that was Clemens's defense, and he stuck with it, and like I say, nothing happened. After the game, Yankees' manager Joe Torre even defended Clemens using the same language. "He thought it was the ball," Torre said. What? It's like everyone was caught up in the madness.

A few days later, Clemens quietly was fined $50,000. He gave that money to charity. It feels like we baseball fans should never ever stop talking about the time Clemens threw a bat at Piazza in the World Series but nobody talks about it. It's so weird.

PHILLIP WELLMAN "LOSES HIS MIND" (JUNE 1, 2007)

Phillip Wellman was content being a baseball lifer. He was a pretty good baseball player growing up in Marlin, Texas, good enough to make it up, briefly, to Class AA. But one day he was at Pittsburgh's spring training, and he looked around at the Pirates' outfielders—including a young Barry Bonds and Andy Van Slyke—and realized, yeah, he probably wasn't going to be a Major Leaguer. He began managing in the minor leagues shortly after that.

He was a pretty good minor league manager, too. Then in 2007, in what should have been just another game, he was managing the Mississippi Braves—Atlanta's Class AA team—against the Chattanooga Lookouts when he found himself griping about ball-strike calls with home plate umpire Brent Rice. A manager isn't allowed to do that. Rice threw him out of the game.

To this day, Wellman doesn't know exactly what came over him next.

He began his protest by throwing his baseball cap at Rice's feet. After a few broadly comical gestures—including holding his hands apart to show just how much Rice had missed the pitch by—Wellman walked over to home plate and began covering it with dirt. After that, he got down on one knee and patted down the dirt on the plate, like he was planting tomatoes.

He was only just getting started. He was no longer angry, exactly. It was more like, hey, he was getting thrown out of the game anyway, and he was mid-rant, so he decided to go all in.

Wellman walked back to the home plate umpire, said a passing word, then went to yell at the third-base umpire. He pulled third base out of the ground, walked a few steps, and threw it into the outfield. He walked toward the pitcher's mound and, halfway there, fell to the ground and began crawling on his stomach, like a soldier hoping to go undetected. When he got to the mound, he grabbed the rosin bag, pulled an imaginary pin from it like it was a grenade, and launched it toward Rice. His aim was true; the bag landed just a foot in front of Rice and sprayed rosin over his pants.

Wellman continued yelling and continued pantomiming his rage. He yanked second base out of the ground, picked up third base, and walked off with them. Before he left through a gate in the outfield wall, he turned back to the cheering crowd and blew them kisses.

"I let my passion get the best of me," he said a decade later. I'll say it again: Baseball is an emotional game. As I write these words, Phillip Wellman manages the San Antonio Missions of the Double A Texas League.

"WHAT'S MY OPINION OF KINGMAN'S PERFORMANCE?" (MAY 14, 1978)

The Chicago Cubs beat the Los Angeles Dodgers 10–7, thanks mainly to their slugger Dave Kingman, who hit three home runs and drove in eight RBIs.

After the game, a Los Angeles radio reporter named Paul Olden asked Dodgers' manager Tommy Lasorda a straightforward question: "What's your opinion of Kingman's performance?"

Lasorda's reply is now a part of baseball lore. I will use the word *honk* in place of, er, other words.

"What's my opinion of Kingman's performance? What the honk do you think is my opinion of it? It was honking honk, put that in! I don't honk . . . opinion of his performance? Jesus Christ, he beat us with three honking home runs. What the honk do you mean, 'What is my opinion of his performance?' How can you ask me a question like that?

"What is my opinion of his performance? Jesus Christ, he hit three home runs. Jesus Christ. I'm honking honked off to lose a honking game and you ask me my opinion of his performance. Jesus Christ. I mean that's a tough question to ask me, isn't it?"

Olden: "Yes, it is. I asked it, and you gave me an answer."

THE LEE ELIA RANT (APRIL 29, 1983)

The biggest Cubs fan I know is a guy named Steve Hirschtick. He lives in a small village somewhere in Thailand—he doesn't like giving out the exact location because he doesn't want people to bother him—and a few years ago, he built his own Wrigley Field.

Steve's Wrigley Field is a sight to behold; it was built by local villagers who had absolutely no idea what they were building. They thought it was a religious structure of some kind. For Steve, it is exactly that.

One of the features of Steve's Wrigley Field is a plaque with the entire Lee Elia rant from 1983.

The Cubs got off to a terrible start in 1983, not unlike most every other year. On a Friday night, in front of 9,391 fans, they blew a lead and lost to the Dodgers. And when it was time to talk to reporters after the game, manager Lee Elia knew just who to blame: Cubs fans.

In this rant, we'll replace some of the words with *quack*.

"All these so-called Cubs fans," Elia began. "I'll tell you one quacking thing. I hope we get quacking hotter than quack just to stuff it up them 3,000 quacking people that show up every quacking day. Because if they're the real Chicago quacking fans, they can kiss my quacking quack right downtown . . . and PRINT IT!

"They're really, really behind you around here . . . my quacking quack!

What the quack am I supposed to do, go out there and let my quacking players get destroyed every day and be quiet about it for the quacking nickel, dime people that show up. The quacking quackers don't even work. That's why they're out at the quacking game. They ought to go out and get a quacking job and find out what it's like to go out and earn a quacking living."

And then, the big finish:

"Eighty-five percent of the quacking world is working. The other fifteen come out here. A quacking playground for the quack quackers."

Elia, remarkably, managed the Cubs for another three months. When he finally got fired in August, he explained himself like so: "My biggest problem is that I might have wanted to win too badly."

NO. 40:
THE PINE TAR HOMER

JULY 24, 1983, BRONX

★ ★ ★ ★ ★

The place: Yankee Stadium.

The game: A Sunday-afternoon matchup between two raging rivals, the Kansas City Royals and the New York Yankees.

The emotions: The Royals' and Yankees' players hated one another; the managers hated each other; the owners were not fond of each other, either. There were many reasons for this, but the main one was that the Royals and Yankees had faced each other in the American League Championship Series four times in the previous eight seasons. The Yankees broke the Royals' hearts three straight years, leaving scars in Kansas City that, in some ways, still have not healed. Then the Royals beat the Yankees in 1980, three straight games, sending Yankees' owner George Steinbrenner into hysterics. He bullied his manager Dick Howser into quitting.

Dick Howser went to manage the Kansas City Royals.

The pitcher: The mustachioed closer, Richard "Goose" Gossage. They called him Goose because of the way he stuck out his neck when looking for the catcher's signs. He was 6-foot-3 and one of the hardest-throwing pitchers who ever lived. While other pitchers threw hard without seeming to exert much effort, Gossage's delivery was a whirlwind of effort and grunts and spite—leg going one way, arm another, eyes never on the target.

"He looks like he's falling out of a tree," said his minor league coach Larry Sherry. "And all limbs are coming at you."

Beyond that: The Goose was mean. He hated everybody he faced. He would get so full of rage and hunger on the mound that his eyes would bulge, his face would contort, and he would feel a thousand hearts beating all over his body.

"I'm like some animal," Goose would say. "I don't know, it's scary. I swear, I scare myself sometimes. I can't believe it's me."

The hitter: The Royals' George Brett. He was only 30 years old, but already everybody knew he was going to the Hall of Fame. In 1980, he almost hit .400—five hits shy. In the 1980 playoffs, when the Royals finally overcame the Yankees, it was clinched by Brett turning around a fastball from, yes, Goose Gossage and planting it in the Yankee Stadium upper deck.

If meanness was Goose Gossage's secret sauce, then fear was the power behind George Brett. He began every game desperately afraid of . . . well, everything. Would he embarrass himself out there? Would he let his teammates down? Would his father, Jack, call him after the game and tell him again that he was no good, that he was wasting his talent, that he had quit on the team and himself?

As the game went on, though, Brett converted that fear into hunger. Nobody played harder. Nobody played with more of an edge. And in the biggest moments, nobody came through more often. Brett did not wear batting gloves, and he painted black under his eyes, and he dared anyone—anyone—to challenge him.

Goose Gossage's fastball?

Bring it on, $&#@#.

"The harder they throw it," he said, "the more I like it."

The manager: The Yankees' manager was a hard-drinking, cigar-smoking, womanizing bantamweight named Billy Martin, who ended so many blurry nights in a fight that it may be easier to name the nights when he didn't get into one.

Martin had been fired by Yankees owner George Steinbrenner twice, and Steinbrenner would fire him three more times, including at the end of the 1983 season. Getting fired was a Martin specialty; he would be fired nine times by five different owners, once for insisting that the music director play John Denver's "Thank God I'm a Country Boy" during the seventh-inning stretch instead of "Take Me Out to the Ball Game."

Another time he was fired after ordering his pitchers to throw spitballs.

Another time he was fired after getting into a fight with his best pitcher outside a bar.

Another time he was fired after getting into a fight with a marshmallow salesman.

To get fired nine times, though, you also have to be hired nine times. Martin was indeed a baseball savant. He had a knack for devising unexpected strategies and finding loopholes in the rules. Foreshadowing.

The home plate umpire: Tim McClelland was in his first full season as an umpire; this was the first time he'd ever been behind home plate for a game at Yankee Stadium, which is a bit like the first time someone performs at Carnegie Hall.

If he was nervous, however, no one saw it. He was a stone-faced and deliberate presence, letting his 6-foot-6 frame speak for itself. They sometimes called him Rain Delay McClelland because of how slowly he made his calls.

The bat: An ash 34½-inch, 32-ounce Hillerich & Bradsby Model T85. The Hillerich in the name was for Bud Hillerich, who in 1885 was in the stands for a game in Louisville when a ballplayer named Pete Browning broke his bat. Hillerich offered to make him a better one, and with the new bat, Browning went on a hitting spree. Soon the other players wanted Hillerich bats.

Pete Browning's nickname was the Louisville Slugger, so that was the name of the company that Hillerich founded. Frank Bradsby helped him build it into the biggest bat company in the world.

The T in T85 stands for Throneberry, as in Marvelous Marv Throneberry, the anti-legendary Met who once had a triple taken away from him because, in his base-running haste, he missed first base *and* second base.

The rule: "The bat handle, for not more than 18 inches from its end, may be covered or treated with any material or substance to improve the grip. Any such material, including pine tar, which extends past the 18-inch limitation, in the umpire's judgment, shall cause the bat to be removed from the game."

This rule came into being because of the Minnesota Twins' cheapskate owner named Calvin Griffith. He was mad that the pine tar on bats were staining so many baseballs. *Hey, baseballs do not grow on trees!*

The situation: The Yankees led 4–3, the Royals had a runner on first, and there were two outs in the ninth.

And now you're ready for the moment.

Brett stepped in. Gossage stared.

The at-bat lasted two pitches.

Pitch 1: Gossage threw a high outside fastball. Brett smashed it foul.

Pitch 2: Gossage threw a high inside fastball. He later said he was aiming for Brett's neck. Brett somehow turned on the ball and knocked it over the right-field wall for a home run. Kansas City had the lead.

"Hitting a home run on *that* pitch," Brett would tell me years later, "is one of the most ridiculous things I've ever done. I look back at that one and go, 'How did I hit that ball out?'"

As Brett triumphantly rounded the bases, Billy Martin unfurled his devious plan. He came out of the dugout and screamed that the bat was illegal—it had way too much pine tar on it. In perfect synchronization, Yankees' catcher Rick Cerone grabbed the bat from the Royals' bat boy so he could show it to McClelland.

When we look back at the video now, it plays out like a silent movie. Martin's pointing and yelling. McClelland's holding the bat and pondering. Brett is back in the dugout pacing and wondering what the heck they are talking about. And Royals' manager Dick Howser is . . . nowhere. You can't even find him in the picture. It's bizarre. Why didn't he go out there?

As the umpires gathered and considered the bat much in the way that

Talmudic scholars pondered passages from the Torah, Brett turned to teammate Frank White: "If they call me out for using too much pine tar," he said, "I'll run out there and kill one of those sons of bitches."

The umpires quickly realized that the bat had too much pine tar, but McClelland wanted to do it by the book. The rule said that pine tar could not cover the bat for more than 18 inches. Home plate is a 17-inch box. McClelland came up with the bright idea of laying the bat parallel to home plate. This was the most dramatic part.

And once he saw that the pine tar went well past the 18-inch mark, he made the ruling of the ages. He took three steps toward the Royals' dugout, pointed the bat handle directly at Brett, raised his right hand as if signaling a right turn, and then clenched his fist.

George Brett was out.

You've seen the reaction, I'm sure. Brett lost his mind and tore out of the dugout, arms flailing, face glowing, looking for all the world like a bull charging in Pamplona. He saw only red and the giant body of Tim McClelland.

"It really wouldn't have been that bad," Brett told me. "I would have just screamed at him for a minute and waved my arms around. I wouldn't have touched him."

Maybe not. We'll never know because umpire Joe Brinkman—"A great friend of mine," Brett says—grabbed Brett, pulled him away, and even choked him a little bit.

The game was over. But the story had only just begun.

The Royals put the game under protest. Normally, protests have virtually no chance of success, but a couple of Royals' front office people had read the rule carefully and realized that Martin and McClelland had misread things. It didn't say anything about calling the batter out for using a bat with too much pine tar. All it said was that if, in the umpire's judgment, that bat had too much pine tar, it was to be removed from the game.

Martin had outsmarted himself. If he wanted to have the bat removed, he would have had to protest *before* Brett hit. But he didn't.

McClelland, meanwhile, had confused two rules. If Brett had used a *doctored* bat—which is to say a bat "altered to improve the reaction or distance factor of the bat"—yes, he would have been out. But nobody ever thought that pine tar improved the bat.

Brett's home run had to count.

And that's exactly what American League president Lee MacPhail ruled. He released a statement that basically said, "Come on, guys, it's just pine tar." And at the end, he added a line specifically for Billy Martin:

"I don't blame the Yankees for doing what they did, and I admire them for being so diligent in their pursuit of the rules."

THE GAME HAD TO BE CONTINUED—THERE WERE STILL FOUR outs left—and McPhail scheduled the finish on August 18. The Yankees took it to court; their lawyer was none other than the infamous Roy Cohn, whose argument was that if the game was continued, there might be a riot at Yankee Stadium. That didn't exactly hold up to legal scrutiny. The decision of Justice Joseph P. Sullivan, the longest-serving Appellate Division justice in the history of New York, was just two words: Play ball.

There were no riots. Heck, almost nobody even came—there were only 1,245 fans in attendance. The teams took the field, a new umpiring crew came out, and the whole thing lasted 12 minutes. In that time, Billy Martin tried numerous stunts. He put pitcher Ron Guidry in center field. He put lefty first baseman Don Mattingly at second base, the first time in 25 years that any team had played a left-handed second baseman.

Martin also tried to get Jerry Mumphrey to come back. Mumphrey had been in the lineup on the original date but had since been traded to Houston. Mumphrey, alas, refused.

The Royals' reliever Dan Quisenberry entered the ninth and put down the Yankees in order to end the game.

There was one more wonderful twist that I just have to mention. During those 12 minutes in August, Billy Martin had reliever George Frazier appeal, claiming Brett had missed first base during his home run trot. When that appeal was denied, Frazier threw to second base, claiming that Brett missed that bag, too. Again, the appeal was denied.

Then Billy Martin, in all his puffed-up glory, stormed out of the dugout and demanded to know how a brand-new umpiring crew could know whether Brett had touched the bases.

With that, new home plate umpire Dave Phillips calmly pulled out a piece of paper and handed it to Martin. It was a notarized affidavit from the previous umpiring crew stating unequivocally that Brett had touched all the bases. They had outsmarted the master.

NO. 39:
STRIKING OUT SADAHARU OH

SEPTEMBER 17, 1968, NEAR KOBE
IN NISHINOMIYA, HYOGO PREFECTURE, JAPAN

★ ★ ★ ★ ★

Here's how my Yutaka Enatsu feature film would begin: It is 1985. Florida. Yutaka Enatsu, a paunchy 37-year-old left-handed pitcher, shows up for his Milwaukee Brewers spring training invitation. He is attempting to become the first Japanese player in the major leagues in two decades, but American reporters barely notice him. What's to notice? He's out of shape. His fastball lacks the first syllable of the word.

"He throws strikes," Brewers' manager George Bamberger says charitably, reminiscent of the time that college football coach Bill Dooley, when trying to think of something magnanimous to say about an overmatched opponent, said, "William & Mary has the finest long snapper I've ever seen."

So no, there's nothing particularly interesting about Yutaka Enatsu.

Except for this: Japanese reporters treat him like he's Elvis, Wilt Chamberlain, and all four Beatles rolled up in one. They shadow his every move. "There are three or four film crews recording his every pitch," the Associated Press reports.

Why do they treat him like royalty? a couple of curious American reporters ask. They learn that Enatsu was once a great pitcher in Japan—"the Walter Johnson of Japan," one Japanese reporter explained. The curosity doesn't go very far, however. It is 1985, and being a great player in Japan simply doesn't interest an American audience; this is long before Ichiro and Hideo Nomo and Shohei. This is at a time when Japanese baseball is considered inferior—when it is considered at all.

As for Enatsu himself, well, he sounds like a man who had done things in his life. When asked if he will learn English to be part of the team, he says flatly through an interpreter: "I came here to play baseball, not to learn the English language."

He is released after only a couple of weeks. And my final shot of the movie's opening scene is of Yutaka Enatsu leaving camp, all the Japanese reporters leaving with him, Brewers' spring training going on as if nothing had happened, and nobody realizing that they had just missed one of the most remarkable players in the history of the sport.

A FEW YEARS AGO, I HAD A FAMOUS EDITOR WHOSE FAVORITE word in the English language was *badass*. He thought it most descriptive and encouraged his writers to use it every chance they could.

Well, Yutaka Enatsu was badass. They called him Lone Wolf—a nickname that was especially flamboyant in a Japanese culture that prized modesty and teamwork—and in his colorful and checkered career and life, he was accused of being connected to the Japanese mafia, he was sent to prison on drug charges, and he struck out more batters than anyone, ever.

How good was he? Well, let's put it this way: He played in the Japanese All-Star Game in 1971, 1972, and 1973. He pitched a total of five innings in those games, going up against the very best Japanese hitters of the time. He struck out all 15 batters he faced.

Hall of Famer Red Schoendienst called him one of the best left-handed pitchers he'd ever seen and said that his own teammate Steve Carlton might learn a thing or two from him.

"At his best," said former Yankees' third baseman Clete Boyer, who had finished his career in Japan, "he was as good as anyone I've ever faced, and that includes Bob Gibson."

Enatsu was not tall—listed at 5-foot-10—and he did not have an es-pecially athletic physique even in his younger days. But he did have two awesome pitches: a rising fastball that, best estimate, he threw in the upper 90s and a 12-to-6 curveball that, as the scouts would say, dropped off a table.

Those, incidentally, were the same two pitches that made Sandy Kou-fax all but unhittable.

Koufax's old teammate Jim Lefebvre called Enatsu another Sandy Koufax.

ENATSU HAD TWO BASEBALL MOMENTS THAT ARE SO STAGGERINGLY awesome, I simply could not choose between them. The Enatsu conun-drum grew to the point where finally, at a dinner in a New York Greek restaurant with friends, I stopped the conversation and asked my friends Ellen, Eric, and Alexis to choose for me.

It was April 30, 1973. Enatsu was pitching for Hanshin against the Chunichi Dragons. He pitched nine no-hit innings.

Unfortunately, Hanshin didn't score in those nine innings, so the game went into the 10th. Enatsu threw another hitless in-ning. But once again, Hanshin failed to score. Enatsu was getting annoyed.

He went back out in the 11th inning and once again held the Chu-nichi batters hitless. This was the longest no-hitter in Japanese history, but this was not Enatsu's concern. He wanted the game to end already. He was not a good hitter, typically, but he'd had enough. He stepped to the plate and hit the walk-off home run—the sayonara home run, as they call it Japan—and won the game.

"I guess one man can win a baseball game by himself," he was quoted saying.

That's pretty good, right?

That's the one my friends *did not* choose.

IN 1968, ENATSU FULLY DEVELOPED HIS CURVEBALL. THAT'S THE pitch that turned him into a strikeout whirlwind. He struck out 401 batters that season, more than even Nolan Ryan or Randy Johnson ever managed.

In September, it became clear that he was going to break the Japanese strikeout record of 353, but being Yutaka Enatsu, he wanted to make it especially memorable. He guaranteed that he would break the record against Hanshin's great rival, the three-time champion Yomiuri Giants.

And even more: He guaranteed that his record-breaking strikeout would be Sadaharu Oh, the greatest player in all of Japan, the man who, to this day, is considered the most glorious Japanese player of them all. Oh had been named the league's MVP three of the previous four seasons and had led the Japanese League in home runs every single year since 1962.

The timing worked out. On September 17, 1968, Hanshin played Yomiuri, with Enatsu needing just seven strikeouts to break the record. It was stiflingly hot. There were 55,000 people in the stands. Enatsu struck out Oh in the first inning. When Oh came up again in the fourth inning, the record was on the line.

Enatsu set him up with curves and then blew a high fastball by Oh for strike three. The record was his alone!

Only, it wasn't. He had miscounted. Or anyway, that's the version I like best.* Oh was his sixth strikeout of the game; he had only *tied* the record. Enatsu, after grasping the situation, made an announcement to

---

* According to other versions, he had decided before the game that he wanted Oh to not only be the player he struck out to *break* the record but also the player he struck out to *tie* the record.

his teammates. Nothing had changed. He would still strike out Oh for the record.

To do that, he would simply let everybody in the lineup make contact until Sadaharu Oh came up again.

I mean—remember that word *badass*? This was a key game in the pennant race. This was a rivalry game. The game was scoreless. But Enatsu did things his own way. And you know what he did? Right: He purposely pitched to contact for the next EIGHT BATTERS.

His stuff was so dominant that even when letting guys hit the ball, he allowed only one hit.

Then finally Oh was up again. Now Enatsu had to finish the job and again strike out the great Sadaharu Oh. Of this, Enatsu had no doubt. Enatsu got ahead in the count 1-2. Then he readied himself, rocked back, and fired a high fastball that blew right by Sadaharu Oh. Enatsu bowed his head in triumph. He had the strikeout record. He still has the record to this day.

How good would Yutaka Enatsu have been in the Major Leagues? We'll never know for sure, but I think it's a pretty good bet that he would have been a star. He had the stuff. But more, he had that something else.

By the way, the game stayed scoreless for 11 innings. Enatsu himself delivered the game-winning single in the 12th.

NO. 38:

"NO WAY I WAS COMING OUT"

OCTOBER 27, 1991, MINNEAPOLIS

★ ★ ★ ★ ★

If you're lucky enough to go to Cooperstown, New York, on the weekend when they induct players into the Baseball Hall of Fame, you probably will see them walking together, Jack Morris and John Smoltz, combatants in the greatest Game 7 duel in the history of the World Series.

They are uncannily alike, Morris and Smoltz, both right-handed, both 6-foot-3, both power pitchers, both from the Upper Midwest. They each, at different times, led their league in wins and innings and strikeouts and wild pitches. They were both pitching bulldogs who would rather eat dirt than come out of a game before it was over.

They both had mustaches.*

But there was something else connecting them, something deep and timeless: Smoltz grew up in Michigan idolizing Morris. "Jack was a guy I watched closely," Smoltz would tell reporters the day before Game 7. "He was a big idol for me. I copied his motion, had it down perfectly. . . . But I copied everything. I tried to go after every hitter the way he did. He was so fierce out there. He battled you on every pitch. I wanted to be just like that."

And Jack Morris's reaction to Smoltz's hero worship?

"I don't want to hear that crap," he told reporters. "That makes me feel old."

---

* As time went on, Smoltz grew his mustache out to a fuller beard.

KIRBY PUCKETT HAD SINGLE-HANDEDLY FORCED GAME 7 IN THE 1991 World Series. He tripled in the first inning, driving in a run, and then came around to score. He made a dazzling leaping catch at the wall on a Ron Gant blast that saved at least one run. Then, at 11:04 P.M. local time in Minneapolis, he stepped to the plate, shut out the manic cheers of the 55,000 people who had stuffed into the Metrodome, and smashed the game-winning home run.

Every Twins fan can recite announcer Jack Buck's call: "Into deep left center. . . . And we'll see you tomorrow night!"

Yes, well, tomorrow night was Game 7, Morris vs. Smoltz.

"How will I pitch?" Morris said back to the reporter who asked him. "I'm not God. I'm not infallible."

Infallible, no. Irascible? Irritable? Yes. He threw his first pitch to Lonnie Smith at 7:38 P.M. Home plate umpire Don Denkinger dared call it a ball. Morris glared hard at Denkinger and for a long time. First pitch.

"He was the last of a breed, somebody who actually comes to the park with anger to beat you," his old Detroit manager Sparky Anderson told *Sports Illustrated*. "I never went near him when it was his day to pitch."

Morris breezed through the first inning, one, two, three.

John Smoltz took the mound. He was just 24 years old then—twelve years younger than Morris—but he was already beginning his own Morris-like reputation. He had pitched three times in those playoffs, and Atlanta had won all three games, including Game 7 of the National League Championship Series against Pittsburgh, when Smoltz threw a six-hit shutout.

Smoltz had expected to feel some nerves, but incredibly he did not. He had napped in the clubhouse before the game. Somehow the pressure relaxed him. He just loved the feeling of a big game. "That," he says, "is where I always felt my best."

Smoltz breezed through the first inning, one, two, three.

And the duel was on.

Things were not easy for Morris in the next few innings. His best pitch, the split-fingered fastball, was not dropping the way he liked. Atlanta put runners in scoring position in four consecutive innings. Morris worked his way out of danger each time.

"Sure, I was a confident pitcher," he says. "But there was something extra special about that day. The Twins could have loaded the bases with nobody out every inning, and it wouldn't have mattered. They were not scoring. That was my mindset."

Smoltz had it easier. The Twins did get a runner to third base in the third inning, but Smoltz ended the threat by throwing a strike-three fastball by Puckett. The game stayed scoreless going into the eighth inning.

Then Lonnie Smith led off with a single against Morris. And what happened next, well, this game is only a pitching classic because of what happened next. Atlanta's Terry Pendleton, the league MVP that year, stepped to the plate, and Morris's 100th pitch of the day was a fastball that caught too much of the plate. Pendleton pounded it the other way, high and deep, and the ball hit the warning track and bounced high off the wall for a double. Lonnie Smith was one of the fastest players in baseball,* and he should have scored easily from first base.

But Smith didn't score. He stopped at third. The announcers and others would say that he was fooled by second baseman Chuck Knoblauch, who had pretended to field the ball. Smith angrily denied that. "If I had been fooled by Knoblauch," he would say, "I would have slid, wouldn't I?"

----

* Lonnie Smith was such an unusual athlete. He was blazing fast—he stole more than 600 bases in his career—but he was, as *The New York Times* wrote, "cursed with a mystifying inability to remain on his feet." He would just fall down for no reason. This caused people to call him Skates, a nickname he found absolutely no humor in. He was a proud man, and when the Phillie Phanatic, the mascot of the Philadelphia Phillies, made fun of his penchant for tripping over himself, Smith tackled the mascot, spraining both of its ankles.

Smith did not slide. Instead, he rounded second base slowly and then stopped. He had lost sight of the ball. By the time he picked up the ball's location, it was too late to score.

"He didn't do very good base running," Jack Buck said, perhaps not with the most stylish English but flawlessly getting the sentiment right.

"What was Lonnie doing?" Pendleton asked Knoblauch when he reached second base. Knoblauch shrugged. When Smith was asked the same question after the game, he replied: "Were you watching the game? That's a stupid $&#^# question."

Atlanta should have led 1–0. Instead, they had runners on second and third with nobody out. And Morris just knew he would get out of the inning without allowing a run. He just knew it. And sure enough, he did, finishing things off when Sid Bream—a hero on a later night— grounded into a double play.

Morris had risen to his eighth-inning challenge. Now Smoltz was ready for his. He allowed a leadoff single to the Twins' Randy Bush, and then after getting an out, gave up a line drive single to Knoblauch to put runners on first and third. Smoltz had the same confidence that Morris had; Smoltz just knew that he would get out of the jam.

Only John Smoltz was not Jack Morris, not yet. He was a brilliantly talented but still inexperienced 24-year-old pitcher. Braves' manager Bobby Cox came out to the mound and told Smoltz he'd done a great job and now it was time for him to come out of the game.

The pure disgust on John Smoltz's face in that moment echoes through the years.

"I just wasn't old enough to fight for myself yet," Smoltz says. "I wasn't old enough to refuse to come out of that game."

The game went on without him: It was now Morris against the Atlanta bullpen, which doesn't have quite the same ring to it. Minnesota had a chance to score in the bottom of the ninth, but Shane Mack hit into an inning-ending double play. In the 10th inning, Morris got the

Braves in order without letting the ball out of the infield. He was getting stronger. Minnesota's manager Tom Kelly asked how he was doing: Morris had thrown 126 pitches. Morris said he had another 126 pitches, if necessary.

"There was no way I was coming out of that game," Morris said.

But he didn't have to. In the bottom of the 10th, Minnesota loaded the bases and a part-time player named Gene Larkin stepped to the plate. Atlanta pulled its outfielders in as far it could.

"You know," umpire Don Denkinger casually remarked, "you could probably hit one over their heads."

And that's what Larkin did. All it took was a routine fly ball to left field, and he hit it, and the ball flew over the head of left fielder Brian Hunter. The Twins won the World Series.

"I cannot describe the feeling I had that day," Morris told me of his 10-inning shutout performance. "All I can tell you is I wish everyone in the world could feel it at least once in their lives."

NO. 37:
THE BO THROW

JUNE 5, 1989, SEATTLE

★ ★ ★ ★ ★

Bo Jackson once ran up the outfield wall. He had caught a long fly ball and was going full speed and didn't want to hit the wall, so he simply ran up the wall and back down again.

Bo Jackson once broke a bat by just swinging too hard. He didn't connect with the ball. The bat broke from the force of the swing.

Bo Jackson once decided to end batting practice by hitting left-handed. *Sports Illustrated*'s Peter Gammons was in town to do a story on him, and maybe Bo wanted to show off. He jumped in the cage, faced one pitch, swung left-handed, and hit a 450-foot home run. "Got some work to do," he said after that, and he ran to the outfield to shag fly balls.

Bo Jackson once asked an umpire for time and stepped out of the box. While he was adjusting his batting glove, he realized that the umpire had not granted him the time-out and the pitch was coming. He jumped back in the box and hit a home run.

Bo Jackson broke his bat on his first professional home run.

Bo Jackson broke his bat on his first major league grand slam.

Bo Jackson's first big-league home run was the longest ever hit at Royals Stadium.

Bo Jackson was an even better football player than he was baseball player.

"I'll always be able to tell people," Bo's teammate Frank White said, "that I really did play baseball with Superman."

Bo was Superman, yes. And his greatest feat of all came in the old

Kingdome, a Monday night, Bo's Kansas City Royals vs. the Seattle Mariners. The game went into extra innings, and in the bottom of the 10th inning, with the score still tied, Seattle's Harold Reynolds reached first base. Harold Reynolds was quite fast. Two years earlier, he had led the league with sixty stolen bases.* Harold planned to run on the pitch, and if the hitter, Scott Bradley, hit the ball into a gap anywhere on the field, he would easily come around to score and the Mariners would win.

Good plan. Bradley ripped a line drive to left field. It bounced high off the artificial turf and hit the top of the wall. Reynolds tore around the bases. He had absolutely no doubt that he would score . . . and nobody else doubted, either. Well, that's not right. One person had doubts.

That one person was Bo Jackson.

What happened next remains a wonderful mystery.

We know that Bo Jackson got to the ball when he was on the edge of the warning track, and he turned and threw.

We know that Reynolds was running full speed and with full confidence as he headed for home—so much confidence that he was shocked when teammate Darnell Coles frantically waved for him to slide.

"Slide?" Reynolds would say. "I thought he had to be joking."

We know that up in the Seattle television booth, Rick Rizzs was quite sure the game was over. "It's up to Bo Jackson to try to stop Reynolds from scoring," he said. "He can't do it."

Only then, abruptly, Rizzs shouted: "YES, HE CAN! I DON'T BE-LIEVE IT!"

Yes, he can. I don't believe it. It was like Rizzs had stopped calling a baseball game and was instead calling a Harry Houdini escape. Between the instant when he had said "He can't do it" and "Yes, he can," the ball

---

* Though it should be added that the *reason* he led the league in stolen bases was because Rickey Henderson was hurt most of the season. The day after the season ended, Rickey called Reynolds, not to congratulate but instead to say: "Sixty stolen bases? You ought to be ashamed. Rickey would have sixty stolen bases at the All-Star Break."

had just appeared on the television screen, as if conjured from thin air, and it was in the glove of catcher Bob Boone—who was as surprised as anyone; he had started walking off the field in defeat—and Boone tagged Reynolds out.

How did it happen? We don't know. We can't know because the person directing the game for Seattle's KSTW 11 television was so sure Reynolds would score, he cut away before Bo Jackson threw the ball. We don't see Bo throw. We don't see the ball speeding to Boone. We don't see the secret.

Neither did Reynolds, who after the game was seen in the Mariners' clubhouse helplessly watching the play over and over again on a little television in a doomed effort to figure out what happened.

"Just a supernatural play," Seattle Mariners' manager Jim Lefebvre would say.

"Now I've seen it all," Bradley would say.

"This," said Bo's teammate George Brett, "is not a normal man."

Predictably the only person who seemed unimpressed by the throw was Bo Jackson himself. "I just caught the ball and threw," he said. "End of story. . . . It's nothing to brag about. Don't make a big issue out of it."

But it *is* a big issue—it might be the greatest throw in baseball history. And even now, more than thirty years later, Harold Reynolds is still slightly haunted by it. He compares seeing that ball show up at the plate to seeing a ghost. Jackson, meanwhile, remains as unimpressed as ever by his own awesomeness. MLB Network's Alexa Datt asked him if, going back in time, he would have any advice for Harold.

"Yeah," Bo said. "Stop at third."

NO. 36:
NOLAN AND THE TABLE LEG

★ ★ ★ ★ ★

Nolan Ryan is the most unhittable pitcher in modern baseball history.

Nolan Ryan also lost more games than any pitcher in modern baseball history.

Tell me: How can anyone explain that? Yes, he pitched a lot of games. But I think the only way to explain it is to say that Ryan was locked in an eternal baseball battle . . . with himself. He struck out more batters than anyone. He walked more batters than anyone. He threw more no-hitters than anyone. He threw more wild pitches than anyone. He allowed the lowest batting average. He made more fielding errors than anyone else.

See, Nolan Ryan's baseball life was a magnificent clash—between light and darkness, control and wildness, strikeouts and walks, dominance and self-destruction. All his career, he had an angel on one shoulder and a devil on the other and it was never entirely clear which would emerge triumphant. Nobody could hit him. But they didn't necessarily have to hit him to win.

Here's what I mean: Ryan walked six or more batters in a game 135 times, far and away the most in baseball history. His team won 68 of those games, lost 67.

Here's what I mean: Ryan allowed three or more stolen bases in a game 77 times. Again, most in baseball history. His team's record in those games: 24–53.

Here's what I mean: Ryan made an error in 79 of his starts, the most for any modern pitcher. His team lost 46 of those games.

Nolan Ryan also did more fabled things than anyone else. He threw seven no-hitters, one of them when he was 43 years old. He broke Sandy Koufax's single-season strikeout record.* He threw 235 pitches in a single game against the Red Sox in 1974, and afterward just shrugged.

"Hell," he said, "I threw 242 pitches in a game in Detroit just last year."

He repeatedly and ferociously punched a batter named Robin Ventura, who had dared to charge the mound against him.

He threw the pitch that the *Guinness Book of World Records* recorded as the fastest ever thrown, 100.9 mph, which might not sound all that amazing, but physicists interviewed for the documentary *Fastball* estimated that because of the archaic way that pitch's speed was recorded, it was actually traveling at 108 mph.

I think Ryan simply had a different goal from other pitchers. They wanted to win games. He wanted to do the unforgettable. They wanted to get batters out. He wanted to make batters throw down their bats and yield.

And that's why I think the closest Nolan Ryan ever got to his ultimate goal was on a July Sunday afternoon in Detroit. It was Cap Day, 1973, and more than 41,000 Detroit fans were in attendance.

That was a big year for Ryan. He had thrown his first no-hitter two months earlier. It was the year he would break Koufax's strikeout record. And yet he felt off-balance coming into the game. He'd been pitching poorly for a month. His control was poor. He needed a big performance, something special to turn things around.

---

* To break Koufax's record, Ryan needed to strike out 16 batters in his last start of the 1973 season. He did just that, striking out exactly 16 (in 11 innings) to finish with 383 strikeouts.

So he went into the Detroit game trying to throw a no-hitter.

That's usually the worst way for a pitcher to think. You don't *try* to throw a no-hitter; you do your best, and if the stars align, it happens. But Ryan, as we know, was built differently, and there was always at least a small part of his mind thinking no-hitter. On this day, he felt like he needed it. A(nother) no-hitter could turn around his whole season.

His first pitch of the game was a curveball to Detroit's Jim Northrup. Ron Luciano was umpiring behind the plate, and he would say that it "broke down as if it had fallen off the edge of a cliff . . . *Uh-oh*, I thought, *if that's his curveball, we're in trouble tonight.*"

By *we* he meant the Tigers. And they were in trouble. They were swinging at shadows. Ryan had 16 strikeouts through seven innings, and no, he had not allowed a single hit. Ryan rarely was impressed with himself; he often said that he was just trying to do his job. But even he couldn't help but notice how much his curveball was breaking that day. "That's the best curveball I ever had," he would say after the game. He looked certain to not only throw a no-hitter but also to break Bob Feller's nine-inning American League strikeout record of 18 and maybe even Steve Carlton's and Tom Seaver's overall record of 19.

Only then the Angels' offense had a very long inning—they got four hits and drew three walks; the Tigers used three different pitchers; the inning lasted almost a half hour. And Ryan's arm stiffened up. It felt dead, the way it normally felt a few hours after a start. "I felt quite concerned," Ryan would admit.

Of course he stayed in the game—that was never a question. But when he went back in, he found that his fastball lacked the pop and his curveball no longer was dropping like it had. He bluffed his way through the bottom of the eighth inning without allowing a hit (and he got strikeout No. 17), but by the time he got back to the dugout, his arm was throbbing.

"Sometimes to be a great pitcher," he would say years later, "you also have to be a great actor. You gotta make the batter think they've got no shot."

And that's what he tried to do in the ninth. His stuff was gone. But dammit, he was still Nolan Ryan. He got Mickey Stanley to ground out. Gates Brown then hit a line drive rocket, a sure single if he had not hit it directly at Angels' rookie shortstop Rudy Meoli.

And that brought Norm Cash to the plate.

Norm Cash was coming to the end of a colorful and fantastic career. He was a Texas farm boy who married his high school sweetheart, was drafted by the Chicago Bears to play professional football, and chose baseball instead. He hit 377 home runs over his career, more than Joe DiMaggio, Gil Hodges, Yogi Berra, or Johnny Mize, among other Hall of Famers.

He was outgoing and fun-loving and wacky. "When you mention Norm Cash," his Hall of Fame teammate Al Kaline used to say, "I just smile."

Cash stepped up to the plate with two outs in the ninth . . . and even though Cash was 39 years old, he was still dangerous. Ryan didn't know if he had enough to finish him off. Only then Ryan noticed something. Cash didn't have a bat in his hand when he came to the plate.

No, he had a table leg.

"You can't hit with that," the umpire, Luciano, barked.

"Ron," Cash said, "I can't hit him no matter what bat I use."*

Then Ryan knew. He was getting his no-hitter. Cash threw away the table leg, got a bat, and dutifully popped up to shortstop to complete the no-hitter. After the game, everybody bowed to the pure awesomeness that was Nolan Ryan. He had to love it.

---

* Funny thing, not a single newspaper reported this story the day it happened. There's video footage of Cash stepping to the plate with that table leg instead of the bat and then having to throw it out of the game. And yet none of the papers mentioned it until a few days later.

"Either that fastball or that curveball should be outlawed," Luciano said. "Nobody should have both of those."

"You just wanted to hit a foul ball," Detroit's Dick Sharon said.

"He struck me out three times," Hall of Famer Frank Robinson said. "And I wasn't even playing."

FIVE
LOUD HOME RUNS

You can rank home runs a lot of ways. Just off the top of my head: You can rank them by importance, by height ("Too high!" the Cleveland fan hoped in *Major League II*), by distance, by exit velocity, by immediacy ("I knew it was gone the instant it hit the bat"), by beauty, and maybe even by the announcer's home run call ("I do not believe what I just saw").

Then there's the sound of a home run.

My friend Buck O'Neil used to say there were three times he heard a home run that sounded different from the rest. The first time, he was young, and he was standing behind the wall during a spring training batting practice. He heard the sound and had to see what it was; he climbed a ladder and looked through a knothole and saw "a big sucker hitting the ball like nobody I'd ever seen." That was Babe Ruth.

In 1938, when he was a young first baseman for the Kansas City Monarchs, he heard the sound for a second time. He was getting dressed for the game when he heard a thunderclap and was so desperate to see who'd caused it that he raced out wearing only a jockstrap. He saw "the most beautiful man I'd ever seen." That was Josh Gibson.

The third time he heard the sound, almost a half century later, he was a scout, and he was in his hometown of Kansas City, where a newly signed prospect was hitting home runs to places that boggled the mind. That was Bo Jackson.

Buck lived to be 94 years old. To his final days, he would go to the ballpark in the hopes of hearing the sound one more time.

BO JACKSON (MAY 23, 1989)

"I'm going to get him this time," Bo told his teammates. He had faced Nolan Ryan six times in his young career. He had struck out all six times. This time would be different, Bo promised. This time.

The situation didn't matter. The Rangers already led the Royals 10–2. But it is moments like these that make baseball sublime. You had a titan on the mound, a folk hero at the plate—yes, this is certainly why we love baseball. They battled back and forth until the count was full.

Ryan then faced a choice. He was set up to throw his knee-buckling curveball. He knew Bo couldn't hit it; Bo had all sorts of trouble against curveballs. All Ryan had to do was flip a curve, get Bo to chase, and that would be the end of that.

But Ryan could read Bo's eyes, which seemed to say: "Come on, old man, you're supposed to have the best fastball ever. Let's see that fastball."

No, Nolan Ryan wasn't about to throw a curveball.

He threw the hardest fastball he had in him. And there was nothing wrong with the velocity; it was plenty fast. But the location was—well, nowadays they call that kind of pitch *middle-middle*. It was right where Bo Jackson wanted it.

"As soon as it left my hand," Ryan would later tell reporters, "I knew I was in trouble."

Bo Jackson swung as hard as he could. He always did. When the bat connected with the ball, the sound was like the liberation of Paris. Jackson hit it to straightaway center field, the deepest part of the ballpark, and none of the outfielders even moved. There was no reason to move.

The ball soared over the fence and two-thirds of the way up the bleachers; nobody had ever hit a baseball there before.

As Jackson rounded the bases, he looked over at Ryan and offered a smile that said: "I finally got you!"

Ryan was not amused. He glared back. After the game, someone asked Ryan if it was the longest home run that he ever gave up. He was not about to give Bo the satisfaction. "You don't pitch twenty-two years and not give up longer ones than that," he said with an edge in his voice.

The next day, though, when Ryan came out to stretch, he looked around the field and couldn't find any of his teammates. Then he looked up in the stands and there they were, sitting way off in the center-field bleachers, where Bo Jackson had hit the home run.

"Hi, Nolan!" they shouted, and he could barely even hear them.

"OK, yeah," Ryan would admit, "he really did hit that one a pretty long way."

JOEY MEYER (JUNE 2, 1987)

Joey Meyer was a big man. How big? *The New York Times*' Dave Anderson reported that when Meyer joined Milwaukee's Class AAA Denver Zephyrs, the only uniform they could find big enough for him was a souvenir shirt hanging in a local sports bar.

Meyer played only parts of two seasons in the big leagues. But before he retired at 29, he hit some very long home runs. And the longest came when he was playing for the the Zephyrs in Denver's Mile High Stadium.

The air was light because of the altitude. The pitcher was a reliever named Mike Murphy. The bat was a Cal Ripken model that Meyer had gotten in a trade from a teammate. There were 1,404 people in the mammoth stadium. There were roughly 75,000 empty seats. The count was 2-2.

Meyer turned on a fastball and sent it soaring into the left-field upper deck. He hit it so high and so far, it went beyond the scope of the camera. "That's got to be more than 450 feet," one of the announcers said, a classic understatement, sort of like saying, "Shaquille O'Neal has to be at least 6 feet tall."

The Zephyrs' general manager Bob Howsam Jr.* ordered a scientific estimate of the homer. The estimate came back at 582 feet.

It is the longest professional home run on record.

ALBERT PUJOLS (OCTOBER 17, 2005)

Sometimes the loudest sound is silence. Maybe that makes sense. Maybe it doesn't. But it's what I think about when remembering Albert Pujols's home run off Brad Lidge in Game 5 of the 2005 National League Championship Series.

Astros superfan Ric Sweeney was there and has a story. Let me set the scene first: Lidge's Astros were one out away from their first-ever appearance in the World Series. They led St. Louis by two runs. The Cardinals had two runners on. Brad Lidge was one of the best closers in baseball. Albert Pujols was the best hitter in baseball.

"It was like an earthquake of noise," Sweeney tells me. "It was the loudest I had ever heard a stadium."

And then Pujols hit the monster, no-doubt home run . . . and all that sound died immediately, suddenly, like someone had hit a mute button on the city of Houston.

"It was so quiet," Sweeney says, "you could practically hear Pujols's cleats hitting the dirt."

So yes, it's hard to imagine a louder sound than that silence.

---

* Howsam Jr. is the son of legendary sports figure Bob Howsam Sr., who was one of founders of the old American Football League and the architect of the Big Red Machine Cincinnati Reds, which won back-to-back World Series in the mid-1970s.

Funny thing is, that home run is not what Sweeney remembers most about that game. Hard-core fans of teams will remember things that everybody else forgets. And what Sweeney remembers is that Brad Lidge walked Jim Edmonds to bring Pujols to the plate in the first place. That still haunts him.

"The absolute worst thing Lidge could have done was walk Edmonds," Sweeney says. "You just can't do that, not with Pujols on deck. You are better off throwing batting-practice softballs right down the middle to Edmonds."

After the Astros lost the game, Sweeney could not stop talking about that stupid walk. In the parking lot, he and his friend, randomly, happened to run into a hero, Hall of Fame basketball player Clyde Drexler, who was as stunned and mortified as every other Astros fan.

"When you get your foot on their neck, you have to break them!" Drexler said angrily. He thought the Astros should have intentionally walked Pujols.

"Well, actually," Sweeney said to him (hardly believing he was talking to one of his all-time sports idols), "the key was walking Edmonds."

The two parted ways. A few seconds later, Drexler chased him down.

"You're right!" Drexler shouted. "You're right! They never should have walked Edmonds!"*

BARRY BONDS (MAY 1, 2000)

There is no winning with Barry Bonds. On the one hand, you can't write a book like this without him. The guy has the career home run record and the season home run record, he stole five hundred bases, he won seven MVPs, and so on. His Baseball-Reference page is an endless delight of wrapped statistical candies.

---

* The Astros did win Game 6 and go to the World Series in 2005. I'm pretty sure this is the only reason Ric Sweeney was even willing to tell his story about the game.

On the other hand, how can you include Barry Bonds in a book called *Why We Love Baseball*? I'm sure some of you grimaced just seeing his name.

But, hey, those splash hits were awesome.

As I write these words, there have been 97 splash hits at Oracle Park in San Francisco. Those are the home runs that clear the right-field wall and splash into McCovey Cove in the San Francisco Bay. There's something so satisfying about seeing a well-struck baseball soaring out of a ballpark and splashing into the water.

The first one happened on a Monday night at the start of May. San Francisco's new stadium—then called Pacific Bell Park—was a few weeks old and utterly gorgeous. The Giants were playing the Mets, and in the sixth inning Bonds came up against Rich Rodríguez. He turned on the first pitch and sent it soaring into right field.

"He hits one high," Giants' announcer Duane Kuiper shouted, "he hits one deep. McCovey Cove! Outta here!"

Several boats went after the now-famous baseball; Joseph Figone's motorized boat won the race, and he scooped the ball out of the water with his net.

Bonds's reaction was pure bliss. Here's how Dennis Georgatos wrote it for the *Napa Valley Register*:

"Barry Bonds clapped his hands, broke into a smile and eased into his home-run trot. He pumped his fists as he headed into the dugout, only to come back out and answer the crowd's rousing cheers and take a bow. It was, after all, no ordinary shot."

No ordinary shot. Ten days later, Bonds hit his second ball into McCovey Cove. In all, he hit 35 splash hits, many more than Brandon Belt's 10 or Pablo Sandoval's 8. Over time, Bonds hit so many splash hits that they began feeling less special and then a little sinister. So goes his story. But that first splash hit was really something.

MICKEY MANTLE (APRIL 17, 1953)

Here's a baseball truism: If you hit a really special home run, some Babe Ruth fan will emerge to tell you that the Babe did it better. This is true, as we will see, of record-breaking home runs. But it's also true of long home runs. Shortly after Mickey Mantle hit what very well might have been the longest home run ever hit in an American or a National League baseball game,* someone obviously insisted that the Babe had hit one even longer.

Mantle's homer in Washington in 1953 is usually called the first tape-measure home run, even though no tape measure was involved. It happened in the fifth inning of a game between the Yankees and Senators. Mantle was batting right-handed against Senators' lefty Chuck Stobbs. The count was 0-1. The pitch was a fastball.

Mantle sent it sailing to right center field, where it clanked off the right-hand edge of the football scoreboard, deflected out of Griffith Stadium, and as the story goes, was found by a 10-year-old kid named Donald Dunaway in the backyard of a house on Oakdale Place NW.

Griffith Stadium was torn down a half century ago.

The house on Oakdale, however, is still standing.

The story continues: Arthur Patterson, the Yankees' publicity director, ran to get an exact measurement of the blast. He found Dunaway holding the ball up in the air. Patterson said he gave Donald a dollar for the baseball (Mantle was thrilled to get the ball!) and asked him to show exactly where the ball was found.†

---

* It seems all but certain that Josh Gibson hit the longest home run in a major league game; perhaps the 600-foot blast he hit at Memorial Field in Belmar, New Jersey, or the ball he almost hit out of Yankee Stadium in 1937 or one of many blasts he hit in Washington's Griffith Stadium.

† In 2010, Jane Leavy of the *Washingtonian* chased down Donald Dunaway, who was 70 years old and in poor health. He told an entirely different story. He said he got $100 for the ball. He said he didn't find it in the backyard. He said he never showed anybody where he did find it. He contradicted himself several times, so it's hard to know exactly what to make of his story; he died a few months later.

Dunaway pointed to the backyard. Patterson walked off the distance, did some math, and calculated that the ball had traveled 565 feet.

"Mickey Mantle," the New York *Daily News*'s Joe Trimble wrote, "the magnificent moppet of the Yankees, today hit the longest home run in the history of baseball."

Enter H. G. Salsinger. He was sports editor of *The Detroit News*, and one of the most influential baseball writers in America. He insisted the longest home run ever hit was not by Mantle but by Babe Ruth, who had hit a 600-foot home run at Detroit's Navin Field in 1926.

As proof, Salsinger claimed to have two signed affidavits from witnesses.

Salsinger's sway was such that newspapers immediately started referring to Mantle's homer as the second-longest home run ever, behind this mysterious 600-foot Babe Ruth homer.

Salsinger's story never did make much sense. For one thing: He had the home run measured at exactly 600 feet. That doesn't seem too likely. But more than that, you can go back to the newspaper accounts. Ruth hit four home runs in Detroit in 1926. None of them was singled out as being especially well-struck, much less a 600-foot rocket ship.

NO. 35:
THE BAT FLIP

OCTOBER 14, 2015, TORONTO

★ ★ ★ ★ ★

The most wonderful part of the Bat Flip is . . . well, the fact that I can use the word *the* and add a fairly common event like a bat flip and you know *exactly* which one I'm talking about. There have been many bat flips in the history of professional baseball—a good number of them by former American League MVP Josh Donaldson after hitting routine fly balls* —but there is only one *the* Bat Flip.

"The Bat Flip," my friend Mike Schur says, "is to contemporary baseball what the David is to sculpture, or the Taj Mahal is to architecture. It's the object that, when one sees it, one is inspired to write, to draw, to paint, to compose an opera, to propose marriage."

Yes, that's right.

The home run that became the Bat Flip did not just happen. It needs context. The game was the fifth and decisive one between the Toronto Blue Jays and the Texas Rangers in the 2015 American League Division Series. The score was 2–2 going into the seventh inning.

Oh, that seventh inning.

The Rangers batted, and a player named Rougned Odor singled. He moved around to third with two outs, and Texas sent a South Korean

---

* This Donaldson joke is the sort that you do not normally include in a book because a book is permanent and the joke is of the moment; I doubt Josh Donaldson's hilarious habit of hitting the ball, flipping the bat in home run triumph, and then watching as the ball is caught without undue effort by an outfielder will be remembered for very long. So, if you are reading this in a distant future where the name Josh Donaldson does not ring a bell, just know that such a man lived, and he often flipped bats on routine fly balls, and it was glorious.

player named Shin-Soo Choo to the plate. Choo was a wonderfully unconventional player who had this weird habit of stretching between pitches by holding his bat way out in front of him like he was holding out a sword for some ceremony. It was odd, but he did it all the time, so everybody got used to it.

He took a pitch, then he held the bat as usual . . . and Blue Jays' catcher Russell Martin, while trying to throw the ball back to the pitcher, instead hit the bat. The ball ricocheted away. Odor raced home.

Nobody seemed to know what to do.

Home plate umpire Dale Scott held out his arms to call a time-out, announced the ball was dead, and sent Odor back to third. That seemed logical enough.

But according to a magnificently specific baseball rule—Rule 6.03a—the ball was *not* dead. Yes, the ball would have been dead if Choo had been *trying* to block the throw with his bat (and Choo would have been declared out).

"However," the rule specifically states, "if the batter is standing in the batter's box, and he or his bat is struck by the catcher's throw back to the pitcher, and in the umpire's judgment, there is no intent on the part of the batter to interfere with the throw, the ball is alive and in play."

The fact there was a rule that *specifically* covered this incredibly odd play perfectly captures another wonder of baseball: There's a rule for everything. After a long discussion with the other umpires, Scott overruled himself and said that Odor had indeed scored.

The game was stopped for 18 minutes as the outraged (and confused) Canadian crowd threw beer cans and bottles on the field and booed darkly. The scene was strange and unnerving. But the Rangers led 3–2.

Then came the bottom half of the inning.

Before the Bat Flip there was more mayhem. The Rangers committed three errors on the first three batters—two of them by Texas shortstop

Elvis Andrus. The tying run scored on a Josh Donaldson blooper. He did not flip the bat.

Up came José Bautista.

He'd already had the oddest career. He was drafted by the Pirates in the 20th round out of Chipola College. And then in an eight-month whirlwind he was:

- Taken by Baltimore in the Rule 5 draft.
- Waived by the Orioles.
- Claimed by Tampa Bay.
- Sold to Kansas City.
- Traded to the New York Mets.
- And then, sure, traded back to Pittsburgh.

Eventually he was traded to Toronto, and he struggled mightily. Then he came upon a hitting secret that, literally overnight, turned him into one of the most feared power hitters in all of baseball. What was that secret? He explained it to me once: He swung the bat earlier. I'm sure there was more to it than that, but that's how I understood it.

When Bautista stepped to the plate that day in Toronto, he was the team's heartbeat and a Canadian hero. The Rangers' pitcher was a hard thrower named Sam Dyson. With a 1-1 count, Dyson threw a 97-mph fastball that tailed inside. Bautista swung.

No verb quite captures what Bautista did to that baseball.

Disintegrated it? Atomized it? Shattered it? Eradicated it?

The sound of the Canadian crowd in that moment was a jet engine in a thunderstorm at a KISS concert. Bautista made a face that said, *I am now emperor of all the land!* And then came the Bat Flip. He threw the bat with his left hand, and it soared through the air, and I'm not entirely sure it has landed still.

Many around baseball didn't like the Bat Flip. Too showy. It's a constant fight in baseball; many believe the sport demands quiet sportsmanship and not barbaric yawps. Many want a more dignified game where home run hitters always run the bases with their heads down, content with a job well done.

I get that. But why can't we have both? Majestic home run trots are wonderful. But so is the Bat Flip. It's a grand statement from a player nobody believed in who, in the biggest moment of his career, unloaded a home run that broke the universe for a moment or two.

NO. 34:
SHOHEI

MARCH 21, 2023, MIAMI

★ ★ ★ ★ ★

On March 21, 2023, pitcher Shohei Ohtani faced Mike Trout with two outs in the ninth inning of the World Baseball Classic Championship. The game between Japan and the United States was in the balance, and the matchup was like something out of a dream. Mike Trout is the greatest hitter of his generation, a right-handed cross between Joe DiMaggio, Willie Mays, and Albert Pujols.

And Shohei Ohtani is simply unlike any player in the history of baseball.

The two battled until the count was full. In everyday life, Ohtani and Trout were Los Angeles Angels teammates and they were great friends. Now, though, they would find out which one would reign.

Ohtani considered his options. He could throw his 101-mph fastball. He could also throw his death-defying slider. Few pitchers in the history of the game have had such options. He chose the slider. And he threw it past Mike Trout for strike three. Chills. Goosebumps.

Two weeks later, in Oakland, Mike Trout hit a 434-foot home run against the Athletics. The next man up was hitter Shohei Ohtani. He hit a 447-foot home run.

What can you say? That man, Shohei, is a nightly miracle.

THERE HAVE BEEN OTHER PLAYERS WHO WERE GOOD AT BOTH pitching and hitting. All baseball fans know that Babe Ruth was one of them. He was a full-time pitcher when he started his professional career with Boston, and he was very good, particularly in the World

Series. It's quite possible that over those three years, he was the third-best pitcher in baseball, behind only Walter Johnson and Pete Alexander. Then, as you might know, he became a pretty good hitter.

There were a few players in the Negro Leagues who successfully hit and pitched, players like Bullet Rogan and Leon Day. The best of these was perhaps the Cuban-born Martín Dihigo, who was called El Maestro. Hall of Famer Johnny Mize would say of Dihigo, "He was the only guy I ever saw who could play all nine positions, manage, run, and switch-hit." Mize saw Dihigo play the outfield at age 41 and called him the best he'd ever seen. As a pitcher, Dihigo threw the first no-hitter in the history of the Mexican League and was widely regarded as one of the best of his day. When he retired, many stopped calling him El Maestro and instead called him El Inmortal.

Through the years, many great hitters started out as pitchers—Stan Musial and George Sisler among them—and quite a few hitters were converted into pitchers, including Hall of Famers Trevor Hoffman and Bob Lemon. But both at the same time? Most considered it impossible. Even Ruth himself was never a full-time pitcher and outfielder at the same time. And when Shohei Ohtani came over from Japan—after five electrifying seasons with the Hokkaido Nippon-Ham Fighters—many felt like his determination to pitch *and* hit would prove his undoing. But he was insistent. When he had graduated high school, Ohtani was challenged by the Ham Fighters' manager Hideki Kuriyama to travel down his own path and try to become the first player to star as a hitter and pitcher at the same time. He signed with the Angels in large part because they were respectful of that dream.

At first the cynics seemed to have a point. Ohtani did win Rookie of the Year in 2018—he hit 22 home runs as a hitter and went 4-2 with 63 strikeouts as a pitcher—but all in all, it was a difficult season. He blew out his elbow and needed Tommy John Surgery. He missed the entire 2019 season and there was considerable doubt about his ever pitching again. "You can't do both," some baseball people said knowingly.

But Ohtani was more committed than ever. He reworked his diet. He changed his workout routine. He developed new pitches. And in 2021, he had a year unlike any other in baseball history. As a hitter, he led the league in triples, led the league in homers per at-bat, he drove in 100 runs, he scored 100 runs, he even finished fifth in stolen bases.

And as a pitcher, he made 23 starts, went 9-2, and struck out 156 batters in 130 innings. He was the league's unanimous MVP.

In 2022, impossibly, he was even better. He did numerical things that boggle the mind. He became the first player to hit 30 home runs and strike out 200 batters in a season. He became the first player to win 15 games and hit 30 doubles in a season. He became the first pitcher with 300 total bases and 150 innings pitched.

Here's one I particularly like: Shohei Ohtani (the batter) was intentionally walked 14 times. Shohei Ohtani (the pitcher) didn't intentionally walk anybody.

He had back-to-back days against Kansas City that are worth pointing out. On June 21, 2022, Ohtani hit two homers and drove in eight runs.

The next day—also against the Royals—the very same Shohei Ohtani pitched eight shutout innings, allowed just two hits, and struck out 13 batters.

There has never been anyone like him.

But here's the question: Could there have been someone like him? That is to say: If someone had been as driven as Ohtani to be both a star pitcher and hitter, could they have done it?

I went to the one guy who, better than anyone else, could answer that question.

I went to Dave Winfield.

///

WHEN DAVE WINFIELD WAS IN COLLEGE AT THE UNIVERSITY of Minnesota, he had two posters on his wall. The first was of slugger Willie McCovey, because "the man just came to the plate with the intention of dominating. That's what I wanted to do."

The other was of pitcher Bob Gibson because "he also intended to dominate, except from the pitcher's mound. I wanted to do that too."

Winfield fulfilled his McCovey dreams. He was one of the greatest hitters in baseball history. There are four players in the Hall of Fame with 3,000 hits, 400 home runs, and 200 steals. They are Henry Aaron, Willie Mays, Alex Rodriguez, and Dave Winfield.

But Winfield did not get to live out his Bob Gibson dreams. He might have, had circumstances been different. Winfield had been a great pitcher. In his senior year at the University of Minnesota—"the one year they let me hit and pitch," he says ruefully—he went 9-1 with a 2.74 ERA during the season and then was almost unhittable in the playoffs. In the District 4 baseball playoffs final against Southern Illinois, he threw a three-hit shutout and carried Minnesota to the College World Series.*

Minnesota's first College World Series game was against Oklahoma, and Winfield threw another shutout, striking out 14. In the ninth inning, Oklahoma loaded the bases with one out, but Winfield finished the job with back-to-back strikeouts.

"My feeling as a pitcher was this," he says. "I would do whatever it takes."

The Gophers lost their next game to Arizona State with Winfield playing left field (with him leaping high and almost stealing the Arizona State homer that won the game).

Then Minnesota played Southern California, and for eight innings, Winfield had his best outing—before it became his worst. He struck out 15 in the first eight innings of the game and allowed just one infield hit. He threw 165 pitches in those eight innings, even though he was pitching on three days' rest. Then when he came out for the ninth inning, Winfield was entirely spent. USC beat him up, and Minnesota

---

* Three days later, he was the fourth pick in the baseball draft. He had already been drafted by the NBA Atlanta Hawks, the ABA Utah Stars, and the NFL Minnesota Vikings. "I have the physical traits for sports," he said modestly.

blew a 7–0 lead, the largest ninth-inning comeback in College World Series history.

Still, Winfield was so incredible overall that he was named the College World Series Most Outstanding Player anyway.

"I only faced him that one time," USC's center fielder and future Red Sox star Fred Lynn would say. "But he threw hard and had a good off-speed pitch . . . You can't teach speed, and Dave had plenty of that. I'm sure Winfield could have pitched at the next level."

Yes, Dave Winfield could have been a star pitcher in the big leagues. He threw in the upper 90s, mixed in a dazzling breaking ball, and he was an intimidating presence on the mound at 6-foot-6, 220 pounds. But pitching wasn't his top priority.

No, his top priority was to never play a single game in the minor leagues.

And that's exactly what he did. He went right up to play with the Padres and became an everyday player the very next year.

Could he have done both? Winfield says he would have loved to try. "I had pitched and hit all my life," he said. "If they had told me, 'We want you to pitch,' I would have been good with that. I would have loved to try it.

"But at the same time, I had so much to learn when I got to the big leagues. I don't think I became an All-Star until my fifth year. Could I have learned how to pitch and how to hit at the major league level? Probably not. I would have needed to go to the minors. And at that point in my life, I didn't want to do that."

I asked him what impresses him most about Ohtani's pitching and hitting brilliance.

"You have to train different parts of your body," he says. "That's a pretty big deal; it's hard enough to stay healthy doing one or the other. And you have to study twice as much. Plus, expectations are so high. Look, some guys can't handle the pressures of expectation just doing one thing. Imagine what it is when you're doing two. Ohtani has handled that so well."

And I ask him again: Could you have done it?

"Look," he says, "I don't want you to think it's something I've lost any sleep over, you know? I haven't. I don't have any regrets. But yes, when I watch Shohei Ohtani play, I see someone who is doing what I was doing for most of my life. I think about it. Could I have done it? If the circumstances were right, yeah, I'd like to think so.

"I was a good pitcher. I don't know how good I would have been against major leaguers. But I'd like to know if I could have dominated. I mean, you always want to know, right?"

NO. 33:
JACKIE AND YOGI

SEPTEMBER 28, 1955, BRONX

★ ★ ★ ★ ★

We were walking around the Yogi Berra Museum in Little Falls, New Jersey, Yogi Berra and me, and he was telling me about his awe-inspiring, movie-magic, too-incredible-to-believe life. He was at Normandy on D-Day. He played for ten World Series champions. He proposed to his first love, and they were married for 65 years. He may have been telling a story about Joe DiMaggio or Mickey Mantle or of the U.S. presidents he met when we walked by a photograph.

"Out!" he shouted suddenly. And then Yogi picked his story back up like nothing had happened.

The photograph was of his applying the tag as Jackie Robinson stole home in Game 1 of the 1955 World Series.

///

THOUGH IT REMAINS AMONG THE MOST INDELIBLE MOMENTS IN baseball history, the steal itself didn't mean very much. The Dodgers were trailing the Yankees by two when Robinson found himself on third base with two outs. His daring steal of home did cut the margin to one,* but the Yankees won the game by that one run.

Still, it is the most famous steal of home in baseball history. I think there are three reasons. One, the players involved are renowned. If this

---

* The man at the plate, Frank Kellert, ended up singling, so we might assume Robinson would have scored anyway.

had been Don Hoak stealing home and Charlie Silvera behind the plate, nobody would be talking about it almost 70 years later.

But it was Jackie Robinson and Yogi Berra.

And the Yankees' pitcher was Whitey Ford, the Chairman of the Board, another Hall of Famer.

Two, this was the Yankees and Dodgers, a rivalry unlike any other. Between 1949 and 1956, the Yankees and Dodgers would play each other in the World Series five times. Up to 1955, the Yankees had won every time, and the Dodgers were desperate and hungry. Robinson's dash was a battle cry.

"The team," Roger Kahn would write of those Dodgers in *The Boys of Summer*, "was awesomely good and yet defeated. Their skills lifted everyman's spirit and their defeat joined them with everyman's existence, a national team, with a country in thrall, irresistible and unable to beat the Yankees."

But it's the third reason that I think best explains why the play is timeless.

We don't know whether Robinson was safe or out.

Oh, you might think you know. Lots of people think they know. Robinson was on third, a nice-sized lead, and he was watching Ford closely. He then took small hops and took off for the plate while Ford was in his windup. Ford's pitch beat him there, Yogi caught it with his left foot on home plate, he reached down with both his glove and right hand and tried to tag Robinson's right foot just before it touched home.

Out? Safe? Home plate umpire Bill Summers did not hesitate: He ruled safe. Berra was sure he'd blown the call, so sure that he stood up and tore off his mask and began screaming at Summers like he never had at an umpire and never would again. Summers just kept stretching out his arms, again and again, a repeat of his safe call, and then turned his back on Berra.

People have been arguing ever since.

There is one surviving film of the play. The replay shows everything . . .

and nothing at all. It is a Rorschach replay. You will see in it exactly what you want. If you want to see Robinson out, he's out. If you want to see him safe, he's safe.

"It was bush stuff," Berra shouted to reporters after the game. "It was showboat strategy, stealing home when you're two runs behind like that. It was a bad play."

Reporters raced over to Robinson for a response.

"The only thing bush about it," Robinson replied, "was Berra's tag."

Reporters raced back to Berra for his response to the response.

"He was out," Berra said. "The call was blown. It was the wrong play, and he was out."

Back to Robinson.

"Tell him to worry about himself," Robinson said. "He didn't tag me until after I crossed."

Back and forth. The Yankees, as you know, won the game. But the Dodgers ended up winning that World Series—they finally beat the Yankees—and Jackie Robinson's stolen base became a symbol of that victory.

WHAT I DID NOT KNOW ON THAT DAY WE WALKED AROUND THE museum was that Yogi Berra yelled, "Out!" at that photograph in the museum every time. His family said he never missed, not even once.

But there's an even better story. Jackie Robinson died in 1972. And for the next 40-plus years, Yogi Berra would often find himself at a banquet or celebration or gathering with Jackie's widow, Rachel Robinson.

They always greeted each other the same way each time.

"Safe," Rachel would say.

"Out," Yogi would say.

And then the two would laugh and hug.

NO. 32:
PERFECTION

SEPTEMBER 9, 1965, LOS ANGELES

★ ★ ★ ★ ★

When he stepped to the mound that day," Vin Scully told me, "the crowd applauded. They did not cheer. There was no yelling, no whooping, no hollering. It was pure applause. It was the sort of appreciation you would hear for the conductor of the Royal Philharmonic Orchestra."

Every day, I miss Vin Scully. I miss the man who became my friend. And I miss baseball's poet laureate, the Dodgers' announcer who simply had a knack for saying things that so beautifully and lovingly captured the essence of the moment.

Take the quote above. That quote was about Sandy Koufax when he stepped to the mound one Thursday evening in September 1965. Could it be more perfect? *The sort of appreciation you would hear for the conductor of the Royal Philharmonic Orchestra.*

When Koufax took the mound that day, he was at the very height of his powers. He was 29 years old and had already been the league's most valuable player and a World Series hero. He had already thrown three no-hitters and 33 shutouts. Vin Scully would say he felt no premonitions that day, but then again, he avoided premonitions. In the booth, he didn't want to anticipate. He wanted the game to wash over him, the way it had when he was a boy.

And it wasn't only Koufax who was at the height of his powers. Scully was as well. He was 37 and had been with the Dodgers since 1950, back when they were in Brooklyn. Vin was living the only life he'd ever dreamed about. There was no such thing as a sports radio broadcaster when he was a boy, and yet he longed to be one ever since the first time he heard the sound of a crowd. He had learned the craft from Red Barber himself, the man who all but invented baseball broadcasting, and he found inside himself a voice unlike any other.

And on that day in Los Angeles, the City of Angels, he called Sandy Koufax's perfect game. The game is one of 23 perfect games. The call, however, is one of a kind. Here is Vin Scully's ninth inning, with a handful of thoughts lodged in.

THREE TIMES IN HIS SENSATIONAL CAREER HAS SANDY KOUFAX walked out to the mound to pitch a fateful ninth where he turned in a no-hitter.

Notice where Vin places the word has. *Only Vin Scully would have the word* has *BEFORE Sandy Koufax rather than after. And that changes everything about the sentence.*

But tonight, September the ninth, 1965, he made the toughest walk of his career, I'm sure, because through eight innings, he has pitched a perfect game. He has struck out eleven. He has retired twenty-four consecutive batters.

And the first man he will look at is catcher Chris Krug, a big right-handed hitter, flied to center, grounded to short. Dick Tracewski is now at second base. And Koufax ready and delivers: curveball for a strike. [The crowd cheers.]

Oh and one the count to Chris Krug.

Out on deck to pinch-hit is one of the men we mentioned earlier as a possible, Joey Amalfitano. Here's the strike one pitch to Krug: fastball, swung on and missed, strike two. [The crowd cheers.] And you can almost taste the pressure now.

"You can almost taste the pressure now." I love that so much.

Koufax lifted his cap, ran his fingers through his black hair, then pulled the cap back down, fussing at the bill. Krug must feel it, too, as he backs out, heaves a sigh, took off his helmet, put it back on, and steps back up to the plate. Tracewski is over to his right to fill up the middle, [third baseman John] Kennedy is deep to guard the line.

The strike two pitch is on the way: fastball, outside, ball one. Krug started to go after it and held up and [catcher Jeff] Torborg held the ball high in the air, trying to convince [umpire Ed] Vargo, but Eddie said, "No, sir!"

One and two the count to Chris Krug. It is 9:41 P.M. on September the ninth. The one-two pitch on the way: curveball, tapped foul off to the left of the plate.

Vin, as you will see, kept going back to the date and time. He hoped that doing so would help the listeners feel the gravitas of the moment.

The Dodgers defensively in this spine-tingling moment: Sandy Koufax and Jeff Torborg. The boys who will try and stop anything hit their way: Wes Parker, Dick Tracewski, Maury Wills, and John Kennedy. The outfield of Lou Johnson, Willie Davis, and Ron Fairly. And there's 29,000 people in the ballpark and a million butterflies. Twenty-nine thousand, one hundred and thirty-nine paid.

This is probably the most perfect line of the inning: "[T]here's 29,000 people in the ballpark and a million butterflies." I asked Vin how, on command, he just came up with lines like that, for he did this his entire life. He said, as modestly as he could, "I really believe God has something to do with it."

Koufax into his windup and the one-two pitch: fastball, fouled back out of play.

In the Dodger dugout, Al Ferrara gets up and walks down near the runway, and it begins to get tough to be a teammate and sit in the dugout and have to watch. Sandy, back of the rubber, now toes it. All the boys in the bullpen straining to get a better look as they look through the wire fence in left field.

One and two the count to Chris Krug. Koufax, feet together, now to his windup and the one-two pitch: fastball outside, ball two. [The crowd boos.] A lot of people in the ballpark now are starting to see the pitches with their hearts. The pitch was outside; Torborg tried to pull it over the plate, but Vargo, an experienced umpire, wouldn't go for it. Two and two the count to Chris Krug. Sandy, reading signs, into his windup, two-two pitch: fastball, got him swinging! [The crowd cheers.]

Sandy Koufax has struck out twelve. He is two outs away from a perfect game.

There was some debate among baseball fans and observers about Scully using the words perfect game *during the broadcast. There's a long-standing tradition in baseball to avoid saying* perfect game *or* no-hitter *to avoid the possibility of jinxing the event. Scully, however, did not believe in jinxes, nor did he keep secrets from his listeners. A perfect game was happening. Vin Scully respected people too much to pretend it wasn't.*

Here is Joe Amalfitano to pinch-hit for Don Kessinger. Amalfitano is from Southern California, from San Pedro. He was an original bonus boy with the Giants. Joey's been around and, as we mentioned earlier, he has helped to beat the Dodgers twice. And on deck is Harvey Kuenn. Kennedy is tight to the bag at third. The fastball, a strike [crowd cheers].

Oh and one with one out in the ninth inning, one-to-nothing Dodgers. Sandy reading, into his windup and the strike one pitch: curveball, tapped foul. Oh and two. And Amalfitano walks away and shakes himself a little bit and swings the bat. And Koufax, with a new ball, takes a hitch at his belt and walks behind the mound.

I would think that the mound at Dodger Stadium right now is the loneliest place in the world. Looks in to get his sign. Oh and two to Amalfitano. The strike-two pitch to Joe: fastball swung on and missed, strike three! [Six seconds of crowd cheers.] He is one out away from the promised land, and Harvey Kuenn is coming up.

Vin never lost his love of a crowd cheering. The sound was like music to him. And when he could, he would stay silent and let that sound tell the story. "What can I say," he used to say, "that could match the sound of a crowd?"

So Harvey Kuenn is batting for Bob Hendley. The time on the scoreboard is 9:44. The date: September the ninth, 1965. And Koufax working on veteran Harvey Kuenn. Sandy into his windup and the pitch, a fastball for a strike. [The crowd cheers.] He has struck out, by the way, five consecutive batters, and that's gone unnoticed.

Vin told me he had only just noticed this himself.

Sandy ready and the strike-one pitch—very high, and he lost his hat, he really forced that one. That's only the second time tonight where I have had the feeling that Sandy threw instead of pitched, trying to get that little extra. And that time he tried so hard his hat fell off. He took an extremely long stride to the plate, and Torborg had to go up to get it. One and one to Harvey Kuenn.

Now he's ready: fastball, high, ball two. You can't blame a man for pushing just a little bit now. Sandy backs off, mops his forehead, runs his left index finger along his forehead, dries it off on his left pants leg. All the while, Kuenn just waiting. Now Sandy looks in. Into his windup and the two-one pitch to Kuenn: swung on and missed, strike two. [The crowd cheers.]

It is 9:46 P.M. Two and two to Harvey Kuenn, one strike away.

While the "million butterflies" line is probably the most perfect, it is this line—"two and two to Harvey Kuenn"—that is most quoted. There's nothing obviously special about the line itself, but the way Vin Scully said it, like a musician, rings through the years.

Sandy into his windup. Here's the pitch: swung on and missed, a perfect game!

Here Vin Scully stays silent for 38 seconds and lets people hear the crowd cheer.

On the scoreboard in right field, it is 9:46 P.M. in the City of the Angels, Los Angeles, California. And a crowd of 29,139, just sitting in to see the only pitcher in baseball history to hurl four no-hit, no-run games. He has done it four straight years, and now he capped it: On his fourth no-hitter, he made it a perfect game.

And Sandy Koufax, whose name will always remind you of strikeouts, did it with a flourish. He struck out the last six consecutive batters. So when he wrote his name in capital letters in the record books, that K stands out even more than the O-U-F-A-X.

NO. 31:
HARVEY HADDIX LOSES

MAY 26, 1959, MILWAUKEE

★ ★ ★ ★ ★

Harvey Haddix woke up that morning in Milwaukee feeling achy and nauseated. He probably had the flu. He looked out his hotel window and saw the clouds and hoped that rain might yet postpone that evening's game. But the rain didn't come. He would have to start the game that night for Pittsburgh against the best team in the National League, the Milwaukee Braves. This was 1959. Pitchers didn't call in sick.

Haddix was 33 years old and already had lived an unlikely life. He grew up on a farm in a tiny community in Central Ohio. He did not pitch a single game until his senior year in high school. After that, he played some semipro ball around town.

One day he saw that the St. Louis Cardinals were holding a tryout in Columbus. When he got there, he filled out a form asking what position he played. "Pitcher, first base, outfield," he wrote, in no particular order. The tryout director looked at it, groaned, and said: "You can only be one thing."

He put pitcher first. So Harvey Haddix was a pitcher.

First came the war: Haddix got a deferment and spent the next three years supporting his family by working on the farm. In 1947, he went to pitch in Winston-Salem, and he was terrific. Then he went to pitch in Class AAA Columbus for three years before he was drafted into the Army in 1951.

Haddix was 26 years old when he made his debut for the Cardinals. He walked the first two batters he faced and hit the third. But he pushed through and pitched a complete-game victory over the Boston Braves.

He was a small and slight man, probably not as tall as the 5-foot-9 and certainly not as heavy as the 170 pounds he was listed. He did not throw especially hard. But Haddix was difficult to hit. He was left-handed, and he had sublime control. He was also a fantastic fielder. That made him useful, even after a severe injury in 1954. ("He was never quite the same after that," his friend and teammate Stan Musial said.) Haddix bounced from St. Louis to Philadelphia to Cincinnati and finally to Pittsburgh. He was pitching for the Pirates on that blustery May Tuesday in 1959.

Haddix, for reasons that are unclear, ate a hamburger and drank a milkshake before that game against the Braves. Considering how sick he already felt, that seemed a particularly poor choice, and one he would regret. But through his nausea he was typically chipper before the game. When asked how he would pitch against the Braves' star Henry Aaron, he smiled and yelped, "High and tight and then low and away!"

OK, what about Eddie Mathews?

"High and tight and then low and away!" Haddix sang.

And Joe Adcock?

"High and tight and then low and away!"

Everybody laughed. "Hey, Harv," his teammate Don Hoak said, "if you pitch those guys that way, you're going to pitch a no-hitter."

///

HADDIX MADE HIS WAY THROUGH THE FIRST INNING DOING JUST what he promised: pitching high and tight and then low and away. He felt terrible. His stomach was wrecked. And what's more, he didn't know that the Braves were surreptitiously stealing his signs. They had a whole system: The relievers in the bullpen used binoculars to catch the sign from Pirates' catcher Smoky Burgess, and then they signaled the pitch to the batter using a towel. "We knew every pitch," Milwaukee's Bob Buhl would later say.

But it didn't matter. Bad stomach. Stolen signs. No problem. He threw it high and tight and then low and away. Haddix felt clarity that day. He didn't second-guess himself. He didn't overthink things. He stuck with his fastball, mixed in his slider rarely, and pitched precisely where he was aiming. When Haddix later found out that the Braves were stealing signs, he shrugged. There was nothing they could do against him on that day.

By the time the fourth inning began, Haddix was already well aware that he had a no-hitter going. In that fourth, Haddix got Mathews and Aaron each to fly out to center field. In the fifth, he got three outs on four pitches. He had a perfect game going. In the sixth, he struck out the opposing pitcher, Lew Burdette, to finish off an eight-pitch inning. In the seventh, he whiffed Mathews and got Aaron to ground out to third. He breezed through the eighth. He got two strikeouts in the ninth. It was so easy.

That was it. It was a perfect game, the first one thrown in the National League in 79 years.*

Only one problem: It wasn't over.

Yes, Haddix had thrown a perfect nine innings. But across the way, Lew Burdette, the pride of Nitro, West Virginia, was pitching his own kind of gem. Burdette threw a ferocious sinking fastball—it might have been more than a fastball; Whitey Ford once called it "the best spitter in the league"—and while the Pirates managed a few hits, they couldn't score a run. They thought they had one in the seventh when Pittsburgh's Bob Skinner hit a long fly ball that seemed a sure home run. Witnesses swear the ball crossed the fence and was then sent back into the park by a gust of howling wind.

---

* You can make a compelling argument that this was the first perfect game ever thrown in the National League, since the previous two were in 1880, when pitchers threw underhand and the mound was 50 feet from home plate.

"That was blown back by a tornado gale!" Pirates' announcer Bob Prince shouted on the radio.

The game went into extra innings. Burdette worked around another single in the 10th inning. Haddix gave up long fly-ball outs to Del Rice and Mathews but pitched another perfect inning.

Thirty up, thirty down.

There had never been a pitching performance like it. Burdette gave up a leadoff single in the 11th but again held Pittsburgh without a run. Haddix again. He needed only six pitches to get through the inning.

Thirty-three up, thirty-three down.

Burdette gave up another hit in the 12th but again kept the Pirates from scoring. One more time for Haddix. Andy Pafko grounded the ball back to him. Johnny Logan flied out to center. Burdette grounded out to third.

Thirty-six up, thirty-six down.

All of this seems so long ago. We now live in a time when starters are often celebrated for pitching five solid innings. That's just how the game evolved. Haddix had no idea how many pitches he had thrown, and for that matter, neither did Burdette. It didn't matter. The game was still scoreless. Burdette allowed yet another hit in the 13th inning—the Pirates' 12th hit of the day—but again Pittsburgh did not score, and Haddix took the mound with his stomach burning and his perfect game intact.

Then the perfect game was gone . . . and in the most unsatisfactory way. Milwaukee's Félix Mantilla hit a ground ball to short, and Pittsburgh's Don Hoak threw the ball wide, pulling first baseman Rocky Nelson off the bag.

"The spell," Haddix would say, "was broken."*

---

* Hoak was a no-nonsense ballplayer, and while he hated making the error, he didn't apologize for it. After the game, he drove Haddix back to the hotel and this is what he said: "I booted 'em before and I'll boot 'em again." Haddix loved that; he had no use for people making excuses.

After a bunt, Haddix intentionally walked Henry Aaron. The no-hitter and shutout were still going, at least. Then those were gone, too. Haddix threw a slider up to Joe Adcock, and that ended things. Adcock smashed it through the wind, over right fielder Joe Christopher's outstretched glove and over the wall.* The game was over.

When told afterward that he had just pitched the greatest game in baseball history, Haddix shrugged. "All I know is we lost," he said. "What's so historic about that?" When they called and asked him to be on *The Ed Sullivan Show,* he declined even though he would have been paid $500.

"How long can I talk about a loss anyway?" he asked.

Well, he would talk about it pretty much every day for the rest of his life. He always handled the conversations with modesty and humor. Of the thousands of letters he received through the years, he always said his favorite came from a fraternity at Texas A&M.

"Dear Harvey," it read in full. "Tough shit."

"It was short and sweet," Haddix said, "but it summed up everything pretty well."

---

* Technically, it wasn't a home run. This is a little bit complicated. Aaron, who was on first base, thought the ball hit the wall, so after Mantilla scored the winning run, Aaron cut across the infield and into the dugout. Adcock, who knew it was a home run, rounded the bases as he normally would. That means he passed Aaron. In the end, Aaron was ruled out and Adcock's homer was reduced to a double. Feel free to use the fun tidbit in your baseball trivia contests.

FIVE
BAREHANDED PLAYS

There were no gloves in the earliest days in baseball. Those were the days—baseball's first great chronicler Henry Chadwick wrote—"when brave men donned neither glove nor mask . . . and left the lemonade drinkers aghast."

When players started wearing gloves in the 1870s and 1880s, they tended to be flesh colored; they didn't want the fans to notice them. The player probably most responsible for making gloves acceptable was A. G. Spalding, a first baseman who not only wore a glove but made it black so that everybody would see it. Soon after, he would sell gloves, as Spalding became one of the biggest sporting goods manufacturers in the world.

Gloves have been an essential part of baseball fielding for almost 150 years.

And yet—who doesn't love a great barehanded play?

THE VIZQUEL REVERSAL (MAY 19, 2011)

There probably isn't a player in modern baseball history who made more barehanded plays than shortstop Omar Vizquel. He learned to use his bare hand while playing baseball with tennis balls on the streets of Venezuela. And numerous times every year, when he felt like a play was going to be close, he would save time by grabbing the ball barehanded and throwing it in one motion.

It's a perfect baseball irony, then, that he was the victim of one of the greatest barehanded plays ever. This happened in 2011, when Vizquel was 44 years old and playing for Chicago. The White Sox were facing Cleveland that day, there was a runner on first, and Vizquel smashed a line drive up the middle that looked to be a sure hit.

But Cleveland pitcher Joe Smith reached up with his glove and somehow managed to deflect the ball to his left. Cleveland shortstop Asdrúbal Cabrera was running to his left, but he managed to stop just in time to reach back and grab the ball with his bare hand. He then flipped it behind the back to second baseman Adam Everett, who fired it to first baseman Matt LaPorta to complete the double play.

It was so good that even in Chicago the fans stood and applauded.

DEWAYNE WISE (JULY 23, 2009)

Dewayne Wise had lived an itinerant baseball life when his moment arrived. He was a good fielder, and he was fast—that's what kept teams taking a chance on him. He was, alas, a struggling hitter, and that's what kept him moving. The Chicago White Sox were his sixth team.

But he was in center field on that glorious Thursday afternoon. Mark Buehrle was pitching for the White Sox, and he was on his game. When Buehrle was on, he created art. He worked fast, and he threw strikes, and everybody loved playing behind him. Buehrle was never better than he was that day; he took a perfect game into the ninth.

Gabe Kapler led off the inning for Tampa Bay and drilled a ball to deep left center field.

"I knew I had to get there, whatever it takes," Wise would later say. "If I had to run through the wall to try and catch the ball, I had to do it."

Buehrle thought the ball was a double for sure, and possibly a home run. Wise was playing pretty shallow, but he got a good jump on the ball and for a time seemed to be running stride for stride with the baseball. They got to the wall at the same time, ball and outfielder, and Wise leaped—he did not have time to set himself—and raised his glove high.

He gloved the ball. Incredible. But that turned out to be the easiest part because then he hit the wall and the ball popped out of his glove as he fell to the ground. He caught it with his bare hand. It was an out. Buehrle finished the perfect game.

"That was every outfielder's dream," Wise would say.

JOHNNY BENCH ENDS THE ARGUMENT (MAYBE MAY 30, 1968?)

OK, Johnny Bench personally told me he did this . . . and so even though I can't find a contemporary reference for it or a precise date, I choose to believe it. This day seems like the most likely one:

Gerry Arrigo was pitching against the Dodgers. Arrigo was a 27-year-old lefty who grew up in Chicago, and by this point in his career he was a veteran. The catcher that day was Bench, who was only 20 years old and a rookie.

Bench noticed early on that Arrigo's fastball was off; he just didn't have the usual zip on it. Bench naturally started calling for curveballs. Arrigo kept shaking him off. As the game went on—and the Dodgers kept on hammering away on Arrigo's fastball—Bench called for curveballs with more and more urgency. Arrigo continued to shake him off.

Finally Bench called time out and went to the mound to tell Arrigo that he didn't have anything on the fastball.

"I'll tell you what, rook," Arrigo said, or words to that effect, "why don't you shut the #$&# up and get behind the #&@% plate and catch whatever I #^#^@ throw."

Or comically profane punctuation to that effect.

Bench shrugged and went behind home plate and called for another curveball. When Arrigo shook him off one final time Bench called for the fastball, Arrigo threw it, and Bench reached out with his right hand and caught it barehanded.

"You should have seen his face," Bench said.

THE LIGHTNING CATCH (AUGUST 16, 1909)

The Giants and Pirates were baseball powerhouses when they faced each other at Forbes Field in Pittsburgh. More than 10,000 people came to the park that Monday afternoon.

As the afternoon progressed, dark clouds rolled into Pittsburgh. The Giants led 2–1 in the eighth inning, but by then the sky had grown scary. It looked like the game would be called at any moment, perhaps simply for darkness.

But it went on. In the bottom of the eighth, the Pirates scored the game-tying run when William Barbeau* doubled in pinch runner Ed Abbaticchio.

That led to the famous ninth inning.

"Nature," the *Pittsburgh Post-Gazette* would write, "the greatest of all stage-setters, gave a scene in that closing inning unequaled."

What happened in that closing inning is that Pittsburgh put two runners on base and sent second baseman Dots Miller to the plate against the Giants' illustrious pitcher Christy Mathewson with a chance to win the game. They called him Dots for the most wonderful of reasons. Earlier in the year a reporter asked the Pirates' great star Honus Wagner who the new kid was playing second base.

"Oh," Wagner said, "that's Miller."

But in his thick accent, it sounded like "Dot's Miller."

---

* Barbeau was universally known in that politically incorrect time as Jap Barbeau because of his 5-foot-4-inch height and because a Columbus reporter decided that he kind of looked Asian. He was not Asian.

He was forever known as Dots.

In his big moment, Dots Miller crushed a long fly ball to right field.

We turn again to the *Pittsburgh Post-Gazette* for some marvelous early twentieth-century baseball writing:

> While raindrops as big as plates were falling, a mystic darkness began to envelop the park. Miller hit for a home run. The crowd went mad. It yelled itself hoarse and went through antics that would give an alienist an easy line on the witness stand.

To explain the last part: An alienist is a psychiatrist who determines the sanity of witness at trial. But I think the point is, Miller crushed the ball, and it looked like a sure home run or at least a double. The Pirates looked like they were about to win.

"Matty's head dropped, and he turned his back," the Giants' manager John McGraw would say of Mathewson. "And I started to turn away."

Only then the Giants' right fielder Red Murray—regarded by many as the greatest defensive outfielder of his day—took off after the ball.

"Suddenly," McGraw continued, "there came the terrific crash of the first bolt of lightning as the storm broke full on. For the brief flash of a second, it lit up the field, and there outlined against the zig-zag frame, his face contorted, leaping high into the air, was our right fielder Red Murray."

The newspapers reported it differently. They did not have Murray leaping in the air. Instead, they had him reaching down and catching the ball just before it hit the ground.

But there were two things everyone agreed upon: One, Red Murray caught Dots Miller's blast with his bare hand rather than with his glove.

And two, a strike of lightning lit up the sky and the ballpark just as he made the catch.

"I NEVER TAUGHT YOU HOW TO DO THAT"
(APRIL 26, 1989)

Kevin Mitchell was not a great defensive player. He is in fact the first person I ever heard described by the expression "Have bat, will travel." But on that April day in 1989, he had his defensive moment.

The game was in St. Louis—Giants vs. Cardinals—and it was the bottom of the first inning. The Cardinals' batter was Ozzie Smith, who sliced a ball down the left-field line. Mitchell ran over to make the play.

Only at the last second, Mitchell realized something inconvenient: He had overrun the ball by quite a bit, and it was about to go over his head. Mitchell would say, "I just reached up with my other hand and tried to catch it. I couldn't think of anything else to do."

The ball landed in the palm of his right hand and stayed there—"like Velcro," Giants' announcer Mike Krukow would say—and he just caught it casually, like that was his plan all along, and he ran gently into the wall in foul ground.

"What he should have done," his teammate Terry Kennedy said, "is rip the cover off with his teeth and thrown it to the crowd."

Instead, he did . . . nothing. He simply did not understand why it was a big deal. He was annoyed when he got back to the dugout and all his teammates were laughing and kidding him and celebrating a catch that people will talk about for as long as there is baseball.

"Hey, it may not have been graceful," he yelled out, "but it got the job done."

After the game, Mitchell got a call from the greatest of all Giants and, I'd say, the greatest defensive outfielder in the game's history, Willie Mays, who had worked a bit with Mitchell in the outfield. Mays's message was simple.

"I never taught you how to do that," he said.

NO. 30:
OZZIE BECOMES THE WIZARD

APRIL 20, 1978, ATLANTA

★ ★ ★ ★ ★

"OK, so here's the thing you have to understand about the Ozzie Smith play," Dale Murphy is telling me. "It's unrepeatable. It's the greatest play in baseball history because no one will ever make another play quite like that ever again.

"And you know why?" he asks.

No. Why?

"Because they will never make a Major League Baseball team play on a field like the one we had in Atlanta."

People talk about baseball being eternal, and it's a lovely sentiment, but the game changes dramatically every era. These days, fielders play on manicured infields that are cared for as lovingly as the ground around a war hero's memorial.

No, it wasn't like that in the 1970s (or before). Infields were rocky terrain, especially in those multipurpose stadiums shared by football and baseball teams. Players used to call Cleveland's infield a car grave-yard because of all the giant humps in it. Dodgers' third baseman Ron Cey insisted that Dodger Stadium had the worst infield in baseball be-cause there was no way to smooth out the red clay. Graig Nettles was partial to Minnesota's Metropolitan Stadium. "I just play for the bad hop," he said. "If the ball ever bounced true, I'd be in trouble."

In 1978, Phillies shortstop Larry Bowa, meanwhile, said the worst infield in baseball, by far, was at Shea Stadium in New York. "What do you expect?" he said. "They built this place on a landfill."

One year later, Bowa said the worst infield he'd ever seen was at

Candlestick Park in San Francisco. "You never know where the ball is going to bounce," he said.

There's more: I looked through 1970s newspapers, and in addition to the above infields, there were complaints from players about the infields in Texas, Milwaukee, Detroit . . .

But by the late 1970s, there was a consensus building that the real worst infield in baseball was in Atlanta's Fulton County Stadium. "The infield is horse manure," Larvelle Blanks said, summing up the complaints of nearly every shortstop and third baseman in baseball.

"It was bad," Dale Murphy says. "Steve Garvey wouldn't even take infield practice in Atlanta. He was like, 'I'm not taking my life in my hands out there.'"

Murph was playing in his first full year with the Braves in 1979—this was before he won his two Most Valuable Player awards, before he made his three appearances on the cover of *Sports Illustrated*, before he was widely regarded as the best player in baseball. He was playing first base for Atlanta—he was a natural catcher but had contracted the throwing yips—and he had so many bad hops hit him that his body was covered with baseball-sized welts.

"When you watch baseball now," Murphy says, "You see infielders making plays on their sides. We couldn't do that. They told us again and again that we had to get in front of the ball; that way when the ball took a bad hop, you could knock it down with your chest."

All of which sets the stage for the greatest Ozzie Smith play.

San Diego was playing in Atlanta. It was just Ozzie's 10th game in the major leagues, before people started calling him the Wizard, but he was already building a reputation as a defensive wonder. Two days earlier, he'd somehow backhanded a ball deep in the outfield grass, turned, and threw out Houston's speedy César Cedeño. "He has the quickest hands and feet I've ever seen," the Padres' general manager Bob Fontaine Sr. said after that play.

That was just the appetizer.

I ask Ozzie to go through his greatest play.

"You know that sixth sense that people talk about," he begins. "Well, it was something I was born with. I've always had this ability to see the whole field, you know? I mean you're seeing everything, from the pitcher to the catcher, to where all the fielders are standing, to how the hitter's waiting on the pitch.

"So, first thing I watched was the pitcher. We can't do anything until he lets the ball go. So all your rhythm and timing is off the pitcher."

The pitcher that day was Randy Jones . . .

"Right. I loved playing behind Randy. He had this slow sinkerball that he'd throw time after time, and you couldn't do anything with that pitch except hit ground balls."

OK, and the batter was Atlanta's Jeff Burroughs.

"Right. Jeff was a good hitter, he hit the ball hard. And he was a pull hitter, so I think I was shading him a little bit toward third base.

"Now Randy's about to pitch. When you get out on the baseball field, in that situation, you don't necessarily want to be in the conscious mind. You want to be in the subconscious mind, if that makes sense. You want to be ready to react to anything that happens. You don't want to be anticipating. You want to be reacting. I was born with the ability to kind of go with the flow wherever the ball is hit.

"Jeff hits the ball hard up the middle. And I react, I take three or four quick steps to my left, and I dive for the ball. That's just pure instinct taking over."

Only then, because this was Atlanta's infield, something crazy happens . . .

"Right. The ball hit a rock or a hole in the infield or something, and it shoots to my right. I'm diving to the left and the ball is going behind me to my right. And I'm parallel in the air. There's nothing I do with my glove hand, so I reached back with my right hand, my bare hand, and the ball just hit me perfectly in my palm and stuck there.

"I had developed this ability to dive and get up at the same time—that's also hard to explain because it's certainly not something you practice all the time. But I bounced up and threw and got him by a step."

To repeat: Ozzie Smith dove left while the ball kicked right. He reached back and snagged it barehanded, fell to the ground, bounced up like he was coming off a trampoline, fired it in time to get Burroughs.

Burroughs immediately called it the greatest play he'd ever seen. So did your manager Roger Craig. What did you think after you made the play?

"I'm just being honest with you, I didn't think anything about it right then. It really wasn't until the next day that I heard somebody on the radio say that this might have been the greatest play they'd ever seen. And I thought, *Wow, that's really something.*"

Yes, it was really something. Dale Murphy was there. His reaction?

"My head exploded," Dale Murphy says. "All of our heads exploded."

NO. 29:
TOUCH 'EM ALL, JOE

OCTOBER 23, 1993, TORONTO

★ ★ ★ ★ ★

J oe Carter was what was called in his time "an RBI man." Those were simpler times, when there were only three hitting statistics that anybody really cared about. There was batting average. There were home runs.

And perhaps most of all, there were runs batted in. RBIs. Ribbies.

His typical line would look something like this: .302, 29, 121.

That was Joe Carter in 1986.

Or: .243, 35, 105.

That was Joe Carter in 1989.

Or .254, 33, 121.

That was Joe Carter in 1992.

Yes, oh yes, Joe Carter was an RBI man. Ten times in his career he had 100 RBIs in a season. Ten times! That's more than Ted Williams or Joe DiMaggio. That's more than Ken Griffey Jr. or Mike Schmidt. It's as many 100-RBI seasons as Hall of Famers Yogi Berra and Carl Yastrzemski had combined.

"I really would get a special feeling when there were runners in scoring position," he says. "I'd feel like, 'OK, it's showtime.'"

That was how he felt when he stepped to the plate on that Saturday night in Toronto: *It's showtime*. It was Game 6 of the 1993 World Series, bottom of the ninth, the Blue Jays trailed Philadelphia by a run, the scene was a tornado of cheers and hope and worry, but Carter remembers feeling in complete control. There were runners on base. This was his world.

"That whole inning sort of went like we thought it would go," he says. The Phillies, as expected with the lead, brought in their hard-throwing left-handed closer, Mitch Williams. They called Mitch Williams Wild Thing because of his habit of losing the strike zone the way the rest of us lose our keys. Rickey Henderson led off the inning for Toronto, and Henderson was famous for folding himself up into a crouch that made his strike zone, in the words of columnist Jim Murray, "smaller than Hitler's heart."

"We knew that he would walk Rickey," Carter says, and indeed Mitch Williams did.

After an out, future Hall of Famer Paul Molitor stepped to the plate with the idea of being the hero himself. "I remember thinking, *Man, you're going to get to live that boyhood dream to hit a home run to win the World Series*," he would tell Canada's Sportsnet. "And then I remember thinking, *Don't let your mind go there*."

Molitor instead rapped a single to put runners on first and second, setting the table for Joe Carter, who remembers stepping to the plate with his mind completely at ease and a fully formulated plan in his head.

"First thing I knew, I was going to take a strike," Carter says.

Mitch Williams needed two pitches. Then Williams got a strike and with a 2-1 count, Carter told himself: "Look fastball." Williams threw him a curve instead, and Carter would say it blended against the white of Philadelphia second baseman Mickey Morandini's jersey. Carter swung at ghosts; he never did see the ball. Blue Jays' writer Bob Elliott called it "the ugliest swing I ever saw."

Someone who didn't know the way Joe Carter's mind worked might have thought the terrible swing would have embarrassed him. But in reality: It clarified his mind. He knew Williams, after making him look so bad on the slider, would try to throw him another one.

Williams, meanwhile, was not sure what he wanted to throw. He shook off a sign. And then he nodded: He would throw a fastball up and away, exactly the opposite of what Carter was expecting. And if Williams had actually thrown that fastball up and away, then this moment would have never happened.

But, alas, he was called Wild Thing for a reason. What began as an up-and-away fastball ended up a pitch that cut down and in, exactly like a slider would. It was just where Joe Carter wanted it and he turned on the ball and he knew that it was a screamer to left field. What he didn't know was if it had the height to clear the fence. He ran up the first-base line and kept jumping up a little bit to see if the ball had gone over the fence.

And when it did go over, Joe remembered losing all sense of time and space and where he was. He leaped high again and again and pumped his fist.

"Touch 'em all, Joe!" Blue Jays' announcer Tom Cheek said. "You'll never hit a bigger home run in your life!"

Well, no, you can't hit a bigger home run than that. Even now, almost 30 years later, people ask Joe Carter about that home run almost every day. He says it's a blessing to talk about; a blessing to be remembered so many years after he retired. I ask if he knew as soon as he hit the homer that his life would completely change. He laughs. His life didn't change.

"Two weeks later," he says, "I remember being at home and my wife said, 'Joe, you need to take out the garbage.' And as I took out the garbage I thought, *Well, yeah, I'll always have that home run.* Life still goes on, though."

NO. 28:

JACKIE MITCHELL WHIFFS THE BABE

APRIL 2, 1931, CHATTANOOGA, TENNESSEE

★ ★ ★ ★ ★

Cast of Characters

JACKIE MITCHELL: Young woman baseball player.

DAZZY VANCE: One of the greatest pitchers ever.

KID ELBERFELD: Temperamental ballplayer who opened up his own baseball academy.

JOE ENGEL: Minor league team owner and flamboyant promoter.

BABE RUTH: The most legendary ballplayer in the world.

LOU GEHRIG: Ruth's sturdier teammate, also one of the best players ever.

Our story begins in Memphis with a young girl named Jackie Mitchell. She dreamed big dreams. When she was 7 years old in 1920, the United States sent a women's swim team to the Olympics for the very first time. They swept the gold medals. Little Jackie Mitchell announced her intention to become an Olympic swimmer.

When Amelia Earhart's name began appearing daily in newspapers for her flying exploits, Jackie announced her intention to become a pilot.

And then, after Joe, her father, taught her to throw a baseball, she announced her intention to become a big-league ballplayer. She spent hours every day throwing a ball against a wall. One day she was doing just that when a tall young gentleman watched her pitch. "What do we have here?" he asked. "A southpaw?"

When she nodded shyly, he smiled.

"I guess I'll have to make a pitcher out of you," he said, and he taught her how to throw his favorite pitch, the drop ball, which, when thrown right, would drop right out of sight.

The gentleman's name was Dazzy Vance. He was then a 28-year-old journeyman pitcher with a bum arm. He was playing in Memphis then, but he had already played in Toledo and Columbus and Rochester and St. Joe. He'd played only briefly in the majors and didn't have any idea when or if he'd get back. Vance didn't know how much longer he could go on in baseball.

His story, like Jackie Mitchell's story, would become legend. He would play in a poker game, and after losing a hand, he smashed his arm on the table. The pain was so intense that he was rushed to a doctor, who somehow fixed it so that for the first time in many years, Vance felt no pain. He joined the Brooklyn Dodgers in 1928 and became the best pitcher in the National League. For the next seven seasons, he led the league in strikeouts. He's in the Hall of Fame.

But this is not his story.

Jackie kept on pitching and kept on getting better as she developed her drop ball. Her father wanted to help her see her dreams through, and when she was 17, Joe Mitchell took her to Kid Elberfeld. They called him Kid after *The Tabasco Kid*, because of his spicy-hot temper.[*] He stood just 5-foot-7 but played 14 years in the big leagues anyway. He was a fine ballplayer with two notable talents. One was getting hit by pitches ("I would have died before I would have jumped back from

---

[*] "I've often been asked whether it did any good to threaten umpires, and occasionally take a wallop at one," Kid said. "I always thought that if I didn't stand up for my rights, they would give me the worst of it."

any pitcher," he would say). The other was for holding grudges, often against those pitchers who hit him with pitches.

After he retired, he opened a baseball camp in his hometown of Chattanooga. He worked with dozens of future major leaguers, including Hall of Famers Luke Appling, Bill Terry, Travis Jackson, and Burleigh Grimes. Joe Mitchell wanted to see if he would take on his daughter.

As it turns out, Kid Elberfeld was a devoted feminist. He raised his five daughters as athletes, at one point putting them together as the "Elberfeld Sisters basketball team."* He saw potential in Mitchell. No, she didn't throw all that hard, but she threw strikes, and her drop ball did drop, and he thought her awkward delivery would trouble a lot of hitters. More than anything, he loved her attitude: Jackie Mitchell was inexhaustibly confident. She felt absolutely sure that nobody in the world could hit her.

After working with Mitchell for a while, Elberfeld decided to introduce her to the man who owned the Chattanooga Lookouts, the one and only Joe Engel.

When Engel died in 1969, the Chattanooga paper wrote a little bit about his life. One paragraph of that will probably suffice:

> You name it, and Joe Engel has done it. He ran away and joined the circus at age 13; went on a vaudeville stage with Al Jolson at 14; was a Washington Senators bat boy at 15 and a major league pitcher at 18. . . . He once led an elephant down Pennsylvania Avenue in Washington; played before a record house at the old Palace Theater in New York; struck out Home Run Baker; owned a horse that raced in the Kentucky Derby; imported bullfrogs from Louisiana so he could hear them sing at sunset and tied coconuts on palm trees to help sell real estate in Miami Beach.

---

* Kid Elberfeld also occasionally had his daughters box and wrestle one another as postgame entertainment. His daughters regularly beat college teams in basketball and were also successful playing tennis and swimming.

Joe Engel had arranged for the mighty New York Yankees to play an exhibition in Chattanooga. And he had a wild idea: What if he had a 17-year-old girl pitch against them?

That would get them talking.

THE BUILDUP TO THE GAME JACKIE MITCHELL PITCHED AGAINST the New York Yankees was a very 1930s combination of laughter and misogyny.

"Curves?" one reporter wrote about Mitchell in the lead-up to the game. "Yes, sir!"

"[She] has a swell change of pace and swings a mean lipstick," wrote another.

When Babe Ruth himself was asked about facing Mitchell, he yawned. "I don't know what's going to happen if they begin to let women in baseball," he said. "Of course, they will never make good. Why? Because they are too delicate. It would kill them to play ball every day."

Rain fell on April Fools' Day, so the game was pushed to April 2. Before the game, Mitchell said something unexpected to her father: "I'll do my best, but I hope they all hit home runs." The last thing in the world she wanted the Yankees to do was take it easy on her. If they did that, she thought, "nobody would believe girls could play against the boys."

She entered the game in the first inning to face Ruth.

Ruth tipped his cap.

And as instructed by Engel, Mitchell powdered her nose.

Her first pitch was high and outside, a nervous one. But the next two were in the strike zone, and Ruth swung wildly and missed both. He turned to the umpire to complain that she was putting something on the ball, but the umpire said play on. With the count 1-2, Mitchell flung a pitch high and outside. The umpire called strike three. Ruth threw his bat to the ground.

Next Mitchell struck out Lou Gehrig on three straight pitches, all swinging strikes. He walked away laughing. She then walked another Hall of Famer, Tony Lazzeri, on four pitches and was pulled from the game.

///

SHORTLY AFTER THE GAME ENDED, JOE ENGEL—HAVING GOTTEN the publicity he craved—released Jackie Mitchell. He said that his hands were tied, that baseball commissioner Kenesaw Mountain Landis made him do it, though it's quite likely that he was telling tales. Landis, to this day, often gets blamed for baseball outlawing the practice of signing women players, but there's no actual evidence to suggest that he ever did.

Mitchell did travel the country and pitch for a while off the publicity of striking out Ruth. "She'll be pitching the World Series someday," her father said. "She'll gain speed as she grows bigger, and she's already got some pretty good speed now."

But traveling was difficult—her father's car was robbed in Atlanta, smaller and smaller crowds attended—and after a while she quit baseball.

"I predict a future for women in baseball," she said in 1934. "The day isn't far off when many women's teams will be organized."

She was right about women's teams being organized: The All-American Girls Professional Baseball League was founded in 1943. Mitchell was invited to play, but she was forty by then and had left baseball behind her.

In 1952, the Harrisburg Senators in the Class B Inter-State League made national news when they tried to sign a local softball star named Eleanor Engle. There was a back-and-forth struggle with the Senators and baseball management over that. Several Hollywood actors weighed in.

"The lady should be permitted to play," Marilyn Monroe told reporters.

"There are lots of women who'd make just as good ball players as men," Doris Day added.

Finally, baseball commissioner Ford Frick stepped in and barred the Senators from signing Engle. It was he, not Landis, who banned women from major or minor league baseball.

"Such travesties as the signing of women players will not be tolerated and the club signing or attempting to sign women players will be subject to severe penalties," Frick said.

The ban lasted for 40 years. It was still in place when Jackie Mitchell died in 1987.

///

JACKIE MITCHELL STRIKING OUT BABE RUTH IS ONE OF MY favorite moments in all of baseball history, and because of that, I've never been too interested in the argument about whether it was on the level or not. It probably wasn't. She was a 17-year-old girl, and they were the two best hitters in the world, and the event was supposed to be an April Fools' Day gag, and even Mitchell in her final interview with *The Atlanta Constitution* said it was a show.

"What was the mystery pitch you threw?" they asked her.

"Mystery pitch?" she asked back. "Lawdy no, there was no mystery about it. All I had was this underhand delivery with nothing on the ball. No speed . . . nothing."

But what of it? This is the story of a 17-year-old girl growing up in the 1920s, only just after women had won the right to vote, with the biggest and most unrealistic dream imaginable: to pitch Major League Baseball. And then one day she stepped on the mound, in front of a big crowd, and she struck out Babe Ruth and Lou Gehrig. Oh, it was real, all right.

"Girls," she told that reporter a year before she died, "can play baseball, too."

FIVE
PITCHING ODDITIES

So far I have never been in the ballpark for an immaculate inning. I've seen a perfect game (in Japan, no less), I've seen no-hitters, I've seen quick pitches and eephus pitches and knuckleballs that appeared to split in two on the way to home plate. But I've never seen an immaculate inning—that is, a pitcher who strikes out the side on nine pitches.

There have been 110 immaculate innings in baseball history—of course baseball people have counted—and it's happening more often now than ever because pitchers are striking out more hitters than ever. Pitchers threw seven immaculate innings in 2022. One of those pitchers was a Chicago Cubs' rookie named Hayden Wesneski. It was in just his fourth big-league appearance. It happened quite suddenly in the fifth inning; he had not exactly been blowing away Pirates' hitters up to that point. But then he struck out Jack Suwinski on three pitches, then struck out Zack Collins on three pitches, then struck out Jason Delay on three pitches.

"You start thinking about it the seventh, eighth pitch," Wesneski said. "And then the ninth one you kind of let it rip and hope it happens."

Someday I'll see one live. It's another reason to go to the ballpark.

Here are five cool pitching oddities.

JOE NUXHALL PITCHES IN THE BIG LEAGUES AT AGE 15 (JUNE 10, 1944)

When I arrived in Cincinnati as a newspaper columnist in the mid-1990s, Joe Nuxhall was the most beloved man in town. The Ol' Lefthander, as he was called, was the Reds' radio announcer, had been for almost thirty years. He had a simple philosophy about baseball and life: "If you swing the bat, you're dangerous."

Before that, well, let's go back to 1944.

In 1944, the Cincinnati Reds signed Joe Nuxhall when he was a 15-year-old ninth grader. He was big for his age—he already stood 6-foot-2—and he threw pretty hard for a freshman in high school. But it was ridiculous. This was during the war, and teams were desperate not only for players but for attention. The Reds had averaged fewer than 5,000 fans per game in '43.

They had Nuxhall on the bench that Saturday afternoon in June as the Reds played the Cardinals. Nobody thought he'd play. But the game got out of hand early: The Cardinals took a 13–0 lead into the ninth inning.

"Joe!" Reds' manager Bill McKechnie shouted out.

Nuxhall jumped up and began to run to the bullpen. There were three steps coming out of the dugout at old Crosley Field in Cincinnati. He easily cleared the first two. The third one, however, caught his foot, and he fell on his face. It was not an especially good omen.

Nuxhall came out to pitch the ninth—the youngest player ever to appear in a major league game. He retired two of the first three batters he faced. He had an 0-2 count on an older Cardinals' player with the unlikely name of Debs Garms. Then—and I can still hear the Ol' Lefthander's voice when he would tell me the story—he realized exactly where he was.

"I had been pitching against seventh and eighth graders," he says. "And suddenly I look over to see who is standing on deck . . . and it's Stan Musial."

The next few minutes were a blur. He threw a wild pitch. He walked Garms. Musial rifled a single. Nuxhall walked the next three batters. He gave up another single. Finally McKechnie went out to rescue Nuxhall. Two days later, Joe was sent to Birmingham for seasoning.

It would be eight years before Joe returned to the big leagues. He still had a fine career; he won 135 games and made a couple of All-Star teams. And as mentioned, he became the most beloved person in Cincinnati. That ain't bad.

TIPPY MARTINEZ PICKS OFF THREE BASE RUNNERS IN THE SAME INNING (AUGUST 24, 1983)

Everything about this inning was wonderful. The Orioles were playing the Toronto Blue Jays, and they trailed by a couple of runs in the ninth. Orioles' manager Joe Altobelli, in a desperation move, pinch-hit for catcher Joe Nolan. When the Orioles tied the game, they had no catchers left.

Altobelli had no choice but to turn to his emergency catcher, infielder Lenn Sakata, who had never played catcher in his professional baseball life. Sakata hated the very idea of playing catcher, but there was nobody else. The game went into the 10th inning and the Blue Jays, well aware that Sakata was back behind the plate, decided to be aggressive on the basepaths. Barry Bonnell singled and was so anxious to steal second that he started to take off way before the pitch. Tippy Martinez, the Orioles' reliever, noticed and tossed over to first. That was pickoff No. 1.

Then Dave Collins walked. Collins was an excellent base stealer—he once stole 79 bases in a season. Blue Jays' first base coach John Sullivan walked over and said to Collins: "Don't get picked off."

Collins got himself picked off anyway. That was pickoff No. 2.

Finally, Toronto's Willie Upshaw singled. Sullivan warned him, too, but at this point, as Humphrey Bogart said in *Casablanca*, destiny had taken a hand. Martinez threw over to first and nailed a sliding Upshaw. And that was pickoff No. 3.

ROKI SASAKI ALMOST THROWS BACK-TO-BACK PERFECT GAMES (APRIL 10 AND 17, 2022)

As I write these words, we don't yet know Roki Sasaki's future. He's only 21. But at this moment, Sasaki—nicknamed the Monster of the Reiwa Era*—is the dominant pitcher in Japan. That has been his fate ever since he threw a 101-mph fastball while still in high school, breaking a high school speed record set by none other than Shohei Ohtani.

In April 2022, Sasaki did something jaw-dropping.

On April 10, while pitching for the Chiba Lotte Marines, he threw one of the greatest games ever thrown, a 19-strikeout perfect game against the Orix Buffaloes. At one point he struck out 13 batters in a row. It was the first perfect game thrown in Japan by a pitcher in 18 years.

Then in his very next start against the Hokkaido Nippon-Ham Fighters, Sasaki threw *another* eight perfect innings. He retired 52 consecutive batters, which—there are no words to describe that kind of dominance.

At that point, his manager Tadahito Iguchi pulled him from the game to protect his arm.

The future is limitless.

---

* The Reiwa Era is the current imperial era on Japan's official calendar; it began in May 2019, when Emperor Akihito abdicated and handed the throne to his son Naruhito. Reiwa means beautiful harmony.

CARL HUBBELL STRIKES OUT FIVE HALL OF FAMERS IN A ROW (JULY 10, 1934)

King Carl, as they called Carl Hubbell, had a long and twisting road to that famous 1934 All-Star Game at the Polo Grounds. He was not signed until he was 21 and was working for an oil company. He kicked around in the minor leagues and seemed about to wash out.

Only then he perfected a pitch called the screwball.

There had been other "screwball" pitchers before Hubbell . . . but not really. Shucks Pruett—a little 5-foot pitcher who was famous in his day for striking out Babe Ruth 13 times in 24 at-bats—was often called a screwball artist. But it's likely his pitch was very different from Hubbell's; he threw it more like a changeup that happened to drift to the left. Another word for that pitch was a fadeaway.

But Hubbell's screwball didn't fade away. No, it broke hard to the left, an anti-curveball, and he threw it by turning his hand inside out upon releasing the ball. It was a painful pitch to throw, an arm wrecker. Jim Murray's line about Hubbell's deformed arm rings through the years: "He looks as if he put it on in the dark."

But few could hit it. In 1933, Hubbell won the league MVP award after going 23-12 with a 1.66 ERA. And in 1934, he started just the second All-Star Game ever held between the American and National Leagues. He started off sluggishly, giving up a single to Charlie Gehringer and walking Heinie Manush.

The next three American League batters were Babe Ruth, Lou Gehrig, and Jimmie Foxx, three of the greatest sluggers in baseball history.

"Brrrr! Nightmares! Shivers! Jitters!" wrote the sportswriter Paul Gallico. "How would you have liked Hubbell's spot?"

Hubbell struck out Ruth looking on a fastball.

He struck out Gehrig swinging on a screwball.

He struck out Foxx swinging, too.

"Now, I am sort of an old-timer at this stuff and used to comport myself with dignity and decorum in a press box," Gallico wrote. "But after this I found myself yelling and running around and slapping colleagues on the back and asking them if they had seen it."

In the second inning, the first two batters were Al Simmons and Joe Cronin. Hubbell struck them out, too, five Hall of Famers in a row.*

JOHNNY VANDER MEER THROWS BACK-TO-BACK NO-HITTERS (JUNE 11 AND 15, 1938)

Pete Rose always likes asking fans, "What's the most unbreakable record in baseball history?" They will usually talk about Joe DiMaggio's 56-game hitting streak or Cy Young's 511 victories.

"No!" Rose will bellow happily. "It's Johnny Vander Meer's record of throwing two no-hitters in a row. Because the only way to beat that is to throw *three* no-hitters in a row."

Johnny Vander Meer had a blazing fastball, but he did have trouble throwing strikes with it. As he used to say about his early baseball days: "I couldn't hit the side of a barn with a handful of peas."

At one point he changed his pitching motion from sidearm to overhand—thanks to advice from one of the greatest pitchers ever, Lefty Grove—and at 23 started to figure things out. On June 11, 1938, when facing the Boston Bees,† he threw a no-hitter. Fans and teammates flooded onto the field and carried him on their shoulders in triumphant celebration.

"I had no idea of pitching a no-hitter," he would say afterward. "I just kept pouring it in."

---

* In the 1999 All-Star Game, Pedro Martínez began the game by striking out Barry Larkin, Larry Walker, Sammy Sosa, and Mark McGwire in a row. At the time it seemed like all four of them would end up in the Hall of Fame; only two are in so far.

† In 1936, in an effort to turn around a moribund franchise, the Boston Braves had a fan contest asking for a new nickname. The winner was Bees. And so for five years, the team was known as the Bees. Unfortunately, the team was just as terrible, and in 1941 they went back to being the Braves.

His next time out, four days later, was against the Brooklyn Dodgers. His fastball was hot that day, but his control was wild. He walked eight Dodgers. Still, nobody could hit him. He went into the ninth inning with the no-hitter very much intact. He walked three batters but still got Leo Durocher to fly out to center field, and that clinched his second straight no-hitter.

"Johnny Vander Meer moved into baseball's hall of fame last Saturday," the Associated Press's Sid Feder wrote. "Now he owns it."

In fact, Vander Meer is not in the actual Baseball Hall of Fame, though he did get quite a few votes through the years. He finished his career with a 119-121 record, led the league in strikeouts three times and in walks twice. But Rose is right: His record will probably never be broken.

NO. 27:
RON NECCIAI STRIKES OUT 27

MAY 13, 1952, BRISTOL, VIRGINIA

★ ★ ★ ★ ★

My friend Jonathan Abrams was 7 or 8 years old when he started collecting autographs. He started with baseball autographs because he loved baseball, but as the years went by, he started collecting autographs of pretty much anybody. Football players. Hockey stars. Authors. He looks back at his binder filled with autographs from politicians and laughs: He's not entirely sure why a young African American in Los Angeles was so desperate for autographs from Trent Lott and Pat Buchanan and Rudy Giuliani.

"I pretty much wanted every autograph," he says. "I didn't care."

Baseball, though, remained his focus, because he loved nothing more than baseball. Jonathan doesn't remember the first baseball player he wrote, but he does remember that after a short while it became an obsession. He wrote to players at spring training because he found that was when he had the most success. He wrote to team owners asking them to help him get troublesome autographs. When he was 11, he decided to get the autographs of every single player on both 1995 All-Star Teams. He finished the job when he got A's reliever Steve Ontiveros. He doesn't remember why Ontiveros was so difficult.

In 1994, when Jonathan was 10, he was reading a magazine called *Sports Collectors Digest* when he came across a story that inflamed his imagination. It began like so: "Here's one record that could stand for another millennium: striking out 27 batters in nine innings. Impossible? Nope. Definitely possible. And Ron Necciai actually did it!"

Ron Necciai?* Jonathan had never heard of him. Not many have. But it's true: Necciai really did strike out 27 batters in a nine-inning game.

Jonathan had bought a used copy of a book that had the addresses of former major league players.† He looked, and sure enough, there was a listing for a "Ron Necciai" living in Pennsylvania. Jonathan wrote a letter to Necciai asking him some of his stock autograph questions‡ and then finishing off with a request: Would Necciai be Jonathan's pen pal?

And Ron Necciai wrote back.

///

BRANCH RICKEY CALLED RON NECCIAI THE GREATEST ALL-AROUND pitcher he ever saw. That's pretty much all you need to know about his talent. Necciai grew up in Monongahela, Pennsylvania, a place that will sound familiar to many sports fans because it's also the hometown of Hall of Fame quarterback Joe Montana. When Necciai was 18 years old, he was discovered by a local barber who "prides himself on the fact that he knows baseball." Necciai signed with the hometown Pirates for $150. He would have taken less.

"Anything," he would say, "beat working in the mills."

He signed as a first baseman, but when he was sent to Salisbury, North Carolina, his manager George Detore saw him throw a ball across the infield and that was that. "Son," Detore said, "you're now a pitcher." Necciai didn't know how to be a pitcher, and to be honest, he did not especially care to learn.

"Baseball," he later told *Sports Illustrated*'s Pat Jordan, "was just something to do."

Necciai got roughed up in Salisbury, and after just three innings, he was demoted to nearby Shelby, where he failed to get even a single out.

---

* Necciai is pronounced "Netch-EYE."
† "How is that even legal?" Jonathan asks.
‡ Who was your best friend in baseball? What do you eat? What's the most important thing to do in order to become a Major League Baseball player? Etc.

He then quit baseball entirely, went home, moved back in with his mother, and got a job at a steel mill. That's when he remembered— yeah, baseball was better than working in a mill. The Pirates still wanted him, much to his surprise, and in 1951 he showed up for spring training and was sent back to Salisbury.

Necciai lost his first seven games and was ready to quit again; this time the Pirates got him to stay by offering him a side job as the team bus driver. "He was a pretty fair bus driver," Detore said. "But he still wasn't much of a pitcher."

Finally, Detore—the man Necciai would later call his second father— lost his patience. He took Necciai to the mound and said, "Just throw the ball as hard as you can." Necciai threw a few unimpressive fastballs, and Detore shook his head.

"Can't you throw any harder than that?" he asked angrily. He had seen Necciai throw harder just playing around in the infield as a first baseman.

"Yes, sir, I can," Necciai said.

"Then why the hell don't you?" Detore asked.

"Because in high school, I broke a guy's ribs," Necciai said. "My coach made me promise not to throw that hard again."

Detore was stupefied. "Just throw it as hard as you can for me," he said.

Necciai unleashed a fastball that Detore later would say had to be 100 mph. He threw it so hard the catcher could not even get his glove up in time and the ball whacked off his face mask. Detore then told him to throw a curveball as hard as he could, and Necciai threw a 12-6 curveball that Detore would say perfectly mirrored what the world would later see from Sandy Koufax, only from a right-handed pitcher.

"Buddy," Detore said, "you've got it."

Not long after that, Branch Rickey Jr.—the Pirates' farm director and son of the legendary Branch Rickey—came to Salisbury and saw him pitch and could barely contain his excitement. "You outta be ashamed of yourself, playing with these babies," he told Necciai. "Your ability is so superior to theirs you should beat them every time out."

In 1952, Ron Necciai beat them pretty much every time out.

///

"NO, I DIDN'T REALIZE UNTIL AFTER THE GAME THAT I HAD struck out 27 batters," Ron Necciai wrote to Jonathan Abrams.

This was May of 1952. He was playing for the Bristol Twins in the Appalachian League in a game against the Welch Miners. There were 1,183 fans at Shaw Stadium in Bristol, Virginia.

Necciai already had been on a roll. In the Twins' home opener, he had struck out 20 Kingsport batters. He struck out 19 in his second start. Three days after that, he came into the game in relief and faced 12 batters. He struck out 11 of them. *Bristol Herald Courier* sports editor Gene Thompson had started calling him "Rocket Ron."

That 27-strikeout day, Rocket Ron was feeling terrible. It's funny how often a pitcher who feels terrible ends up pitching the best game of his life. Harvey Haddix felt sick and nauseated leading into his 12-inning perfect game. Many have said that Don Larsen was a little bit hung over when he threw his World Series perfect game.*

And Necciai barely slept the night before the game. He was dealing with painful ulcers. He came to the park looking so miserable that Detore offered to pitch someone else. Necciai downed some antacid pills and said he would try his best.

In the first inning, he struck out all three batters he faced.

In the second, he struck out two—allowing a ground ball to short between the strikeouts.

In the third, a batter reached on an error. Necciai struck out the next three.

His stomach hurt so much between innings that Detore made him

---

* Larsen always insisted he was not, but we'll get back to that in Larsen's chapter.

eat some cottage cheese and drink some milk. These were primitive days for dealing with ulcers.

In the fourth, Necciai hit the first batter and then struck out the next three swinging.

In the fifth, he struck out all three batters he faced.

In the sixth, he struck out all three batters he faced.

That's 17 strikeouts through six innings and only two batters had put a ball in play. Necciai's fastball was popping, obviously, but it was his curveball that left hitters breathless. It seemed to be falling out of the sky. "I'm not talking four or five inches," Welch's Frank Sliwka would say about how much the ball dropped. "I'm talking a foot."

By the seventh inning, fans started singing the number after each strikeout. "Eighteen!" they sang when Billy Hammond struck. "Nineteen," they sang when Bob Kendrick* struck out. After a walk, Necciai struck out Welch catcher John Barry. "Twenty!" they sang.

In the eighth inning, Necciai once again struck out all three batters he faced. The Miners even tried to bunt the ball, but they couldn't.

If you're keeping count, you know that he had 23 strikeouts going into that inning. He was well on his way to striking out more batters in nine innings than anyone ever had . . . but 27 strikeouts seemed mathematically out of reach. Except this was a day for miracles.

Frank Whitehead was the first Welch batter in the ninth. He hit a high foul pop-up that seemed an easy play for Bristol catcher Harry Dunlop. "Drop it!" first baseman Phil Filiatrault shouted. The crowd picked up on the cue and also screamed for him to drop it. Dunlop did. Necciai struck out Whitehead for No. 24.

A pinch hitter named Joe Uram came into the game. He struck out less dramatically. "Twenty-five," the fans sang.

---

* This is not my friend Bob Kendrick, famous for being president of the Negro Leagues Baseball Museum in Kansas City. But this is just a friendly reminder: If you are anywhere near Kansas City, you must go to the museum. It's amazing.

Finally, Billy Hammond stepped up again—he'd already struck out three times. And he stood no chance on Necciai's curveball; he swung about a foot over the ball for strike three. That was strikeout No. 26.

And that should have been the end of the game. Except, you know how if the catcher drops a third strike, then the runner is allowed to run to first? Well, yeah, the ball got by Harry Dunlop. People would always ask him: "Did you do that on purpose?" And he always said no.

"The way his ball was dropping that day," Dunlop would say, "I was just trying my best."

Hammond made it to first, and that brought up Bob Kendrick. Necciai struck him out, completing a 27-strikeout no-hitter, just maybe the greatest game anyone has ever pitched in professional baseball.

"I just did my best," Necciai said after the game. "I'm just learning to pitch."

"PLAY HARD," RON NECCIAI WROTE TO JONATHAN ABRAMS. "AND study hard."

In each of his letters to Abrams, Necciai made a point of saying how important it was that Jonathan got his education. "Baseball may be more fun," he wrote at one point, "but school is more important."

Ron Necciai kept striking out batters in 1952. That was his year. In 148 innings for Bristol and Burlington, he had struck out 255 batters. His ERA was 1.28. On August 6, the Pittsburgh Pirates called him up to the big leagues, news so massive that *The Pittsburgh Press* put it at the top of the front page. A big crowd was there for his big-league debut on August 10.

Necciai was just 20 years old.

"He was shaking so bad on the mound," his catcher Joe Garagiola said, "he could not see my signals."

Yeah, that day was rough: Necciai gave up seven runs. But his next time out, against Cincinnati, he pitched three hitless innings in relief and struck out five. Cincinnati's Ted Kluszewski said Necciai threw the best curveball he'd ever seen.

Alas, that's where the fairy tale ended. Necciai pitched 10 more times and the Pirates lost nine of the games. Pittsburgh thought he could regain his confidence in the off-season, but then the Army drafted him, and his ulcer reemerged. He weighed just 150 pounds when he got back to Pittsburgh. He blew out his shoulder trying to work his way into shape. He missed the whole 1954 season. He tried to make it back in 1955, but he could not. He retired at 23.

Even then, Rickey talked about how Necciai could have been another Dizzy Dean.

Necciai went to work for a sporting goods company and later became a co-owner of his own. The letters he wrote to Abrams were all on Hays, Necciai & Associates stationery. In one, he talked about a trip he took to the Panama Canal. In another, he wrote that Stan Musial was the best hitter he ever faced. All the while, he reminded Jonathan: "Study hard, play hard and listen to Mom," he wrote.

Jonathan did not become a big-league ballplayer. Instead, he became a *New York Times* sportswriter and a bestselling author. In 2022—almost 30 years after exchanging letters with Ron Necciai—Jonathan went to Belle Vernon, Pennsylvania, to talk to his old pen pal about what it means to be famous, even for a short while. Necciai was 90 years old.

"I'm surprised at the people that still remember," Necciai told him. "I haven't played in 70 years. I still get fan mail every week."

NO. 26:
ALEXANDER STRIKES OUT LAZZERI

★ ★ ★ ★ ★

There's an argument to be made that between 1911 and 1920, Grover Cleveland Alexander—everyone called him Pete—was the greatest pitcher in the world. They even called him the Great Alexander. He led the league in wins and strikeouts six times.

But by 1926, Pete was hollowed out. World War I had wrecked him. He had lost hearing in his left ear and took shrapnel on his right ear. He injured his right arm while operating a howitzer. He returned from war shell-shocked and an alcoholic. He suffered from epilepsy.

He kept on pitching. He'd lost much of the speed off his once great fastball, and his curveball no longer broke as it once had. But he still had his almost supernatural control, to the end he could pitch a ball exactly where he wanted.

"He might decide to throw that next one right to the batter's known strength," his contemporary Bill Doak said, "but just off enough to make it a bad ball to hit."

Midway through that 1926 season, the Chicago Cubs waived Alexander. Manager Joe McCarthy believed his drinking and erratic behavior were hurting the team. The Cardinals' manager Rogers Hornsby rather famously did not drink,* but in the words of sportswriter Westbrook Pegler: "He is broadminded as to the application of horse lotion and

---

* Hornsby also didn't smoke or even go to the movies. He thought it was bad for his batting eye.

doesn't care what time a fellow gets to bed just so he's up in time to play in the afternoon."

Alexander kept on drinking, but he showed up to play. He was a key pitcher for St. Louis in the pennant race, outdueling Cincinnati's ace Dolf Luque in perhaps the most important game of the season. St. Louis won the pennant by two games and faced the Yankees in the World Series. The 1927 Yankees Murderers' Row lineup is still regarded as perhaps the best in baseball history. The 1926 Yankees that St. Louis played had exactly the same lineup.

But Alexander was reborn. In Game 2, he pitched nine strong innings and, remarkably, struck out ten Yankees. He had struck out only 47 batters all season.

"Grover Cleveland Alexander, one of baseball's old masters," the Associated Press reported, "uncurled the mighty power in his ancient right arm to pitch the Cardinals to victory over the Yankees today."

In Game 6, the desperate Cardinals—down 3–2 in the Series—pitched him again. Nobody thought Alexander had another good outing in him. "You might have thought that the Yankees, being a hitting team by reputation, would get on Aleck this time and blast him out of there," Pegler wrote.

Instead, Alexander threw another complete game and won again.

Game 7 was the next day.

The Cardinals led 3–2 in the bottom of the seventh inning when the Yankees loaded the bases against St. Louis starter Jesse Haines. Rookie Tony Lazzeri, a future Hall of Famer who drove in 117 RBIs that season, was the next batter.

Hornsby had a decision to make. Haines had pitched well. He would end up in the Hall of Fame. But Hornsby's gut told him he should turn to Pete Alexander, despite two seemingly disqualifying facts:

Fact 1: Alexander had pitched a complete game the day before.

Fact 2: Hornsby suspected that Alexander was drunk.*

Alexander entered the game. He may or may not have warmed up—accounts differ. He then walked around the mound for a moment in order to, in his own words, "let Lazzeri stew."

And the duel began. Alexander threw a curveball that broke down and away. Lazzeri watched it go by, and home plate umpire George Hildebrand called it a strike.

Alexander then went for the pitch that made him famous: a low and away fastball. Some people even called him Old Low and Away Alexander. But for once Alexander's control failed him. His pitch was up, and Lazzeri crushed it to deep left field. It had the distance of a home run, but it curved foul. How far foul? In the atrocious movie *The Winning Team*—where Alexander is played by an actor named Ronald Reagan—the ball was *just* foul. That might have been an exaggeration.

Still, it was close enough that Alexander famously said: "A few feet made the difference between a hero and a bum."

On the third pitch, Alexander threw a low and away curve one more time. Lazzeri flailed at it for strike three. The Cardinals won the World Series. And Alexander's strikeout of Lazzeri was instantly hailed as perhaps the greatest moment in baseball history. It is specifically referenced on Alexander's Hall of Fame plaque.

He pitched for four more years, but after that, Alexander's life would take a sad turn; he lived on for 24 heartbreaking years where he battled with alcohol, money troubles, and health issues. For a time, he was paid a few bucks to relive his famous strikeout on a vaudeville stage. He gave that up after a few weeks. When a friend asked him why, he shook his head sadly.

"I'm tired of striking out Lazzeri," he said.

---

* Hornsby would say for the rest of his life that Alexander *was* drunk but this was probably just to make the story better. Alexander, for his part, insisted he was not drunk or hung over.

FIVE
FUNNY THINGS

Whenever I told people I was writing this book, they would inevitably recommend a favorite moment. The one they recommended most happened March 24, 2001. On that day, in Tucson, Hall of Fame pitcher Randy Johnson was facing San Francisco Giants' center fielder Calvin Murray. He fired a fastball.

Three-quarters of the way to home plate, the ball hit a dove that had flown in its path.

"I'm expecting to catch this ball," Arizona catcher Rod Barajas said, "and all I see is an explosion."

For months, I went back and forth about the moment. "You have to," one friend told me. "It's the funniest moment in baseball history."

Is it, though? I mean, I guess you could make the argument if you don't think too hard about the bird. In the end I decided to not include it—or at least not to give it more space than this.

Here are five funny moments:

DAVID HULSE'S FOUL BALLS (OCTOBER 3, 1992)

The Rangers and Angels, two going-nowhere teams, were playing out the season. Ninth inning. Texas trailed 4–2 with one out. Rangers' rookie David Hulse stepped to the plate against Angels' closer Joe Grahe.

Hulse, a left-handed batter, was late on the first pitch and he fouled it hard into the Angels' dugout on the third-base side. The Angels' players scattered a bit and then, as players often do when foul balls come flying in, made various hand gestures toward Hulse as if to say, "Hey, what did we do?"

On the next pitch, Hulse slapped the ball hard into the Angels' dugout again. More silliness. A security guard waved a white towel in surrender and an Angels' player got up to get his glove for protection.

This sort of thing happens now and again.

But on the next pitch, Hulse smashed ANOTHER ball into the Angels' dugout. And that doesn't happen. Three in a row? Now all the Angels' players and personnel, every last one of them, moved into the other corner of the dugout. The announcers were laughing so hard they couldn't even broadcast the game.

"Look at them all bunched up over there," one said.

Hulse smiled and shook his head. He was still a rookie trying to prove he belonged in the major leagues. He needed to concentrate. Grahe's next pitch was up. Hulse swung . . . and he fouled the ball hard into the Angels' dugout for the fourth time.

"Obviously, I didn't do it on purpose," he would say. "Hell, if I could do it on purpose, I'd be in the Hall of Fame."

It was wonderful. Hulse received a standing ovation from the crowd when he grounded out on the next pitch. He would say it was the only standing ovation he ever received.

Not long after, *Saturday Night Live* did a baseball skit where mayor Rudy Giuliani's son, Andrew, kept getting hit in the head with foul balls. The batter in the skit? Right. It was David Hulse.

CANDLESTICKS MAKE A NICE GIFT
(1988, MOVIE *BULL DURHAM*)

I believe the mound visit scene in *Bull Durham* is the funniest scene in any baseball movie. And it almost didn't make it into the movie. Why not? Producers didn't think it "forwarded the plot." They seemed unmoved by director Ron Shelton's explanation that *Bull Durham* didn't exactly have a plot.

Setting up the scene: Nuke LaLoosh was struggling. The infielders all gathered on the mound, and they ended up talking about a cursed glove and a teammate's wedding and Nuke's father in the crowd. Hey, we've all wondered what these mound visits are like.

Finally, Durham Bulls coach Larry Hockett—played by Robert Wuhl—was sent out to the mound to break things up. "Excuse me, what the hell's going on out here?" he asks.

"Well," says Crash Davis, played by Kevin Costner, "Nuke's scared cause his eyelids are jammed and his old man's here. We need a live rooster—is it a live rooster?—we need a live rooster to take the curse off Jose's glove, and nobody seems to know what to get Millie or Jimmy for their wedding present. That about right? We're dealing with a lot . . ."

"Well, uh," Hockett says, "candlesticks always make a nice gift. And maybe we can find out where she's registered, maybe a place setting or, I guess, silverware pattern. OK? Let's get two!"

Perfect. And Robert Wuhl came up with it on the spot.

Here's what happened: The scene was shot at four A.M., it was freezing, and everybody was ready to call it a night. Shelton said, "OK, last one, Robert, this one's yours," meaning Wuhl was free to say whatever he wanted.

His line was supposed to be: "Oh, I thought there was a problem." But this time, Wuhl was thinking about how a few weeks earlier he'd asked his wife what they should get a friend for their wedding. "Candlesticks make a nice gift," she said. He used it, ad-libbed the rest, and ended it with the classic baseball phrase "Let's get two!"

Wuhl never thought they would use it in the movie. But the next day, when everybody was watching the dailies, the scene played and the whole room broke up. And later, focus groups called it one of their favorite scenes in the movie.

ADRIÁN BELTRÉ PULLS OVER THE ON-DECK CIRCLE (JULY 26, 2017)

Adrián Beltré was very funny. For years and years, he didn't let that part of his personality show—baseball does ask its players to be stoic. But as he grew older and more comfortable in the big leagues, he let his personality out. He would get in rundowns and then just run off the field, heading for nowhere. He would tease infielders by taking his hand off the base, daring them to tag him. He would lose his mind whenever anyone touched his head.

His funniest moment was probably in the late innings of a lopsided Rangers–Marlins game. Florida was leading the game by a dozen runs in the eighth inning, when Beltré began taking a few warm-up swings near the Texas on-deck circle. Unfortunately, in the eye of umpire Gerry Davis, he was not near enough. Davis demanded Beltré move closer.

Beltré seemed sure that Davis was putting him on. But Davis was serious. He kept barking at Beltré to move closer to the on-deck circle.

So Beltré did. He dragged the on-deck circle closer to where he was standing.

"I just did what he told me to do," Beltré said.

Davis then threw him out of the game, which only made the whole thing funnier.

KEN GRIFFEY MAKES THE PLAY IN FRONT OF KEN GRIFFEY (SEPTEMBER 21, 1990)

It was the ninth inning of a close game between the Chicago White Sox and the Seattle Mariners. A young White Sox player named Sammy Sosa lifted a fly ball to left field. The ball was headed directly at the

Mariners' left fielder, a 40-year-old Ken Griffey. This was Griffey's 18th season in the big leagues. He'd been a star on the famous Big Red Machine Reds of the mid-1970s. He'd played in three All-Star Games. He'd caught thousands of fly balls.

This was no different. He held out his arms, the universal sign for "I got it."

And just as he was about to catch it . . . his 20-year-old son Ken Griffey Jr., with the biggest Bart Simpson smile on his face, jumped in front of him and caught the ball first.

It was so funny and, more, so lovely. The Griffeys were the only father-and-son combination to ever play in the same game. They had several wonderful moments together; they once hit back-to-back home runs. But this was my favorite, especially for the look on Ken Griffey's face afterward, the look fathers know, the look that says: "You've got to be kidding me."

GIBSON PLUNKS LACOCK (SOMETIME IN 1986)

On September 3, 1975, a Wednesday evening in St. Louis, the Cardinals and Cubs played a game that didn't matter much. The Cardinals were only just in the pennant race. The Cubs were long gone. Only 15,000 or so diehard fans came out.

The game took on new meaning in the seventh inning.

That's when the Cardinals sent Bob Gibson to the mound for the final time.

They didn't know for sure that it was the last time, but they had a pretty good guess. Gibson was 40 and had already announced he was retiring at the end of the year. Two days earlier, the team held Bob Gibson Day, complete with tributes and gifts and a message from President Gerald Ford.

"Most of all," Gibson said to the crowd, "I'm proud of that fact that whatever I did, I did it my way."

He might have retired right then, but he decided to stick it out a little longer. He wanted to believe that he still had a little something left, even at age 40. There was never anyone who competed harder than Gibson. He pitched with radiance and verve and a salty disposition. He'd glare hitters into dust.*

"Don't dig in against Gibson, he'll knock you down," Henry Aaron told Dusty Baker. "He'd knock down his own grandmother. Don't stare at him. Don't smile at him. Don't talk to him. He doesn't like it. If you happen to hit a home run, don't run too slow and don't run too fast. And if he hits you, don't charge the mound. He's a Golden Glove boxer."

No, Bob Gibson didn't leave much room to operate.

That day, Gibson came in to pitch relief, and he just didn't have it. He walked a batter, gave up a hit, walked another batter, threw a wild pitch, and intentionally walked a batter to load the bases.

Up stepped left-handed pinch hitter Pete LaCock. If anyone else had been on the mound, Cardinals' manager Red Schoendienst would have brought in a lefty reliever. But he had too much respect for his old friend and teammate to pull him.

"This is Gibby's out to get," Red told everyone on the bench.

LaCock was feeling a bit salty himself. He was 23 then, and cocky and sure that the Cubs were not treating him with the respect he deserved. Before the game, he yelled at Cubs' manager Jim Marshall for 45 minutes.

"Pete is a very ambitious young man," Marshall told reporters. "He needs a lot of time for someone to explain to him what it's all about."

LaCock stepped in and worked his way to a full count. Gibson threw a fastball, down and in. In his younger days, he had thrown that fastball by Mays and Aaron and Clemente. Now, though, it just sat there. LaCock turned on it for a grand slam, the first and last of his career.

---

* Gibson always said that he wasn't glaring at hitters at all, it's just that he didn't wear his glasses on the mound and so needed to squint to see the catcher's signs. Nobody—and I mean nobody—bought this.

Gibson retired that day.

Wait, you say: There's nothing funny about this.

Well, for the next decade, Gibson stewed about that pitch he threw to Pete LaCock. He could barely stand the fact that LaCock got the better of him and there was no second act. He fought back by taking shots at LaCock. "When a hitter like Pete LaCock hits a grand slam off you," he told one reporter, "it's time to hang them up."

In 1986, there was a series of old-timers' games played in ballparks across the country. It was fun. Gibson played in a couple of them. And, as it turned out, so did LaCock. In fact, there was a game in Kansas City, and Bob Feller was pitching when LaCock came up.

Suddenly, and without warning, Feller stepped off the mound, and Bob Gibson raced in. He had not been scheduled to pitch. He took only a few warm-up pitches.

And on the first pitch, he drilled LaCock in the back.

Now, *that's* funny. Many years later, announcer Bob Costas asked Gibson if the story was true, if he had really come in just to hit Pete LaCock with a pitch in an old-timers' game. Gibson gave him the famous stare.

"Robert," he said, "the scales must be balanced no matter how long it takes."

NO. 25:

BALL CONKS OFF CANSECO'S HEAD

MAY 26, 1993, CLEVELAND

★ ★ ★ ★ ★

There was a time when José Canseco seemed destined to be the player of his generation. He had Reggie Jackson's power. He had startling speed. He had charisma and good looks and a burning ambition to be an all-time great player. The ambition mostly came from his hard-driving father, who would yell, "You stink!" at him for motivation.

Once in the big leagues, Canseco hit three homers in a game.

"Yeah," his father asked afterward. "What did you do in your other at-bat?"

Later, there would be steroids admissions and player accusations and bizarre turns in his personality. But in 1988, he was the first player to hit 40 homers and steal 40 bases in a season. Annie Leibovitz photographed him shirtless for a magazine cover. He started hanging out with Madonna.

"Why are you so popular?" he was asked on ABC's *Primetime Live*.

"I'm José Canseco," he said. "I do things out of the ordinary."

Over time, though, his popularity turned sour. It wasn't any one thing. Canseco was reportedly a difficult teammate. He dealt with some nagging injuries. Steroids rumors began surrounding him. He was standing in the on-deck circle in a game between Oakland and Texas when he got traded to the Rangers.

Canseco did not understand at all why people had turned on him. "I'm the most exciting player in baseball," he insisted.

Fewer and fewer people seemed to believe. Canseco got hurt in 1993 and played in only 60 games. But in one of those games, he played the key role in the funniest play in baseball history.

It was a Wednesday night in Cleveland. Kenny Rogers was pitching for the Rangers. The Cleveland hitter was Carlos Martínez, who lofted a fly ball to deep right center, where Canseco was playing.

Canseco drifted back toward the wall. He looked a little bit unsteady as he went back; he seemed to think he was closer to the wall than he actually was. Canseco was not, in the best of circumstances, a graceful fielder. He turned back toward the ball and lifted his glove to catch it.

And then—no other way to say it—the ball conked him on top of the head and bounced over the wall for a home run.

Here's what makes the play so special: You can watch it endlessly on a loop and it will never not be funny. I personally have watched that ball hit his head at least 500 times in my life and fully expect to watch it 500 more times. I think it comes down to timing. You can see Canseco kind of stumbling about, and then he seems to have the ball, and then it clanks on his head and then he reaches up with his hands in the universal sign for "Ow! Owee! That hurt!"

Then he looks around helplessly for the ball, which has already popped over the fence.

It's the most perfect piece of slapstick comedy.

"Did you ever see anything like that?" someone asked Canseco's teammate Julio Franco after the game.

"Yeah," Franco said. "In cartoons."

EVERY YEAR, ON THE ANNIVERSARY OF THE PLAY, JOSÉ CANSECO would put something on social media about it. Here are a few of those anniversary thoughts; taken together they paint a pretty good portrait of the man, José Canseco:

> **2014:** I see today is the 21st anniversary of the ball off my head game. Poor ball was never the same.

2015: A ball bounced off my head a million years ago. Find something else to make fun of me about. Time for new material, guys. Plenty to pick from.

2016: Twenty-three years ago today, I bounced a homer off my head.

2017: I have decided to have my entire upper body tattooed while watching the Athletics play.

2018: Canseco says if you milk a one-teated goat you will have a friend for life.

2019: King Kong ain't got nothing on me, but Sasquatch is a different story.

2020: I am one of the lucky ones that got to play in the major leagues.

NO. 24:
MR. OCTOBER

★ ★ ★ ★ ★

Most people think that Reggie Jackson got his famous nickname Mr. October *because* he hit three home runs in Game 6 of the 1977 World Series against the Los Angeles Dodgers. That's sort of true.

And it's also not true at all.

By the time he hit those three home runs, there were some people already calling him Mr. October. It's just that they didn't mean it as a compliment.

Baseball nicknames have often started out as insults. Mickey Mantle and Whitey Ford called Pete Rose Charlie Hustle, because they were annoyed by the way he ran to first base on walks and never stopped talking or moving during spring training. "Hey," Ford said to Mantle sarcastically, "look at Charlie Hustle over there." Rose later embraced the name.

Shoeless Joe Jackson hated his nickname all his life. Negro Leagues star Turkey Stearnes got the nickname because he ran like a turkey, and he didn't like that one, either. They called Ted Williams "Kid," because he didn't like being called a kid. They called Eddie Collins "Cocky." They called Charlie Keller "King Kong," because, as Lefty Gomez said, "Keller wasn't scouted. He was trapped." Keller so loathed the nickname that people knew better than to say it to his face.

So: Mr. October. That sounds complimentary, right? Well, let's start here: The 1977 Yankees were a complete mess. They had signed Reggie during the off-season, and probably the quickest way to explain him is to use the words he used about himself in his autobiography, *Reggie*: "My name is Reggie Jackson, and I am the best in baseball. This may sound conceited, but I want to be honest about how I feel."

Reggie was hardly the only strong personality with the Yankees. The newspapers called owner George Steinbrenner "King George." The manager, Billy Martin, was always getting fired and always getting in fights. The catcher and captain, Thurman Munson, was a proud Ohioan who always felt like the team was disrespecting him.

Jackson gave an interview early in the season that questioned Munson's leadership skills.

"I'm the straw that stirs the drink," Jackson said.

There were problems all season. At one point, Jackson refused to high-five the rest of his teammates after a home run and claimed it was because his hand hurt.

"He said that?" Munson asked incredulously. "He's a liar."

Later, Martin and Jackson almost came to blows on national television. Later still . . . well, hey, why don't we just let the *New York Post*'s Henry Hecht summarize it for us. He wrote this on the day that the Yankees clinched the American League East.

> **Reggie Jackson can't stand Billy Martin. He has an uneasy truce with Thurman Munson. He wants to do well for his ego and for George Steinbrenner. Thurman probably wishes Reggie would disappear. He hates Steinbrenner over a small matter of some $1.3 million. Martin has no use for Steinbrenner, little use for Reggie except when Reggie hits a home run.**
>
> **See how much fun it is being around the Yankees?**

But hey, the Yankees did make the postseason, and Reggie guaranteed that he would be the difference maker. He was, you see, Mr. October. That's the name he gave himself. "People with the strongest character usually succeed in the biggest moments," he told a reporter. He meant himself.

It might have gone unnoticed except Jackson promptly had a terrible American League Championship Series against Kansas City. He went 0-for-4 in Game 1 and misplayed a ground ball. He went hitless again in Games 3 and 4. He was so bad that Billy Martin benched him for the decisive Game 5. Jackson did come in later as a pinch hitter in the seventh inning, but the bottom line is that he hit .125 for the series and the Yankees had won in *spite* of him, not because of him.

It didn't get much better in the early part of the World Series against the Dodgers. Reggie was pulled for a defensive replacement in Game 1. He went 0-for-4 with two strikeouts in Game 2, and then after the game, he angrily second-guessed Martin's decision to start Catfish Hunter, who had been injured and had not pitched for more than a month.

"How could he pitch him?" Jackson complained. "In a World Series, how do you make a decision like that on a guy like Hunter? It's not fair to Cat, and it's not fair to us."

Martin was furious: "This guy has a lot of growing up to do," he raged. "As long as I'm the manager here, I'm gonna do things my way, and no player will ever tell me what to do. If he wants to come into my office and make a suggestion, I'd love it. I'd like to teach him. Maybe he'd make a good manager someday."

But as angry as Martin may have been, it was Thurman Munson who had reached his breaking point. He was angry about the mayhem surrounding the team, angry about his contract, and most of all, he was angry at Reggie Jackson for, well, everything.

"We're trying to win a damn World Series and somebody's stirring," Munson told reporters. "If I was hitting .111 or whatever, I wouldn't be second-guessing the damn manager. I'm going to stop talking here because the more I talk the angrier I get."

But he went on . . .

"Don't call me Captain Yankee. Call me ex–Captain Yankee. There are so many things going on. I've just got to laugh. Reggie hasn't been doing all that well. Still, he keeps talking. I guess Billy doesn't realize that he's Mr. October!"

There it was. There was the introduction of Mr. October. Munson meant it as the biggest dig he could imagine. Jackson was hitting .136 in the playoffs. He was causing endless problems. He was dragging the Yankees down. And yet he was calling himself Mr. October.

That was the joke.

Only . . . the newspapers didn't really get the joke.

Over the next days, they started referring to Reggie Jackson as "Mr. October." Some put quotations around the words to indicate irony. But others liked the sound of the name. It does have a ring.

In Game 4, Reggie Jackson doubled and homered and the Yankees were suddenly just one win away from the World Series title.

"While Ron Guidry held the spotlight," the Associated Press wrote, "a great deal of credit for the triumph must go to Reggie Jackson, the man his teammates call 'Mr. October' because of his record of performing well in postseason play."

The man his teammates call Mr. October.

Poor Thurman Munson. His joke had backfired. Jackson did not, at that point, have a record of performing especially well in the postseason. Going back to his days in Oakland, he was only a .254 lifetime postseason hitter with five total home runs. But the power of Reggie's personality made him seem greater. People were really beginning to call him Mr. October.

And then came Game 6 and the name would be his forever.

THE YANKEES WERE DOWN BY TWO RUNS WHEN REGGIE STEPPED to the plate in the second inning. Dodgers' pitcher Burt Hooton walked him on four pitches.

Reggie came up again in the fourth, again against Hooton. The Yankees still trailed. But on the first pitch, Reggie Jackson swung with all his force—nobody swung the bat harder than Reggie—and he hit a home run that soared into the second deck at Yankee Stadium. "Goodbye!" Howard Cosell screamed on national television, as if the ball were an unwanted party guest.

Reggie's third time up was in the next inning, this time against Dodgers' reliever Elías Sosa. The Yankees led 5–3. Again, first pitch, Jackson turned on it and this time hit a screaming line drive to right field, and it was over the fence in what seemed like an instant. The first home run was majestic. The second was violent.

And the third . . . well, the third home run was unforgettable. The Yankees led 7–3. The Dodgers' pitcher was knuckleballer Charlie Hough. Jackson went to the plate with only one thought: Hit a home run. "And when I saw that first pitch," Jackson would say, "I thought, *Oh boy!*"

Oh boy. Brian Koppelman, writer and creator of the television show *Billions,* was 11 years old and in the crowd that day. The memories of the night stay vivid, but none more than the sight of Reggie's home run taking flight toward center field.

"It seemed like it would go forever," Koppelman says.

It has, in many ways, gone on forever. It jolts the senses even now. The Yankees won the World Series and Reggie won the thing he wanted more than anything: his place in baseball history.

"Now I believe him," his teammate Mike Torrez said. "Now I know why he calls himself Mr. October. Now we'll all call him that."

NO. 23:
MR. NOVEMBER

NOVEMBER 1, 2001, BRONX

★ ★ ★ ★ ★

What I remember most was feeling numb. It was a Thursday morning in New York, a little bit after midnight, and everybody around me was singing and hugging and, yes, crying a little bit, too. I stared at a blank computer screen that demanded I somehow put all of it into words.

I do not remember even writing the words.

NEW YORK—THAT'S THE GAME I FELL IN LOVE WITH. SOMETIMES YOU HAVE TO WONDER ABOUT BASEBALL. . . . YOU WONDER IF TIME HAS JUST PASSED BASEBALL BY.

AND THEN, WEDNESDAY NIGHT HAPPENS AT YANKEE STADIUM.

THAT WAS THE BEST BASEBALL GAME I EVER SAW.

EVERYTHING ABOUT THE 2001 WORLD SERIES FELT JUST A BIT surreal, starting with the fact that the Arizona Diamondbacks were in it. The team was only three years old—we were all still getting used to the idea that there was an actual baseball team in Phoenix. It felt like something you would see in a bad baseball movie: "OK, sports fans, we have the Arizona Diamondbacks facing the San Antonio Mustangs in the Baseball Super Series."

But no, the Diamondbacks were very real, and they had perhaps the two best pitchers in all of baseball in Randy Johnson and Curt Schilling. They led the three-time defending World Champion Yankees two games to one. And they led Game 4 with two outs in the ninth inning.

But before we get there, we must first talk about the time. This was less than two months after 9/11. Nothing felt quite normal in America, and that was particularly true in New York, where the smoke still rose from Ground Zero. Baseball, in that charged moment, felt both unimportant and more important than ever.

Curt Schilling started that game for Arizona . . . and he was pretty much unhittable. Schilling had made himself the centerpiece of the series with his brilliant pitching, and perhaps even more, with his bluntness.

"How will you deal with the mystique and aura that surrounds the New York Yankees?" he was asked.

"When you use words like *mystique* and *aura*," he said, "those are dancers in a nightclub. They are not things we concern ourselves with on the ball field."

He then backed up his words by dominating the Yankees in Game 1, allowing just three hits and one run over seven innings. Then he did *exactly* the same thing in Game 4, going seven innings and allowing three hits and one run. Even the boos at Yankee Stadium were laced with admiration.

"What a horse," Yankees' manager Joe Torre would say.

So yes, the Diamondbacks led the Yankees 3–1, with two outs in the ninth inning and their closer Byung-Hyun Kim on the mound. I wrote columns for *The Kansas City Star* in those days, and I was on what we called a "game over" deadline, meaning "send in your column the second the game is over."

I had a whole thing written. I will never forget how I started it:

NEW YORK—The Yankees are dead.

That's when Tino Martinez stepped to the plate for the Yankees. He represented the tying run, and he went to the plate with the sole intention of hitting a home run. He was pretty good at doing that; he hit 339 home runs over his career.

"I was hoping I would see something down the middle," he said. "And I would swing as hard as I could."

Second pitch, Kim threw him a fastball down the middle.

Martinez swung as hard as he could.

The ball flew to deep center field and cleared the fence for the game-tying home run.

I stared at my computer screen and all those useless words on there. What would I do now? I changed the lede ever so slightly.

NEW YORK—The Yankees are not dead.

A clever change, sure, but in fact we didn't know if the Yankees were dead or not; the game was only tied, and it went on into extra innings. Yankee Stadium was engulfed in cheers and wails and hope and panic, and Arizona failed to score in the 10th, and my deadline came and went, and the clock struck midnight, and up stepped Derek Jeter to the plate.

As I look back now, sure, it had to be Jeter. He's not the *greatest* Yankees player, no, not for a franchise with Babe Ruth and Lou Gehrig and Joe DiMaggio and Mickey Mantle and Yogi Berra. But in many ways, he might just be the most *Yankees* player ever based on what he represented, what he meant to his teammates and the city. Most of all, how his mere presence set off opposing fans.

This last part, by the way, is best expressed in one of my favorite ever *Saturday Night Live* bits, a point-counterpoint between Red Sox fan Seth Meyers and Derek Jeter.

> **SETH'S POINT:** Derek Jeter sucks.
>
> **DEREK'S COUNTERPOINT:** No, I don't.
>
> **JETER:** I know my good friend Seth here is a Red Sox fan, and that's great. The fans really are what keeps Major League Baseball going. But I hope Seth can see that I play hard all the time and I always do the best for the team.

TINA FEY: Seth? Counterpoint.

MEYERS: YOU SUCK!

"That week was actually the *worst*," Meyers told me; he really is a big Red Sox fan. "I wanted to hate him so much, but he was such a gentleman that it was impossible not to like him."*

Yes, that was Jeter. He was a great player, obviously, but so much more than that: He was the most persistent, most beloved, most loathed, and most enduring player of his time, as well as the most overhyped and most underappreciated player. Jeter contained multitudes.

Yes, it had to be Jeter in that moment, as October turned to November in New York City, a city still reeling. Kim was pitching. He left his first pitch up, and Jeter punched it to right field. It would have been an out in a lot of places. But Yankee Stadium had a short right field. And nobody knew that better than Derek Jeter.

He'd measured it just right and the ball flew over the right field wall. The Yankees won.

As Jeter rounded first base, he thrust his right arm into the air.

I do not like the Yankees. It is a deep animosity that goes back to my childhood in Cleveland. And yet I'll tell you, that Derek Jeter home run was the greatest baseball thing I've ever seen live. The crowd made a sound I've never heard before and never heard since: a blend of delight and hope and joy and also this shared melancholy for what America had lost.

My next few minutes were spent trying to find words for what had just happened, and as mentioned my only memory is of the numbness I felt. The Frank Sinatra version of "New York, New York" played over the Yankee Stadium loudspeakers. This was tradition, the song the

---

* Meyers says he has one regret about that bit. Mike Shoemaker, a *Saturday Night Live* producer then, suggested that during the point-counterpoint he pay homage to Dan Aykroyd's line by saying, "Derek, you ignorant slut." Meyers thought that was hacky and didn't add the line. "In the years since," he says, "I have come to appreciate how much that would have killed and how wrong I was."

Yankees always played after victories. As I recall, for a time, they would play the Liza Minnelli version of the song when they lost.

This night, Derek Jeter had summoned Sinatra, and the crowd sang along, and then the song ended. And it started again, and the crowd was still singing along, and the song ended. And then it started again. Nobody would leave. People were weeping and people were singing.

> I want to wake up in a city
> that doesn't sleep

The Yankees hater in me obviously needs to mention that the Diamondbacks ended up winning that series in Game 7 when a broken-bat single by Luis Gonzalez scored Jay Bell in the bottom of the ninth. That's one of the best baseball moments ever.

But this moment was something different. No, I don't know how many times they played "New York, New York" that night, but it felt like a hundred. And everybody stayed and sang until a man with a megaphone explained that they had to get Yankee Stadium ready for the next day's game.

"Do me a favor," he said in a voice thick with New York. "Go home."

NO. 22:
DAVID FREESE LIVES HIS BEST LIFE

OCTOBER 27, 2011, ST. LOUIS

★ ★ ★ ★ ★

> **"**The majority of American males put themselves to sleep by striking out the batting order of the New York Yankees.**"**
>
> —AUTHOR JAMES THURBER

I cannot tell you that baseball inspires more dreams than other sports. But I can tell you that baseball dreams, yes, they're at the heart of the game. Tell me: Did you ever practice the pose you would strike for your baseball card? I thought this was something ridiculous that only I would do, but then I put up a poll on Twitter and found that more than 70 percent of people who voted used to do this, too.

In 1952, the Topps Company invented the modern baseball card. The John and Paul of baseball cards were two men who apparently didn't care much for each other, Sy Berger and Woody Gelman. Together they came up with pretty much all the features that would thrill young baseball fans for generations: new designs every year; statistics on the back; obscure facts about the players; autograph replicas, etc.

I don't believe that Berger and Gelman came up with all the baseball card poses themselves, but in time there were five that emerged as the go-to poses for ballplayers.

> Pose 1: A pitcher with his arm stretched out in front, as if he had just thrown a pitch.
>
> Pose 2: A batter on one knee with a bat on his shoulder.

Pose 3: A batter in hitting stance directly facing the camera.

Pose 4: A pitcher holding his glove and pitching hand above his head.

Post 5: A fielder holding out his glove as if asking an infant to toss the ball.

I preferred Pose 3, and I practiced it often, dreaming not of one specific thing, but of a million little things, a million big-league ballplayer things of making a diving play, of punching a single up the middle, of chattering with the stars in the dugout, of hearing the roar of the crowd, of seeing my own baseball card in the same pack with Tony Gwynn, Dan Quisenberry, and Jack Fimple.*

And like everyone, I dreamed of being the World Series hero for my hometown team.

But dreams like that don't ever really come true, do they?

DAVID FREESE GREW UP IN WILDWOOD, MISSOURI, ABOUT 30 minutes west of St. Louis via I-64. The family attended many Cardinals games. A 16-year-old David was in the crowd when Mark McGwire hit his 500th home run. That was a good day for dreaming. David did a lot of dreaming when he was that age; he wanted to be a hero for the Cardinals.

Freese was a good slugger himself for Lafayette High School. In his senior season, he hit a school-record 23 home runs. But after that, he was kind of tired of baseball. He'd spent his entire childhood on traveling teams, in batting cages—he'd had enough. He went to the

---

* In 1984, the Topps Company, without telling anyone, printed four times as many Jack Fimple cards as the others, guaranteeing you would get at least one in each pack. I don't know if that was a true statement, but I do know I got a lot of 1984 Jack Fimples.

University of Missouri to study computer science. The school offered him a full baseball scholarship. He turned them down.

"I was burned out," he would say. "And I'd lost my love of baseball."

He spent a year away from the game. Then the summer after his freshman year, he was back at Lafayette, working on a school maintenance crew. As he walked around the school, he watched the baseball team practice. And he felt it. He wanted to play again. He called the baseball coach at local St. Louis Community College at Meramec and asked if he could try out for the team. He then left Missouri, played at Meramec, became a Junior College All-America, went to the University of South Alabama, hit like crazy, was named conference player of the year, and was drafted in the ninth round by the San Diego Padres.

Yeah. That was fast.

And before he ever played a single game for San Diego he was traded to, yes, his hometown St. Louis Cardinals.

Freese just kept on hitting through the minor leagues, and in 2011, at age 29, he won himself a starting spot as the Cardinals' everyday third baseman. He crushed the ball. It was all happening. And then on May 1, he was hit by a pitch, it broke his hand, and he missed the next two months. When he came back, he was a shell of himself. The Cardinals were playing uninspired baseball. It looked like a lost season.

Then all sorts of weird things happened. The Cardinals started playing better—they won 12 of 14 at one point. It shouldn't have mattered: The Atlanta Braves seemed to have the wild-card slot all wrapped up. But the Braves collapsed, losing their last five games, and St. Louis sneaked into the postseason on the final day of the year.

The Cardinals were supposed to be easily dispatched by the Philadelphia Phillies, who boasted what many had hyped as the greatest starting rotation ever. Instead, St. Louis won with great pitching, and the Cards were underdogs again when they faced Milwaukee in the National League Championship Series.

Cue: David Freese. He put on a six-game light show, hitting .545. He carried the Cardinals to the World Series against the Texas Rangers. In the decisive Game 6, he went 3-for-4 with a double, a homer, and three RBIs. The Cardinals were going to the World Series. Hometown hero David Freese had led them there.

"What can I even say?" he gushed after the game. "It's a dream come true."

Right. How can anything beat that?

RAIN DELAYED GAME 6 OF THE 2011 WORLD SERIES BY A DAY. That gave the Cardinals' players time to reflect on how they were blowing the series. The Cardinals had lost a ninth-inning lead in Game 2. Their bats failed to show up in Game 4. And in Game 5, they squandered another lead and then failed to come through in the biggest moment.

Specifically: David Freese failed to come through. In the seventh inning, with the score tied, Freese came up with the bases loaded. On the first pitch, he lofted an easy fly ball to end the threat.

"If he sees a good pitch, it's his job to swing at it," Cardinals' manager Tony La Russa insisted. "He needs to keep swinging."

Foreshadowing.

Game 6 of the 2011 World Series was a freewheeling carnival of a game, one of the wildest and weirdest and funnest in baseball history. Was it a great game? Maybe not. It was more like the description film critic Pauline Kael had for *Star Wars*: "A box of Cracker Jack which is all prizes."

Top of the first inning, the Rangers took a 1–0 lead.

Bottom of the first, St. Louis took the lead themselves.

Top of the second, Texas tied the game.

The Cardinals committed a brutal error in the fourth and Texas took the lead 3–2.

The Rangers committed a brutal error, and the score was once again tied.

The Cardinals committed *another* error—this time it was David Freese dropping an easy pop-up—and Texas had the lead again.

Texas committed an error in the sixth, and the score was tied.

Finally in the seventh inning, the Rangers seemed to put an end to the nonsense. Third baseman Adrián Beltré launched a long home run to right field. Nelson Cruz followed with an upper deck shot of his own.

And the Rangers carried a two-run lead into the ninth. They sent in one of the hardest throwers in baseball, Neftalí Feliz, to clinch the game and a Rangers championship. Feliz gave up a double to Albert Pujols and walked Lance Berkman.

David Freese came up with two outs and two runners on.

Neftalí Feliz threw a 98-mph fastball on the outside half of the plate. David Freese poked it to right field.

What strikes me about the moment now, looking back, is that when the ball left the bat, nobody knew how it would turn out. Freese hit it well but not *too* well. When he hit it, the ball had a chance to be anything—a home run, a routine fly out, a double, a triple, a fantastic catch . . .

All any of us could do was watch.

Texas right fielder Nelson Cruz drifted back on the ball. He seemed to have a play. But something about the trajectory of the ball fooled him. He reached up, but the ball carried over his glove and crashed into the wall, ricocheting back to the infield. By the time the Rangers chased it down, the Cardinals had scored the tying run. And David Freese stood on third base.

He'd already lived his biggest dreams.

And now this!

But the game went on. Freese had only tied it. In the 10th inning, the Rangers took the lead right back on a two-run home run by Josh Hamilton. In the bottom of the inning, the Cardinals scored two runs of their own on a barrage of bloops and grounders.

A Cracker Jack box with all the prizes.

Then it was the bottom of the 11th inning, the score was tied, and David Freese stepped to the plate. He told himself: "Just put the ball in play."

Rangers' reliever Mark Lowe threw him a 3-2 fastball over the heart of the plate.

Freese put the ball in play. He hit it some 420 feet to center field.

And THAT was the dream.

"We'll see you tomorrow night," broadcaster Joe Buck said, echoing the call his father Jack Buck had made in Game 6 of the World Series 20 years earlier. Goose bumps.

The Cardinals won the World Series the next day; Freese was named World Series MVP.

⁂

IN THE END, DAVID FREESE HAD A FINE CAREER. IT WAS NOT A Hall of Fame career. But he got a thousand hits and hit more than a hundred home runs. He made an All-Star team. A fine career.

But those are just numbers. David Freese lived the dream. Do you know how many players grew up rooting for a team and then ended up playing for that team and then led that team to the World Series, then saved that team from defeat and then hit the walk-off home run that won the biggest game? I can think of only one. I suspect David Freese wouldn't trade places with anybody.

NO. 21:

DOTTIE DROPS THE BALL

★ ★ ★ ★ ★

Did Dottie drop the ball on purpose at the end of the movie *A League of Their Own* so that her younger sister, Kit, could finally have her moment?

This has become one of the great questions in baseball history.

I'm going to give you the answer here . . . but you won't believe me. You will believe what you choose to believe because that's the beauty of art and movies and baseball. The right answer is the one in your heart.

///

LET'S SET UP THE SCENE BY FIRST TALKING A LITTLE BIT ABOUT *A League of Their Own*, Penny Marshall's brilliant homage to the women who played in the All-American Girls Professional Baseball League (AAGPBL). The league was founded in 1943 by Cubs' owner and gum magnate Philip K. Wrigley, among others, to promote baseball while the best major league players were fighting in World War II.

Marshall was a big sports fan, so it really jolted her when she was given a little documentary about the AAGPBL called *A League of Their Own*. She had never heard of it. And she realized that if she had never heard of women playing professional baseball, neither had anyone else. She wanted a woman to write the script but, according to her autobiography, *My Mother Was Nuts,* she couldn't find one. Instead, she handed the script to lifelong baseball fan Lowell Ganz and his writing partner Babaloo Mandel.

They wrote a script around two competitive sisters, Dottie and Kit, who end up getting scouted to play in the new league, for the Rockford Peaches. Dottie, played by Geena Davis, would become the best player in the league. And Kit, played by Lori Petty, is a fine player, too, but she's ceaselessly jealous that at no point in her life has she ever been as good as her sister.

All of which leads to the final scene, the final game of the World Series, and Kit (now playing for the Racine Belles) hits a ball into the gap and then tears around the bases. She runs right through the coach's stop sign at third and heads for home, where Dottie is waiting with the ball. Throughout the movie, we have been given scene after scene showing how strong Dottie's hands are. She caught a ball barehanded to prove a point. She held on to the ball when another player had tried to run her over. Now she stood there with the ball and Kit bore in on her, and the collision was fierce, and Dottie put on the tag . . . but when her hand holding the ball hit the ground, it rolled out.

"Safe!" the umpire yelled.

And we ask the question again: Did Kit knock the ball out of her hand through sheer will? Or did Dottie drop the ball on purpose because she knew how much it meant to Kit to finally have her moment?

OPINIONS ARE EVERYWHERE ON THIS ONE. BITTY SCHRAM, WHO played Evelyn in the movie,* said she dropped the ball on purpose. Lori Petty says she didn't. "I kicked her ass," Petty says.

Helen Callaghan—who was called the "Feminine Ted Williams" in the real AAGPBL and who inspired her son Kelly Candaele to do the documentary that inspired Penny Marshall—thought Dottie dropped the ball on purpose and it really bothered her. "Nobody would do that!" she shouted at her son.

---

* Evelyn is the outfielder who manager Jimmy Dugan tells, "There's no crying in baseball!" See Five Meltdowns.

Baseball writer Molly Knight thinks Dottie was flustered and lost focus but she would never actually drop the ball on purpose.

Young adult book author Jennifer Iacopelli is enraged that anyone would ever even suggest that she dropped it on purpose and says, not without merit, that such a charge would never be made about a male baseball player.

"Ultimately what I would say happens," actress and obsessive baseball fan Ellen Adair says, "is that Dottie allows Kit to knock the ball loose."

King Solomon would be proud of that answer.

"Those two characters were always so competitive," says Tom Hanks's son Colin, who grew up with the movie, "that saying she dropped the ball on purpose is like saying Jordan threw a game."

There seem to be cues and hints spread throughout the movie. For instance, at the very beginning, there's a scene of the older Dottie telling her grandson to let his younger brother play basketball. And then she tells her other grandson, "Kill him!" That clue suggests to me that maybe she did drop the ball on purpose.

On the other hand, just before Kit bats, Dottie goes over to the pitcher and tells her to pitch the ball up in the zone; Dottie knows this is Kit's weakness. This points us in the other direction.

Back and forth it goes. I put up a couple of different polls asking the question: Did Dottie drop the ball on purpose? In both, the vast majority voted that she did. Geena Davis, who says she knows "because it was me," refuses to answer.

But I found someone else who was willing to answer the question.

Someone who definitely knows.

And this is what Lowell Ganz, who wrote the scene, told his daughter Allie: "I always thought that Kit just wanted it more."

In fact, Ganz and Mandel never even considered that Dottie dropped the ball on purpose. They were surprised when people started even suggesting it—so much so that even they started wondering if they had their own character right.

But surely, they did have it right.

Dottie did not drop the ball on purpose.

I feel 100 percent certain that this did not convince anyone.

A FEW WEEKS AFTER SHOOTING FINISHED, MARSHALL AND company brought Davis and Petty back to shoot one more scene. It was the sisters meeting in the concourse of the stadium after the game ended.

"Sorry I knocked you over," Kit said.

"No, you're not," Dottie said.

"You were blocking the entire plate . . ."

"You beat me," Dottie said. "You wanted it more than me."

The studio president himself told Penny Marshall that she should end the movie right there . . . but she had a different idea. Marshall ended the movie in Cooperstown, at the Hall of Fame, with the real players of the All-American Girls Professional Baseball League playing a game of baseball.

It was a beautiful ending to what I believe is the best baseball movie ever made, an ending that soars above the whole question of whether Dottie dropped the ball. In fact, it inspired a different filmmaker, just some guy named Steven Spielberg, to end *Schindler's List* by gathering together the real survivors that Oskar Schindler was able to save from the Holocaust.

"He asked if I would mind if he used that type of ending," Marshall wrote. "I said, 'Of course not. You're entitled.' And the truth was, it didn't belong to me. In the same way that the end of Steven's movie belonged to the survivors, mine belonged to all the women who had played the game."

FIVE

HEARTSTRINGS

ARCHIBALD GRAHAM ENTERS THE GAME (JULY 29, 1905)

66 The Giants' great little manager got desperate indeed and pulled Browne out of the game, putting Dr. Archie Graham in his place. He then hunted around for his bat boy. 99

—*BROOKLYN CITIZEN*

Yes, there was a real Moonlight Graham. If you have seen *Field of Dreams*—and I suppose even if you have not—Burt Lancaster plays Archibald Graham, a man they called Moonlight. He played in only one major league game and never got a chance to bat. Instead, he went to Chisholm, Minnesota, and became a doctor.

It's all true. Well, most of it, anyway.

The real Moonlight Graham was put into a game between the Giants and the Brooklyn Superbas.* The Giants were winning 10–0, which is the only reason Graham entered the game in the first place (you can see

---

* Brooklyn was a star-studded team, and so sportswriters were looking for a flashy name. They settled on Superbas because of a flamboyant vaudeville acrobatics act called Hanlon's Superbas.

how the *Brooklyn Citizen* joked that manager John McGraw wanted to put in his bat boy next).

Graham was already a part-time doctor by then. Nobody is entirely sure why they called him Moonlight, but the best guess is that, yes, he moonlighted as a doctor. Or maybe it's better to say he was a doctor who moonlighted as a ballplayer. He played two innings that day—"two joyous innings in the right garden," *The New York Evening Telegram* reported—but did not make a play and, as the movie indicates, did not get a chance at the plate. He was on deck when the game ended.

All of this would have been forgotten . . . except this is baseball, and nothing is forgotten in baseball. Two things happened. In 1969, *The Baseball Encyclopedia* was published. It was an enormous, heavy book that had the statistics of every single player in the history of baseball. And it was a publishing sensation. Every baseball fan had to have one.

The second thing was that one of those baseball fans was a writer named W. P. Kinsella, who scoured through the *Encyclopedia* and came upon that single entry for Archibald Graham.

"I thought, *How could anyone come up with that nickname?*" Kinsella would later say. "I was intrigued, and I made a note that I intended to write something about him."

In *Field of Dreams*, Ray Kinsella—played by Kevin Costner—goes to Chisholm to learn all he can about Moonlight Graham. In real life, that was exactly what W. P. Kinsella did. He found out the basics and he wrote them in his magnificent novel *Shoeless Joe,* and in a most unlikely turn, the book was adapted into a movie.

"I want to ask you a question," Moonlight Graham says to Ray Kinsella. "What's so interesting about a half inning that would make you come all the way from Iowa to talk to me about it fifty years after it happened?"

The answer is simple. This is baseball.

JIM ABBOTT THROWS NO-HITTER
(SEPTEMBER 4, 1993)

Jim Abbott was born without a right hand. When he showed interest in sports as a boy, his parents tried to guide him toward soccer. That seemed to make the most sense. But it was baseball he truly loved. So he developed his own way. He pitched, and what he would do was tuck his glove away and then, after releasing the ball, slip it on his pitching hand to field.

"I never felt limited," he would say. He also never felt special. When he was named the Most Courageous Athlete by the Philadelphia Sports Writers Association, he modestly accepted the award but refused the label.

"It's hard calling it courageous to do what I have fun doing," he said. "Courage is getting up every day and facing a life-threatening situation. It's much more than fielding bunts."

Abbott was one heck of a pitcher. At the University of Michigan, he became the first baseball player to win the James E. Sullivan Trophy as America's finest amateur athlete. The Angels took him in the first round of the 1988 draft. The very next year, he was a regular starter for the Angels. In 1991, he finished third in the Cy Young voting after going 18-11 with a 2.89 ERA.

His best day came for the Yankees on a Saturday afternoon in 1993. The Yankees played Cleveland, and Abbott felt right from the start that he had good stuff but not his best control. He walked five batters on the day. But he had fortune. Cleveland batters just kept hitting balls directly at fielders, including two double plays.

"A no-hitter takes luck," Abbott would say. Then again, to quote the line from the movie *The Color of Money*, "for some players, luck itself is an art." Cleveland's Carlos Baerga made the final out of the no-hitter, and the Yankees swarmed Abbott. He made a curtain call for the fans. Then he found his trembling wife in the tunnel below the dugout, and they embraced. "Can you believe it?" he kept saying.

"Sometimes," Mike Lupica wrote for the New York *Daily News*, "the cheer does not just come from the ballpark. Sometimes there is a moment in sports and the noise seems to come from the whole spread-out place that is New York."

STAN MUSIAL HITS FIVE HOMERS IN A DOUBLEHEADER (MAY 2, 1954)

It is hard to describe just what Stan Musial meant to baseball fans in the 1950s. Maybe the best way is to recount his 3,000th hit, which came in Chicago when he was sent in to pinch hit against the Cubs in May 1958. He lined a double into the gap. Cubs fans, who quite famously loathe the Cardinals, stood and cheered for the longest time.

Then Musial went to the train station for the ride back to St. Louis. Hundreds of people were there to celebrate with him. And then all along the train route, at every stop, people kept showing up just to get a glimpse of Musial, to sing "For He's a Jolly Good Fellow," to wave to him. Harry Caray, the Cardinals' announcer at the time, would call it the greatest thing he ever saw in baseball.

I've got a different Musial moment in mind.

On a May Sunday in 1954, the Cardinals played a doubleheader against the New York Giants. Musial always loved hitting against New York teams, and never more than on this day. In the third inning of Game 1, he hit a ball on top of the right-field pavilion roof. Two innings later, he hit another ball on the roof. Three innings after that, he did it a third time.

In the second game, he hit a home run over that roof off knuckleball wizard Hoyt Wilhelm. And then he hit his fifth home run in a doubleheader, something that had never been done before, and he laughed joyfully as he rounded the bases.

"I still can't believe it," he told reporters. "You mean real sluggers like

Babe Ruth, Lou Gehrig, Ralph Kiner—men like them—never hit five homers in a doubleheader?"

So that was great. But what makes it eternal is this: There was an 8-year-old boy in the stands that day. He was there with his father. Both idolized Musial. The father, Nate Colbert, had played some semi-pro baseball, and every time the two of them went to a game, Colbert would say to his son: "Watch how Stan handles himself out there."

Well, the son, Nate Colbert Jr., became a ballplayer himself. After high school, he fulfilled his dream and signed with the Cardinals. But it wasn't meant to be. The Cardinals didn't see his potential. He bounced around a bit and found himself on an expansion team, the San Diego Padres. It wasn't exactly what he had hoped, but the Padres gave him a chance to play every day and he became one of the game's top power hitters. He made the All-Star team three straight years.

On August 1, 1972, a Tuesday, the Padres played a doubleheader in Atlanta. You might see what's coming here. Colbert hit two home runs in the first game.

Then in the second inning of Game 2, Colbert hit a fly ball that landed just beyond the outstretched glove of Atlanta's Ralph Garr. "I measured that one just right," Colbert would say.

In the seventh, he hit his fourth home run of the day. When he came up in the ninth, absolutely, he was thinking about Musial. And he was thinking about his father.

Atlanta's Cecil Upshaw's first pitch was a high fastball.

Nate Colbert did not miss. There are two men in baseball history who have hit five home runs in a doubleheader. One is Stan Musial. The other is that kid in the stands, Nate Colbert Jr.

"I don't believe it!" Colbert shouted to umpire Bruce Froemming as he rounded second base.

"Nate," Froemming responded, "I don't believe it either."

CURTIS PRIDE GETS A HIT (SEPTEMBER 17, 1993)

❝ The ovation came rolling out of the seats, louder and louder, reaching out to a man who is deaf. One minute. Two minutes. Curtis Pride never knew he had this many friends. **❞**

—MICHAEL FARBER, *MONTREAL GAZETTE*

When Curtis Pride stepped to the plate on that Friday night in Montreal, the pennant race was on. More than 45,000 fans had stuffed their way into Stade Olympique to see if their second-place Expos could cut into the division lead of the first-place Philadelphia Phillies. The Expos took an early lead. But the Phillies scored seven runs in the sixth inning.

Things looked pretty bleak when Pride came to bat with two runners on in the seventh inning and Philadelphia up three runs. Few knew much about Pride. He was 24 years old. It was his third major league game and only the second time he'd ever come to the plate.

Few knew that Pride had been born deaf.

Athletically, he said, it all came pretty easy to him. He was a prodigy. He was named one of the world's best young soccer players after a dominating performance at the FIFA U-16 World Championships. He was offered a basketball scholarship at William & Mary. But baseball was his favorite thing, so he signed with the New York Mets when they drafted him in the 10th round. He kicked around the minor leagues for seven frustrating years. Then the Expos signed him to a minor league deal.

He stepped to the plate to face Phillies' reliever Bobby Thigpen.

"This fella can't hear," one of the Phillies' broadcasters said.

"He's a deaf player, that is correct," another broadcaster, Harry Kalas, confirmed.

Thigpen threw a change-up and Pride crushed it to left center field, scoring two runs. It was a double, his first major league hit.

And the crowd started cheering. And they kept cheering. As the Phillies made a pitching change, Pride walked over to third-base coach

Jerry Manuel, who motioned for him to tip his cap. Pride did not realize that the fans were still cheering.

And they would not stop. Most of the loudest cheers ever heard in Montreal were obviously for hockey stars—for Rocket Richard, when they closed the Montreal Forum; for Guy Lafleur's return; for Soviet goalie Vladislav Tretiak, when he put together perhaps the greatest goaltending performance in hockey history against the Canadian team on New Year's Eve in 1975.

The cheers for Curtis Pride were like that.

"It became a standing ovation, as word circled that he was deaf," says Tom Tango, the analyst who invented Wins Above Replacement. "And that ovation thundered, with the stomping of our feet on that concrete reverberating throughout Olympic Stadium. . . . It lasted minutes on end . . . for that one moment, a journeyman player transcended the legends."

After the game, Curtis Pride was asked what it felt like.

"I could hear it here," he told reporters as he pointed to his chest. "The vibrations."

DEE STRANGE-GORDON HOMERS FOR A FRIEND (SEPTEMBER 26, 2016)

José Fernández was a pitcher, young and brash and thrilling and gifted beyond imagination. He grew up in Cuba, and three times he and his mother, Maritza, attempted to defect to the United States. The fourth time, they made it . . . but only after a three-day boat trip that at one point required José to pull his mother out of the water.

Fernández wanted only to become the greatest pitcher in the world.

"I stand in front of the mirror every day," he told *Sports Illustrated*'s Albert Chen, "doing *this* 10,000 times." *This*, in the sentence, meant holding his right arm high in the air and pulling it through to mimic the pitching motion.

And, in quick order, he was on his way to becoming the greatest pitcher in the world. He was unlimitedly gifted and confident and irresistible. Once in 2013, Colorado's Troy Tulowitzki ripped a line drive up the middle. Fernández somehow pulled it in.

"You caught that?" Tulo asked in disbelief.

"Abracadabra," Fernández said.

Abracadabra! He was that kind of magical. He smiled all the time, and you couldn't get a hit off him and he struck out the world and he was only getting better.

Any time an athlete dies young, it's a jolt. But it was particularly shocking and awful when José Fernández died in a boating accident. He had seemed invincible.

"I'm still waiting to wake up from this nightmare," Marlins' outfielder Giancarlo Stanton said. Another teammate, Dee Strange-Gordon, simply went to a corner of the clubhouse and cried.

"I'm just numb," was all he could say to reporters.

The Marlins did not play the day José Fernández died. The next day was a Monday . . . Fernández had been the scheduled starter. Everyone on the Marlins wore No. 16, José's number. None of the Marlins felt ready to play. But games go on.

Strange-Gordon led off. He did not want to play, but he felt like he had to in honor of his friend. He stepped into the box as a right-handed hitter and tried his best to imitate Fernández's batting stance. Side-by-side photos later show he got it almost exactly right.

Strange-Gordon then switched back to his natural lefty stance.

Strange-Gordon had not hit a home run all season. He'd hit only nine in his entire career up to that point. Home runs were not his game.

The Mets' Bartolo Colón threw the ball over the heart of the plate, and Strange-Gordon swung as hard as he could. He remembered how the crack of the bat sounded. Pure.

"I never hit a ball like that," Strange-Gordon would say. "Not even in batting practice."

The ball soared to right field. It sailed into the upper deck. And Strange-Gordon, feeling as if in a dream, rounded the bases.

"It seemed like it took forever," he said. As the crowd cheered and cried, as his teammates banged the top railing in front of the dugout, he looked up to the sky.

"I kept hearing his voice," he would say.

When he got to home plate, he broke down and sobbed.

"I don't have kids," Dee Strange-Gordon said. "So hitting a home run for José Fernández is the best moment of my life."

NO. 20:
JOHN MCDONALD HOMERS
ON FATHER'S DAY

JUNE 20, 2010, TORONTO

★ ★ ★ ★ ★

My father taught me baseball. That's a common story. Baseball is a game of fathers, some domineering, some distant, some ebullient. Jack McDonald was the sort of dad who never knew a stranger. Everybody called him Jack Mac.

By day (or night, depending on the shift), Jack Mac was a fireman in the Connecticut coastal town of East Lyme. But that was just his job. His life was serving as president of the local Little League, home plate umpire for Little League games, and referee for pee wee football. His life was in the backyard, where he would play long games of catch with his son, John.

"Hit me in the chest," Jack Mac would say, and John loved the challenge.

All of it feels so familiar, right?

"Baseball is fathers and sons," the poet Donald Hall wrote. "Football is brothers beating each other up in the backyard."

John McDonald played baseball with a near-obsessive passion. He will tell you that he was working with pretty limited attributes— he wasn't fast, had only a so-so arm, and would grow to be only 5-foot-9—but he made himself into a brilliant defensive shortstop and he built up enough strength so that pitchers weren't just knocking the bat out of his hands.

He was pretty shocked when Cleveland made him a 12th-round draft pick. Shocked and delighted. He and Jack Mac celebrated the triumph. John was going to be a professional ballplayer. It was beyond their dreams.

"I'm not going to lie to you: I wasn't even thinking about making the major leagues," John says. "But I didn't care. I loved it. When I played in the Carolina League, I thought, *If this is the end, I'm still so happy.* And then I went to play in Akron, so close to Cleveland, and I thought, *If it stops here, I'm fine with that.*"

But he kept on going up, and in 1999, at age 24, he made it to the big leagues. On Independence Day, he got his first big-league at-bat against Kansas City. Jack Mac and John's mother, Joanne, were in the crowd five days later when he got his first start.

Jack Mac constantly reminded his son to enjoy every step of the journey because it was all so unlikely and wonderful. "I kept telling myself, 'This could end tomorrow,'" John says. But it didn't end. Some team always wanted his defensive brilliance and his spirit. He went from Cleveland to Detroit, Detroit to Toronto, Toronto to Arizona, then Pittsburgh and Philadelphia and Boston and Los Angeles.

All the while, John took Jack Mac along for the ride. He took his father on the field at Yankee Stadium, where they had watched Don Mattingly take ground balls. He flew him in every year on Father's Day and they would share their story with kids. It was marvelous.

In 2008, Jack started feeling sick and constantly exhausted. It took a long while for doctors to figure out the full scope of what was wrong. In time, they found he had liver and kidney cancer. And it was advanced. The doctors prescribed aggressive chemotherapy. Jack Mac said the cure was exponentially worse than the disease.

In 2010, John was at spring training with the Blue Jays. One evening he was in a restaurant with friends when he got a call from his father.

"I'm not going to take my medicine anymore," Jack said. "I don't want to live like this."

John felt his heart plummet . . . but he knew it was best. Jack Mac had suffered enough. As the season went on, John kept telling his father to hang on; he wanted them to have one more Father's Day together at the ballpark.

Jack Mac said, "I'll try. But I can't make any promises."

Jack would not make it to Father's Day. Near the end of May, John got a call that his father's death was imminent. He left the team to spend the last days with his father.

Those final days turned out to be three weeks. They were filled with agony, yes, but also laughter; fear, yes, but also hope.

"You will hear people say, 'I wish I had said this or that,'" John says. "That wasn't the case. I said everything. Dad said everything. We didn't leave anything out. It was a gift.

"I wrote my dad's eulogy while we were in the hospital room. And I read it to him. . . . He actually changed two small things."

That was the raw honesty between Jack Mac and his son. Every day, they asked each other: "Is there anything else to say?" And one day, near the very end, Jack Mac did have one more thing to say.

He said: "Next time you hit a home run, when you cross home plate, point to the sky for me."

That was not like Jack Mac. He loathed anything showy or brash. But when John tried to make a joke about it, he realized his father was serious.

"OK," John said, "I'll do it. But it will take me a while. I might have to go back to the old-man adult league in town to be able to hit it. You know, I just don't hit too many."

True. He'd hit only 13 home runs in the major leagues.

Jack McDonald died on Tuesday, June 15, 2010—five days before Father's Day. On that Friday, John delivered the eulogy his father had edited. Then, knowing that it was what Jack Mac would have wanted, he went back to Toronto on Saturday. He was on the active roster on Father's Day. He addressed the team. He took part in a special Father's Day event for kids who had brought their fathers to Rogers Centre for the game against San Francisco.

"It was so therapeutic," John says. "Some of the dads there had cancer.

Some had gone through hard things. . . . To them, I wasn't a ballplayer; I was a son."

He did not expect to play in the game. But in the ninth inning, with the Blue Jays hopelessly behind, manager Cito Gaston sent him in as a defensive replacement. John was the second batter in the bottom of the ninth. Before his at-bat, he restlessly paced in the dugout.

"It's OK—relax," one of his teammates said.

"Oh, I'm relaxed," John said. "It's just that I'm about to go deep."

That was so unlike Johnny Mac.

Jeremy Affeldt, a hard-throwing lefty, was pitching for the Giants. On the first pitch, Affeldt threw a fastball. McDonald took a mighty cut and fouled it straight back to the screen.

"I thought, *Oh, man, I missed my chance,*" John would say.

The next pitch was a curveball that hung just a touch. This time John McDonald did not miss. He hit it as hard as he had ever hit a baseball. He took off running; he never expected a ball he hit to go over the fence. But this one did. He was so emotional, he could barely take it all in.

"I wish I could go back and slow down that one moment," John said. "I wish I could see that ball go over the wall and feel everything. But . . . I put my head down and ran."

When he got to home plate, John pointed to the sky, just as Jack Mac had asked. He felt countless feelings, some of them happy, some of them terribly sad, and he made sure to take them all in, every last emotion, because that's what Jack Mac always wanted him to do.

NO. 19:
JOE GOES SHOELESS

MAY 1908, GREENVILLE, SOUTH CAROLINA (PROBABLY)

★ ★ ★ ★ ★

> "An apothecary down in [Greenville], who had previously written me some good tips in regards to young prospects, kept urging me to give this fellow a trial. But what intrigued me most was that this prodigy played without shoes. 'He doesn't wear spikes or in fact any kind of covering for his feet,' came the tip. He's so fast that he can tear around the bases without any such help. They call him 'Shoeless Joe.'"

—HALL OF FAME MANAGER CONNIE MACK

Nobody knows the day it happened, the team it happened against, or any of the particulars. The story has been told a hundred different ways—many of them by Joe Jackson himself. What we do know for sure is that in 1908, while playing either semiprofessional baseball or minor league baseball in and around Greenville, a prodigy named Joe Jackson played a baseball game without shoes.

And baseball was never quite the same after that.

Lolly Gray, the man who discovered Jackson, said it happened when he was playing ball for the Brandon Mill baseball team. Gray said he would regularly play while wearing just socks (with his toes sticking out through holes). But he insisted that once Joe Jackson started playing professionally, he never played even a single game without shoes.

Tommy Stouch—who signed Jackson to his first professional contract—disagreed. He said that Jackson did not play the outfield without shoes, but he did *pitch* in his stocking feet because that helped him get better traction on the wooden slab on the mound at Greenville games.

"When he was still in the minors, he bought a new pair of spikes and they hurt his feet," Kevin Costner's Ray Kinsella told his daughter in *Field of Dreams*. "About the sixth inning, he took them off and played the outfield in just his socks. The other players kidded him, called him Shoeless Joe, and the name stuck."

And the newspapers, well, they told all sorts of tall tales about a brilliantly talented player down south—another Ty Cobb, they called him—who ran around rock-strewn outfields in his bare feet.

"I've read and heard every kind of yarn imaginable on how I got the name," Joe Jackson said.

The story Jackson told most consistently is that it happened while he was playing for the Greenville minor league team. He did in fact get a new pair of spikes that hurt his feet. But he did not just take them off. Instead, he played through the pain and then asked for the next game off so he could deal with the blisters. Stouch refused and reminded Jackson that when he signed for the princely sum of $75 per month, he promised to "play his head off."

That's why Jackson played without shoes. And he would always remember hitting a triple and as he slid into third base, someone in the crowd yelling, "Oh, you shoeless wonder!"*

"I guess every baseball fan in the country heard him," Jackson said, "for I have been called that ever since."

Jackson told other versions of the story, so we'll likely never know for sure.

But to me, a question that is even more interesting than "How did he get the nickname?" is "Why did a man playing without shoes fascinate America so much?" And it did. Within a couple of months, even before he signed a big-league contract, newspapers all over the country

---

* More frequently quoted as, "Oh, you shoeless bastard!"

were talking about the shoeless wonder. From the start, there was rarely a reference that did not refer to Jackson playing shoeless, and it would be that way for the rest of his life.

Here's what I think it is: I think people were (and are) forever drawn to the story of Joe Jackson because it starts with the innocent exuberance of a boy who plays baseball for the pure joy of it. Jackson's father, George, like so many fathers of the day, worked long and miserable hours. Joe worked in the mill, too, but he had a titanic gift for baseball. Connie Mack said he was faster than Cobb. Babe Ruth called his swing "the perfectest."

He was a natural. Nobody taught him how to play ball. He just knew.

I think that's why the image of a brilliantly talented man playing baseball without shoes is so captivating.

SHOELESS JOE DID NOT WANT TO GO TO THE BIG LEAGUES. HE was plenty happy playing for $75 a month plus his cotton mill pay in Greenville. He made some extra money because fans threw money at him after he hit a long home run, something he did with regularity. Even when Connie Mack offered him $900 to play for the Philadelphia Athletics, Jackson was reluctant.

"I hardly know as how I'd like it in those big northern cities," he told Stouch.

Well, Stouch told him he'd be crazy to pass up on the chance to play for the Athletics . . . and this was not just because Stouch was set to make some money himself off the deal. He liked Jackson a lot. He thought Jackson owed it to himself to play in the big time. He put Shoeless Joe on the train to Philadelphia and even traveled up there on the same train.

But when Stouch got to Philadelphia, Jackson was gone. He was concerned something had happened to him, but then Mack showed him the telegram that had just arrived:

AM UNABLE TO COME TO PHILADELPHIA AT THIS
TIME. JOE JACKSON.

Jackson had hopped off the train in Charlotte.

Mack wasn't ready to give up. He sent his injured star Socks Seybold to bring Jackson to Philadelphia, even if it meant getting "his whole family to come back with you." But Jackson hated Philadelphia as much as he had expected. The big city frightened him. Teammates cruelly mocked him, particularly because of his inability to read. Shoeless Joe went home again.

"Shoeless Joe Jackson has returned to his home in Greenville," *The Washington Post* reported. "Big league life just wasn't to the young man's liking. . . . Joe had just about one week of mingling with city folk when he concluded that he was never cut out for the major league. He told Connie Mack that he'd rather be a star in the bushes than struggle for a regular place on a big-league team."

We know, of course, that Jackson did not stay in the bushes. He was too good for that, and the temptation of making a lot of money was too strong. He went up to Cleveland in 1910, and in 1911, his first full season, he hit .408. The next year, he led the league in hits and triples. The year after that, he led the league in hits and doubles.

And at that point, Joe Jackson was no longer that small-town kid who played the game for fun and to get out of the mills. No, he was one of the best players in all of baseball, and he felt sure that they were not paying him what he deserved. He demanded a trade out of Cleveland and said he would quit baseball entirely and go perform in vaudeville if he didn't get his wishes.

That's how he got traded to the Chicago White Sox, where his dark destiny awaited. That story is well known. He and seven teammates were banned from baseball for whatever role they played in throwing the 1919 World Series. Jackson himself would say he did not throw any games himself, though he admitted taking cash from the gamblers.

Anyway, of all their stories, Shoeless Joe's felt the most tragic because it felt like a greater loss.

"A bunch of kids stood outside the criminal courts building in Chicago when Joe Jackson left," the newspaper reported. "One kid asked: 'It ain't true, is it, Joe?' Jackson hung his head. 'I'm afraid it is,' he said."

The boy's plea would later be prettied up by the newspapers to: "Say it ain't so, Joe."

And that has become one of the most famous phrases in baseball history.

Joe Jackson never played in the big leagues again. But he did play. He returned to the small southern towns, and he played in various sandlot leagues around the South until he was fifty. This has usually been painted as the sad ending, but I'm not so sure: Joe was always happiest on those fields, playing ball for a few. When he wasn't playing, he taught kids in the neighborhood how to play ball. Sometimes he and his wife, Katie, bought them all ice cream.

"I gave baseball my best," he said.

NO. 18:

PETE ROSE CATCHES COBB

SEPTEMBER 11, 1985, CINCINNATI (OR NOT)

★ ★ ★ ★ ★

Some years ago, I was in Las Vegas sitting outside a sports memorabilia store in Caesars Palace called Field of Dreams. Two young and, in memory, rather enormous men were standing nearby, and they were shouting at people walking by: "Come see Pete Rose! Come see the Hit King!* Live and in the flesh!"

Inside the store—indeed live and in the flesh—Pete Rose himself sat on a metal folding chair behind a card table and a velvet rope and a woman named Sarah and a large box of baseballs awaiting his signature. This was not an uncommon occurrence. Quite the opposite. Pete was appearing at Field of Dreams in Las Vegas four or five times a week in those days.

"Are you sad?" I asked him that day. It seemed the right question to me.

"Sad?" he asked back incredulously. "Hell no, I'm not sad. I get paid a lot of money. . . . I get paid seven figures. . . . It isn't just barely seven figures, either. I get paid a $^#&#* of money."

IF YOU ARE OLD ENOUGH, YOU PROBABLY REMEMBER PETE ROSE broke Ty Cobb's hit record by whacking an opposite-field single off a

---

* Let's get this out of the way: If you add up Ichiro Suzuki's hits from Japan and the United States, you come up with 4,367 hits, which is more than Pete Rose. But this is not how the records are tabulated, and unsurprisingly Rose himself has been entirely unsympathetic to the argument that anyone else is the Hit King. "I had 427 minor league hits," he says. "Are we counting those now, too?"

rather unhappy Eric Show on September 11, 1985. It was a huge deal, front-page news across America.

Technically speaking, he did not break Cobb's record that day.

He broke it three days earlier with a hit off Reggie Patterson at Wrigley Field in Chicago.

This is a good one to use in your trivia games.

See, in 1985 it was widely accepted that Cobb had 4,191 hits. We now know—and to be fair, some people knew it even in 1985—that Cobb actually had two fewer hits. It's a great story. Maybe you've heard it, but maybe you won't mind hearing it again.

It happened in the summer of 1910, when Cobb was just 23 years old and still something of an arrogant upstart (though he had won the batting title each of the previous three years). The grand old hero of the American League in those days was the regally named Napoleon Lajoie, Nap for short. He was the league's first true star, and he was so beloved and admired that when he went to play for Cleveland, they simply named the team the Cleveland Naps.

Lajoie was 35 that year, and it was his last great season. He and Cobb were locked in the most famous batting race in baseball history. In those days, the batting average races were watched almost as closely as the pennant races; there were daily updates in the papers. This race was of particular significance because the winner was promised a Chalmers Detroit Model 30 automobile, a big deal in 1910.

Cobb was so sure he had the race wrapped up that he sat out the last two games, claiming that he was having problems with his eyesight. But even with all the emphasis placed on the batting race, nobody was exactly sure where it stood going into the final day. Record-keeping was primitive then. You had to wait until the league released the official numbers to get a final total.

Lajoie's Naps were playing the St. Louis Browns in a doubleheader, and all anybody knew was that Lajoie needed a bunch of hits to win the batting race. How many? Nobody was entirely sure, but his first time up he hit a fly ball that most observers thought was catchable by St. Louis's Hub Northen. Instead, the ball went over his head for a triple.

And then came one of the most shameful displays in early baseball history. The Browns ordered their third baseman Red Corriden to play very, very deep—in the outfield, essentially—allowing Lajoie, who no longer had much speed, to bunt safely for hits *seven times*. Why did the Browns do this? Some said it was because the Browns' players hated Ty Cobb and admired Nap Lajoie. It's more likely that they bet some money on Lajoie winning the batting title.

"Never before in the history of baseball," *The Washington Post* wrote, "has the integrity of the game been questioned as it was by the 8,000 fans this afternoon."

When the numbers were added up, Lajoie had the higher batting average, .383 to .382. But American League founder and President Ban Johnson could not just let that stand. So he secretly manipulated the record book to give Cobb two extra hits. Those hits were still on the books in 1985; that's why Rose's record-breaking number was 4,192 rather than 4,190.

IN RECENT YEARS, COBB'S LEGACY HAS SOMEWHAT IMPROVED AS various researchers have found that he was perhaps not the monster that sportswriters like Al Stump portrayed him to be.

In recent years, Rose's legacy has taken even more of a hit as various problematic bits of his private life have been revealed.

But Rose and Cobb played the game alike, which is to say they played baseball with a boundless fury and all-consuming determination. They were both obsessed. You don't get to 4,000 hits without obsession. Rose's entire life was driven by obsession, off the field and on. He was an obsessive gambler. He was an obsessive womanizer. He was a convicted tax evader, and he was accused of sexual misconduct with a minor. He was obsessive about making money and also about spending it.

And in baseball, he was obsessive about collecting hits. They gave his life meaning. When he had two hits in a game, he needed three. When he had four hits in a game, he needed five. It didn't matter the score. It didn't matter the month. It didn't matter who was pitching. When managers asked him to take a day off, Rose angrily refused. You can't get hits sitting on the damn bench. He missed a total of five games between 1972 and 1980.

At age 40, Rose hit .325 and again led the league in hits, and that was when he started to think about passing Ty Cobb. He was still about 500 hits away from Cobb's record, but he did the math in his head. Rose was always good at math. He always knew his up-to-the-minute batting average. He just knew it: Pete Rose was destined to be the Hit King.

It was a bumpier road than he expected. As he approached 43, Philadelphia no longer wanted him. He went to play in Montreal, and that wasn't looking too promising. Then came an opportunity to not only play again in his Cincinnati hometown but to manage the Reds at the same time. He could put himself in the lineup whenever he wanted.

//

ON THAT DAY IN LAS VEGAS, I ASKED PETE ROSE WHAT HE remembered most about breaking Ty Cobb's hit record. We had plenty of time to talk; autograph seekers were coming in only sporadically. Rose seemed untroubled by this. He also seemed untroubled when someone asked him to sign the Dowd Report, which had led directly to his permanent ban from baseball. It was no big deal. I have seen him sign the mug shot he took before serving five months in prison for tax evasion. Pete will sign anything.

"Why wouldn't I?" Rose said. "If they pay the money, why not?"

I asked him about that day he broke the record, and he went through a fairly pat answer that he'd undoubtedly used many times before. It was like a dream for him. It was so great to hug his son Pete Jr. He looked into the sky and saw his father and Ty Cobb looking down on him.

"I know people don't believe it," he said, "but I really saw them."

The hawkers were still out there trying to get people to come get their Pete Rose autographs. Rose, while he was talking, signed some baseballs for stock. I thought about what a conundrum he is. When he was off the field, his addictions were destructive and ruinous. He got thrown out of baseball. He lost his certain place in the Hall of Fame. Every now and again, some new and terrible accusation comes out against him, and as one of his old running mates told me, "Anything you hear about Pete is probably true."

But the man did love baseball—loved it like perhaps no one in the long history of the game. He lived baseball, breathed it, played games with his whole heart and then sat in his car and listened to West Coast games on the radio. To watch Pete Rose run to first on a walk and take the extra base on a line drive and dive headfirst into bases was to see the game played at its most joyous. Baseball brought out the best in Pete Rose, and Pete Rose brought out the best in baseball. It was the rest of his life that was ruinous.

"Best day of your life?" I asked Rose of the day he broke Ty Cobb's record.

"I had a lot of good days," he insisted.

NO. 17:

"WAVING AT THE BALL
LIKE A MADMAN"

OCTOBER 21, 1975, BOSTON

★ ★ ★ ★ ★

There was something about the movie *Good Will Hunting* that Reds' pitcher Pat Darcy really didn't like one bit. If you've seen the movie, you'll remember the scene. Robin Williams's Sean Maguire—a psychology teacher—is trying to get through to the brilliant but troubled Will Hunting, played by Matt Damon.

Will asks Sean when he knew that his wife was the one.

"October twenty-first, 1975," Sean says.

"You know the $@%& day?" Will asks.

"Oh yeah, it was Game 6 of the World Series," Sean says. "Biggest game in Red Sox history."

Sean explains that he and his friends slept outside all night to get tickets. Then they were in a bar before the game, and that's when he first saw his future wife.

"Bottom of the 12th, in stepped Carlton Fisk," Sean says, moving to the game action. "Ol' Pudge steps up to the plate, you know, he's got the weird stance . . . and then BOOM, he clocks it, you know, high, high ball down the left-field line, 35,000 people on their feet yelling at the ball. And that Carlton Fisk, he's waving at the ball like a madman, he's like 'Get over! Get over!' And then it hits the foul pole, oh, he goes ape, and 35,000 fans, you know, they charge the field . . . and he's like, 'Get out of the way! Get out of the way!'"

"Did you rush the field?" Will asks excitedly.

"Naw, I didn't rush the field," Sean said. "I wasn't there."

"What?"

"Naw, I was in a bar having a drink with my future wife."

And scene.

So, what's Pat Darcy's problem with that? Well, see, he was the pitcher who gave up that home run to Fisk. He's OK with that, OK with his place in history. But what he is not OK with was the way the movie kept showing him pacing the mound and kicking the dirt, like he was nervous.

"I wasn't nervous, not even a little bit," he tells me. "Why would I be nervous? I'd already thrown two scoreless innings. Everybody forgets that. I wasn't nervous at all. They shouldn't have tried to make it look like I was nervous."

He pauses for a moment.

"I *was* gassed," he says.

//

YES, THEY WERE ALL GASSED, ENTIRELY SPENT, AT THE END OF Game 6 of the 1975 World Series, the best game ever played. Too much happened. Even while it was happening, it felt like too much was happening. Great catches. Monumental home runs. Brilliant throws. Too much, all of it. Pete Rose got hit with a pitch and he ran to first base, where Carl Yastrzemski stood. You couldn't get men much different than the bouncy and frenzied Pete Rose and the stoic and taciturn Carl Yastrzemski.

"This is the greatest game I've ever played in," Rose cried out happily.

And Yaz, despite himself, couldn't help but nod.

How do you even sum up such a game? The Reds were one victory away from taking the World Series. The rain postponed Game 6 three straight days. The anticipation was too much to bear. When it was finally played, scalpers charged their highest ticket prices to that point.

Games 6 and 7 would become the highest-rated back-to-back baseball games in television history.

What happened? What *didn't* happen? Boston's Fred Lynn hit a three-run homer. His teammate, the wonderful Luis Tiant, pitched with all sorts of early-inning swagger.* Ken Griffey hit a long triple as Lynn crashed into the wall and, for a time, appeared to be unconscious. Johnny Bench hit an epic single off the giant Green Monster in left. George Foster hit a double off the center-field wall. Light-hitting César Gerónimo hit a home run that seemed to seal the game for Cincinnati. Boston's Bernie Carbo homered to tie the game. Boston's Denny Doyle got thrown out trying to score the game-winning run because he heard third-base coach Don Zimmer yell, "Go, go, go!" when Zimmer was *actually* yelling "No, no, no!" Dwight Evans made a ludicrous catch in deep right field and then doubled off a Reds' runner and . . .

It's like I said: Too much. It was a sprawling Russian novel of a game with too many characters and too many stories and too many pages.

Let us pause, though, for one moment on the Bernie Carbo homer. That home run—like Nikola Tesla, the Nicholas Brothers, Antonio Meucci, and Sybil Ludington—should be so much more famous. It has a whole backstory.

The most important person in Carbo's career had been a hotheaded young minor league manager named Sparky Anderson, the very same Sparky Anderson who was managing the Reds in that World Series.

Before Anderson, Carbo seemed destined to waste his extraordinary talent and never make it out of the minor leagues. But with Anderson as his biggest booster, Carbo turned his game and life around. He made it to the Reds at 22. He had a fantastic rookie season. But then he began

---

* Luis Tiant's father, Luis Sr., was in the stands watching. He had never seen his son pitch in the Major Leagues before that series. Luis Sr. was a great pitcher himself in Cuba and the Negro Leagues; some say he had the best pickoff move of any pitcher ever.

goofing off again and Sparky Anderson felt he had no choice but to trade him away.

"I never loved a player more than I loved Bernie Carbo," he said.

Then, in the bottom of the eighth inning, with the Reds up by three runs, Carbo came to the plate with two runners on base. Everybody thought Anderson would bring in his lefty reliever Will McEnaney.

But for reasons he was never able to fully explain, Anderson stayed with his right-hander Rawly Eastwick. Eastwick got ahead in the count but then left a fastball over the plate and Carbo blasted it to deep center field for a three-run homer that tied the game. Fenway Park shook like it never had before.

Without Carbo's homer, there's no Carlton Fisk homer.

CARLTON FISK LED OFF THE BOTTOM OF THE 12TH WITH THE score tied 6–6. Darcy had nothing left by that point. Johnny Bench would remember catching his warm-up pitches and thinking: "There's no way we get out of this inning."

And they didn't. Darcy's second pitch had nothing on it, and as soon as Fisk hit the ball, he knew it was long enough. What he did not know was if it would stay fair. As Robin Williams described, Fisk began to wave at the ball, asking it to straighten out and stay fair.

On command, the ball straightened out and stayed fair.

"Everybody should have a moment like that," Fisk said.

In Charlestown, New Hampshire—Carlton Fisk's hometown—the church bells rang.

To this day, many people think Fisk's home run won the World Series. It did not. The homer forced a Game 7, which the Reds won with their own heroics. Still, the Fisk home run is more famous than anything else in that series . . . and I think I know why.

It's the camera shot of Fisk jumping up and down the line waving the ball fair.

It's one of the most iconic television moments in baseball history . . . and it almost wasn't on television at all. Lou Gerard was NBC's cameraman. He was set up inside the left-field scoreboard. He was not supposed to train his camera on Fisk. He was supposed to follow the baseball.

But he noticed a rat closing in on him while Darcy was throwing the pitch. And he got flustered, could not pick up the ball, and so he focused on Fisk instead. And he got the shot of a lifetime.

NO. 16:

THE SHOT HEARD ROUND THE WORLD

OCTOBER 3, 1951, NEW YORK

★ ★ ★ ★ ★

I'm not going to read your book," Chicago White Sox owner Jerry Reinsdorf told me.

"OK," I said.

"Aren't you going to ask me why?"

"Sure. Why aren't you going to read my book?"

"Because you're going to have the worst moment of my life in there."

"Who knows? Maybe I won't have it in there."

"Oh," he said, "you'll have this moment in there for sure."

WELL, JERRY REINSDORF WAS RIGHT. THE MOMENT IS HERE. YOU can't leave it out. The Shot Heard Round the World has been dissected, it's been exposed, it has even been at least partially debunked. On top of that it was, as Reinsdorf rightfully points out, the worst moment to at least as many people who think of it as the best.

But Bobby Thomson's home run is utterly unforgettable.

The Giants trailed Brooklyn by thirteen games. They raced back in the standings to force a three-game playoff. They trailed the Dodgers in the ninth inning of the decisive playoff game. Ralph Branca came in to pitch for the Dodgers. Bobby Thomson stepped up.

You, no doubt, can hear Russ Hodges's famous call ringing in your ear.

"Branca throws . . . there's a long drive . . . it's gonna be I believe—THE GIANTS WIN THE PENNANT! THE GIANTS WIN THE PENNANT! THE GIANTS WIN THE PENNANT! THE GIANTS WIN THE PENNANT!

*Bobby Thomson hits into the lower deck of the leftfield stands! The Giants win the pennant! And they're going crazy! They're going crazy! Waa-WOO!"**

Goosebumps. Every time. Everything else goes away when you hear that call.

Well, not for everybody.

"I hate Bobby Thomson," says Jerry Reinsdorf, who was 15 and in Brooklyn when the home run happened. "And I always will."

///

BASEBALL FANS ARE FICKLE ABOUT CHEATING. SOME PLAYERS have been endlessly celebrated while bending and breaking rules. Others have faced a fierce campaign to write them out of the game's history entirely. Some illegal drugs bother fans more than others. The 2017 Houston Astros have had their World Series championship questioned and, in some circles, invalidated because of their covert sign stealing.

The 1951 Giants, though, endure.

Joshua Prager's seminal book *The Echoing Green* makes it clear that not only was the Giants' epic pennant race comeback aided by an illicit sign-stealing system created by their amoral manager Leo Durocher,[†] but it's very likely that Bobby Thomson himself knew what pitch was coming from Branca on the Shot Heard Round the World.

Prager was able to pinpoint the very day—July 19, 1951—that Durocher pulled all his players into a meeting and explained to them the new sign-stealing plan. On that day, the Giants were 47-41 and trailed

---

[*] I have never quite known how to spell the sound Hodges makes at the end of that call. WAA-oo? WEHHH-yooo! Whatever the spelling, it might be the most joyous sound a baseball announcer has ever made.

[†] Durocher on cheating, in his 1975 book: "If you get away with it, fine. If you don't, what have you lost? I don't call that cheating. Win any way you can as long as you can get away with it."

the Dodgers by 7½ games. They would go an incredible 55-17 the rest of the way.

The system worked like so: A coach, Herman Franks, set up in Durocher's office beyond the center-field wall and swiped the catcher's signs using a telescope. Then, using a specially installed buzzer system, he relayed the pitch to bullpen catcher Sal Yvars, who alerted the players with various ever-changing signs. In one iteration, Yvars tossed a baseball up in the air if a breaking ball was coming. When he held on to the ball, it would be a fastball.

How big a difference did it make? It's sometimes hard to quantify cheating. For instance, we know the 2017 Astros had an elaborate home-park camera system for stealing signs and then they hit garbage cans to relay them—but that team still hit better on the road. The 1951 Giants as a whole hit better *before* July 19.

But it can be said that one player in particular hit a lot better after July 19.

And that one player was Bobby Thomson.

Before July 19, he hit .237 and slugged .482.

After July 19, he hit .357 and slugged .652.

Game 3 of the Giants–Dodgers playoff was in fact in New York's home park, the Polo Grounds. And the Giants were held down all game long by Brooklyn's Don Newcomb. The Dodgers led 4–1 after eight innings. Newcombe gave up back-to-back singles to lead off the ninth inning, and then after getting an out, he gave up a double to Whitey Lockman.

In came Branca. Up stepped Thomson.

Thomson always said he didn't know what pitch was coming. Branca, who became friends with Thomson, never quite seemed to believe him.

There were three Hall of Fame broadcasters calling the action that day. Ernie Harwell was calling the game for television. He remembers his call being simple: "I just said, 'It's gone,'" he told me. "I didn't think anything else needed to be said."

Red Barber was announcing for the Dodgers. His call, too, was succinct: "A curve, swung on and belted, deep shot to left field, it is a home run!"

And then there was Hodges's call. Barber loathed that call, thought it unprofessional. Maybe it was. But it remains the most famous call in baseball history.

///

I'VE SEEN THE BOBBY THOMSON HOME RUN AT LEAST 500 TIMES. But it wasn't until time No. 497 or so that I noticed the first-base coach going bonkers.

Once you see it, you cannot unsee it. The first-base coach was just having a party all his own, jumping up and down. Then he throws his cap up in the air like he just graduated from Yale, and he runs around looking for somebody to hug, and it's all quite wonderful.

That guy, I thought, must have his own story.

And he does: That guy is Fat Freddie Fitzsimmons.

He grew up in Mishawaka, Indiana, not far from the University of Notre Dame, and all his life he wanted to be a ballplayer. When he was 15 years old, he learned how to throw a knuckleball, and he spent the next 25 years of his life learning how to control that incorrigible pitch, how to make his delivery more deceiving, how to field his position better, and how to outsmart everybody.

"He was a whiz at giving you the pitch you weren't looking for at that particular time," his catcher Gabby Hartnett said.

Fat Freddie would do anything to get batters out. He developed an awkward delivery, one where he turned his back on the hitter, and he threw what most people believe to still be the fastest knuckleball in big-league history.*

"The batter watches the ball," he said. "But if you turn your back on

---

* It's an odd categorization; knuckleballs by their very nature are not intended to move fast. They flutter. But the speed of Freddie's knuckleball was consistently mentioned, making it sound more like a fastball with a wiggle.

him as I do, he loses sight of it. When he gets his next glimpse, the ball is already traveling toward him. From his viewpoint, it is disconcerting. That, of course, is what the pitcher wants."

Fat Freddie wasn't actually fat. He was a remarkable athlete, the best fielding pitcher of his time. But he LOOKED fat because he had an odd body type, and sportswriters never tired of mocking him. Freddie didn't walk, he waddled. He didn't pitch, he "threw his girth around." He was called burly and plump, portly and rotund, stout and potbellied.

"'Fitz' was 'out to lunch' when necks were handed out," the sportswriter Bob Broeg wrote. "His head plumps squarely between wide shoulders of a bulging torso that dwarfs short legs."

Freddie himself never seemed to mind any of it. He was a supremely nice man. After he retired, he became manager of some terrible Philadelphia Phillies teams during World War II, and that didn't work because those teams didn't have any talent and because he was too nice to be the manager. He was better suited as a coach, and in 1949 he joined the New York Giants.

How nice a guy was he? This nice: There were many stories in all the newspapers about how he would stop whatever he was doing to teach young kids how to pitch.

"I try to help the kids all I can," he said modestly when caught in the act of teaching a young stranger. "This boy may never make a pitcher, but showing an interest in him might help him some other way in life, no matter what career he follows. He'll understand he isn't fighting a lone battle, that there are people willing to help him."

Fitzsimmons loved being part of those '51 Giants. They were destined to win. He always loved telling the story about how before the season, he and Durocher went to see a fortune teller. She told them the Giants would get off to a bad start but would be right there at the end of the season.*

---

* She also told Fitzsimmons to change his uniform number from 5 to 6. He did.

He later called the Thomson home run the most exciting baseball moment of his life. "That team played for each other," he would say. "Bobby was the man who happened to come up to the plate. But it could have been anybody on that team, and Bobby would be the first person to tell you that."

The pure joy he felt as Thomson's ball sailed over the fence at the Polo Grounds still echoes—as much for me now as Russ Hodges's famous call. There's a lot about that home run and story that leaves a bad taste, but it's pure joy seeing baseball lifer Fat Freddie Fitzsimmons jump up and down, throw his hat in the air, and run to hug anyone he could find.

NO. 15:
THE BABE HITS 60

SEPTEMBER 30, 1927, BRONX

★ ★ ★ ★ ★

The sixty home runs that Babe Ruth hit in 1927 hasn't been a record in more than a half century. And yet it endures because the Babe endures. Five other players have hit more home runs in a season than Babe. And yet you could argue, none of them really surpassed the Babe.

That's a baseball thing completely and thoroughly. No other North American sport clings so utterly to a player from a century ago. This is in part because other sports were still in their infancy then, but it also speaks to the timeless appeal of the Bambino.

WHEN ROGER MARIS BROKE RUTH'S RECORD THE FIRST TIME— he hit home run No. 61 off Tracy Stallard on October 1, 1961—it was the end of a miserable experience. Part of this was simply Maris's humble and solitary nature; he loathed being in the spotlight. The daily repetitive questions from reporters, the constant pressure placed on him, the New York fans' preference for his teammate Mickey Mantle— all of it weighed so heavily on him, he began to lose clumps of hair as the season wound down.

Some of the misery, though, was caused by a man named Ford Frick.

Frick was baseball commissioner then. He also idolized Ruth to an unhealthy degree; Frick had been a ghostwriter for Ruth. And in July, he had a decision to make. See, 1961 was the first year that teams played 162 games. Ruth had only played in 154.

Everybody wanted to know: What would happen to Ruth's record if Maris hit his 61st home run AFTER Game 154?

Frick did not hesitate. He announced in July that Maris had to break the record in 154 games or else Ruth's mark would still stand.

"Standard yardsticks might suffice for ordinary mortals," Frick would say. "Not for Babe. He was different!"

Frick probably did not really have the power to make such a decision. There was no official record book at the time. But he had a lot of sway, and most baseball writers in those days were Ruth fans like him, so it simply became accepted that Ruth's record would keep on going after Maris failed to break it in the season's first 154 games.

It's hard to fully capture just how unhappy Maris was in those final days, first as he fell short of the artificial deadline, then as he went into the final day looking for No. 61, even though he knew it would be saddled with an asterisk. "Maybe I'm not a great man," he told reporters that last day. "But I damn well want to break it."

He broke it in front of a two-thirds-empty Yankee Stadium. He planted the ball in the right-field bleachers. A mechanic named Sal Durante ended up with the ball and offered it back to Maris. "Nah," Maris said. "You make whatever you can out of it."

Many years later, Roger Maris was asked how he felt about his baseball career.

"It would have been a helluva lot more fun," he said, "if I had not hit those 61 home runs."

///

MARK McGWIRE WAS NEXT. HE BROKE MARIS'S RECORD IN 1998. He did it in his team's 144th game, so even the ghost of Ford Frick couldn't complain. It seemed magical at the time. None of us had ever seen anyone like Mark McGwire that year, and it's likely we never will again. People piled into stadiums two hours before game time just to watch him take *batting practice*.

He and Sammy Sosa both hit more than 60 homers that year.* They each hit titanic blasts all over America, and it was a baseball party unlike any seen in decades. I specifically remember a home run McGwire hit off Kansas City pitcher Glendon Rusch that was so majestic, Rusch himself felt like cheering.

A baseball party, yes. But it didn't turn out that way. As time went on, it became clear that performance-enhancing drugs—particularly steroids—had become rampant in baseball, a not-unexpected consequence of a sport that didn't even test for steroids. When Barry Bonds hit 73 home runs in 2001, the veil was beginning to be lifted. A year later, Ken Caminiti admitted to *Sports Illustrated* that he used steroids and estimated that at least half of baseball did. José Canseco began naming names. Congress got involved. McGwire himself admitted using steroids in a tear-filled interview with Bob Costas.

And all the joy of 1998 was washed away.

///

ON OCTOBER 4, 2022, AARON JUDGE HIT HIS 62ND HOME RUN off Texas's Jesús Tinoco. What a joy Aaron Judge is. He's probably the largest everyday player in the history of baseball. He's listed at 6-foot-7, 282 pounds, and it's likely he's bigger than that.

But beyond his sheer size—he's bigger than NFL tight end Rob Gronkowski—he's also a superior athlete, a good base runner, a fine outfielder. He has a great arm, and he hits for average. His awesome power is his greatest attribute, and as obvious as that might seem, it still comes as a constant surprise. His fly balls just tend to soar fifteen or twenty or thirty feet longer than you expect. He also has a great smile.

His home run chase should have been entirely joyful . . . except it

---

* Sosa topped 60 home runs THREE times in his career, which leads to a wonderful bit of trivia: he didn't lead the league in home runs any of those three seasons. Mark McGwire outhomered him the first two times, and Barry Bonds outhomered him the third.

wasn't. For one thing, it was never entirely clear what record he was even going after. Technically, he was challenging Roger Maris's American League record. But so many people wanted to make it about something more. They wanted to wish away Barry Bonds and Mark McGwire and Sammy Sosa, so they made Judge's chase about words like *legitimacy* and *authenticity*, and it felt less fun.

Maris's own son, in a bitterly ironic twist, said that Bonds's record (along with the big home run seasons of Sammy Sosa and Mark McGwire) should have an asterisk next to it. Numerous people wrote when Judge hit his 62nd homer that he was the "authentic" home run champion of all time, and there are many who concur.

Judge did not want to play that game. He grew up watching Barry Bonds hit all those home runs. "I saw him do it," he said. No matter how many people tried to tell him that he was the legitimate home run king, he refused to accept the crown.

//

ALL OF WHICH, INEVITABLY, BRINGS US BACK TO THE DAY BABE Ruth hit home run No. 60. That home run record felt boundlessly joyful. All of America celebrated.

Ruth was 32 years old that year, 1927, and there was a powerful sense before the season started that he was beginning to fade a bit. There was a new kid in town, a 24-year-old slugger named Lou Gehrig, and he seemed like the new king.

On September 5, the Yankees had a 16-game lead in the American League.

And on that day, the American League home run leaders were:*

Lou Gehrig, 44

Babe Ruth, 44

"The most astonishing thing that has ever happened in organized

---

* Another Yankee, Tony Lazzeri, was third on the list with 18 home runs.

baseball is the home run race between George Herman Ruth and Henry Louis Gehrig," the famed novelist and sportswriter Paul Gallico wrote.

Ruth, it should be said, did not love having Gehrig as a rival. He'd never had anyone challenge him as a home run hitter before. But he responded as only Babe Ruth could: While Gehrig's pace slowed, Ruth put together the greatest home run show the game had ever seen. He hit three home runs in a doubleheader on September 6 and two more on September 7.

The *New York Times*' John Kieran wrote a couplet for the occasion.

> *With vim and verve, he has walloped the curve, from Texas to Duluth*
> *Which is no small task, and I beg to ask: Was there ever a guy like Ruth?*

Ruth hit No. 50 on September 11. The next day he was in court defending himself against an assault charge from an artist who said Ruth had socked him in the eye. The next day Ruth hit two more home runs in a doubleheader and the Yankees clinched the pennant.

"No one figured he would ever come close to his 59 mark," Grantland Rice wrote of Ruth's 1921 record. "But even this isn't beyond him now."

On September 15, he was found innocent of all charges in the assault case, and the next day he hit home run No. 53. Two days later, he crushed No. 54.

He now had eight games left to hit six home runs.

He went about his business. He homered off Detroit's Sam Gibson on September 21. He hit a walk-off homer the next day. On September 27, he hit a grand slam off Philadelphia ace Lefty Grove. That left him with 57 home runs and three games left to play.*

On September 29, Ruth mashed two home runs against Washington.

---

* On the same day, a white leghorn hen in Omaha named Babe Ruth laid her 152nd egg in as many days, setting a different sort of record. Aren't you glad you check in on the footnotes?

That gave him 59 home runs, tying his own mark. There were some rumblings that Washington pitchers grooved pitches to him, but one sportswriter saw nothing but glory.

"Twice the Babe swung with all his gigantic force and twice he sent home runs screaming into the stands," the sportswriter wrote. "And now the thing they said couldn't be done has transpired. This morning the Babe stands alone as the champion of swat."

That sportswriter's name? You guessed it: Ford Frick.

On September 30, 1927—in front of only 8,000 or so people at Yankee Stadium—Babe Ruth stepped to the plate in the bottom of the eighth inning against the Washington Senators' pitcher Tom Zachary. Zachary threw a fastball. Ruth pulled it into the right-field seats.

Zachary threw his glove to the ground and screamed, "Foul ball! Foul ball!"*

But it was not foul. And Ruth was elated; he would call it the biggest home run he ever hit. When he got back to the clubhouse, according to Robert Creamer's wonderful biography *Babe: The Legend Comes to Life*, Ruth shouted, "Sixty. Count 'em. Sixty. Let's see some other son of a bitch match that!"

Others have hit more home runs. But in a way Ruth was right. No one has matched it.

---

* Ruth never forgave Zachary for his tantrum. Twenty years later, when he saw Zachary again, Ruth said, "You crooked-arm SOB, are you still claiming that ball was foul?"

NO. 14:
TED WILLIAMS HITS .400

SEPTEMBER 28, 1941, PHILADELPHIA

★ ★ ★ ★ ★

The two most memorable moments of Ted Williams's remarkable career both happened on September 28. The second of those was September 28, 1960, Baltimore at Boston, in what turned out to be his final game in the big leagues.

That was not a day for a left-handed batter to hit a home run at Fenway Park. The weather was cold, the air soggy and dense, the wind was blowing in. Williams did have the thought of homering in his final game, it seemed the right way to go out, and he swung for the fences. In the fifth inning he hit a rocket that he said was as hard as any ball he'd ever hit.

"We thought he had it," Red Sox fan John Updike wrote in his *New Yorker* story "Hub Fans Bid Kid Adieu." "He smacked the ball hard and high into the heart of his power zone, but the deep right field in Fenway and the heavy air and a casual east wind defeated him. The ball died."

Williams had one more chance in the eighth inning facing Baltimore's Jack Fisher. And he got hold of it again, but this time nothing could hold it back, not wind, not heavy air, not anything. The ball traveled 450 feet according to one measurement, and Williams ran quickly around the bases "as if our praise were a storm of rain to get out of," Updike wrote. He then disappeared into the dugout. The 10,454 fans who had come to see this very thing cheered for four minutes in the hopes of a curtain call.

But there was no curtain call, not even as teammates and coaches urged Williams to acknowledge the crowd. But Williams had not tipped his cap since 1940. In those days, fans regularly booed him for various reasons, and he promised himself that he would *never* acknowledge them after that. He was not a man to let go of grudges.

"To hell with them," Williams said.

"Gods," Updike wrote, "do not answer letters."

"Ted Williams was in character to the end," Harold Kaese wrote in the next morning's *Boston Globe*. "He hit a home run in his last time at bat. He took a dig at the sports writers. He did not tip his cap or otherwise acknowledge the applause . . . but as long as baseball is played, Ted Williams's last home run will be epic."

///

THE OTHER MOMENT HAPPENED SEPTEMBER 28, 1941. IT WAS the final day of the season, and the Red Sox played a doubleheader against Connie Mack's Philadelphia Athletics.* The games themselves meant nothing; the Yankees had long clinched the pennant.

What mattered was that Ted came into the game batting .3995. He was trying to become the first American Leaguer since Harry Heinemann back in 1923 to hit .400. And he wanted it.

"He'd get on the same kick every day," his teammate Charlie Wagner told author Leigh Montville. "'I'm going to hit .400! I know I can do it! I'm determined to do it!' He was obsessed with the challenge."

In many ways, this story has been told wrong through the years. The common version—the one I grew up hearing—is that Williams was given the option to sit out that final day and have his batting average round up to .400. Lots of great players, including Ty Cobb, sat at the end of seasons just to win batting titles. Nobody would have blamed

---

* I mention Connie Mack because it blows my mind that he was still managing a baseball team in 1941. He began as a player in 1887. But here's the kicker: He managed NINE MORE YEARS after that. In all, Connie Mack was in baseball for 65 years; 11 different men were president during his time in baseball.

him for sitting out to hit a magical number like .400. But Ted Williams chose to play!

Trouble is: That's not *exactly* right.

Williams's final day is legend, absolutely, but he *had* to play that day.

See, to hit .400, you actually have to hit .400—there's no rounding up.

In fact, it was big news when Williams's average dropped to .3995. It was the first time in two months that his average had dropped below the line. For most of those two months, he was well above .400; he was hitting .413 on September 9, for example. But then he stopped getting any pitches over the plate, and he grew anxious, and the average slowly dropped. When he went 1-for-4 against a Philadelphia knuckleballer named Roger Wolff on the season's penultimate day, the headline that appeared in papers across America was "Ted Williams Slips Below .400 Average" or some close variation.

In other words, it wouldn't have counted as an official .400 season if he had not played that last Sunday.

But all he needed was one hit.

And in the very first inning, he got that hit off a pitcher named Dick Fowler. Williams got ahead in the count 2-0 and then lined a single off the glove of first baseman Bob Johnson. That gave him a .401 batting average—.4008, if you want to be exact—and *now* he could have rested. In later years, he would sometimes say that if he'd known that he would be the last .400 hitter,* he would have rested.

But in the moment, he felt too good to stop. He faced Fowler again and homered. Now, he was swinging freely; even a couple of outs would not drop his batting below .400. He singled off Porter Vaughn twice to push his batting average all the way up to .405.

And then, why not, he played the second game too. There was no

---

* By "last .400 hitter," we are talking about the American and National Leagues. There would be three .400 hitters in the Negro Leagues after Ted: Tetelo Vargas of the New York Cubans in 1942; Williams's hero Josh Gibson in 1943; and Artie Wilson of the Birmingham Black Barons in 1948.

danger of his average dropping below .400 by that point and he just felt so good. He went 2-for-3 in the second game, his last hit a ringing double that smashed a loudspeaker.

That made him 6-for-8 for the day, and he batted .406, a number that is now as much a part of his legacy as any of his many nicknames—Splendid Splinter, Teddy Ballgame, Kid, Thumper, Mister Wonderful, Gorilla Ted, etc.

Ted Williams didn't love being the last .400 hitter because that means every single time anyone came close—Rod Carew in 1977, George Brett in 1980, Wade Boggs in the mid-1980s, Tony Gwynn in 1994, Larry Walker in 1999—reporters called. And Ted Williams loathed reporters. But he was always positive when talking about someone hitting .400 again.

"I'm rooting for him," he said in 1977 for Carew.

"I was rooting for him," he said of Gwynn in 1994 after the season ended prematurely for a player's strike.

"I remember Ted Williams told me that he really wished I had hit .400," George Brett told me. "I thought that was nice. Then he said, 'Yeah, that way every time some #&@$^! gets close to .400, they can call you instead of me.'"

FIVE
BLUNDERS

Babe Herman was a great hitter for Brooklyn in the 1920s and 1930s. He was also famous for his blunders. One of the best happened at Ebbets Field in August of 1926; Herman tried to stretch a double into a triple and found when he got to third base that there were already two other Dodgers there.

But, technically, one of those runners—Chick Fewster—was entitled to the bag. So only two outs were recorded. He did not triple into a triple play as so often was reported. Instead, he doubled into a double play.

No sport celebrates its blunders like baseball does. One more Babe Herman story before we go on: He was a famously clueless outfielder and a danger to himself; writers often talked about balls conking him on the head. It got to the point where he had to protest.

"Let me tell you this," he told a reporter. "If I ever stop a fly ball with my bean, I'll walk right off the field, out of the park and out of baseball, and never come back."

"What happens if a fly ball hits you on the shoulder instead of the head?" the reporter asked.

"No," Herman said. "Shoulders don't count."

JEREMY GIAMBI FAILS TO SLIDE
(OCTOBER 13, 2001)

Most refer to this as the Derek Jeter Flip Play . . . but I call it the Jeremy Giambi Didn't Slide Play. It happened in Game 3 of the 2001 American League Division Series between Oakland and New York. The Athletics—this was Billy Beane's first *Moneyball* team—were threatening to knock the three-time defending champions out of the playoffs.

Bottom of the seventh inning and the Yankees led 1–0. With two outs, Jeremy Giambi—younger brother of league MVP Jason Giambi—singled. Teammate Terrence Long followed with a double into the right-field corner. Giambi was off with the pitch, which should have made scoring from first pretty easy.

But Giambi was notably slow. He rounded third and headed for home, and it looked like he'd make it. Yankees' right fielder Shane Spencer had overthrown the cutoff man. Only then Jeter, displaying the astonishing field awareness that marked his career, raced over, grabbed the off-line throw, and flipped it to catcher Jorge Posada. Giambi tried to score standing up and Posada placed the tag on the back of Giambi's leg. The Yankees went on to win the game and the series.

Now, I readily admit I come at this from the perspective of someone who has loathed and feared the Yankees all his life, but Giambi blundered by not sliding. His teammate Ramón Hernández was standing behind home plate *wildly signaling* for him to slide, but Giambi went in standing up.

Why didn't he slide? "I didn't want to slow down," Giambi would say, hardly much of an explanation. "Maybe it was my mistake."

"Yeah, it might have made a difference if he'd gotten dirty," Hernández said. "Who knows?"

I know it in my heart: Jeremy Giambi is safe if he slides.

THE A.J. PLAY (OCTOBER 12, 2005)

A minor league manager called A. J. Pierzynski into his office one day and said this: "A.J., if you want to make it in this game, you need to do one thing."

"What's that?" Pierzynski asked.

"You've got to be a prick," the manager answered.

Pierzynski didn't need to be told twice. He had a first-rate career—he had 2,000-plus hits; he caught two no-hitters; he made a couple of All-Star teams—and he will tell you the key was his willingness to be the bad guy, the instigator, the meddler.

The best example came in Game 2 of the 2005 American League Championship Series between A.J.'s White Sox and the Los Angeles Angels. The score was tied 1–1 in the bottom of the ninth. There were two outs. Pierzynski came up. And he struck out. Home plate umpire Doug Eddings made the out signal. The Angels' backup catcher Josh Paul rolled the ball to the mound. Everybody prepared for extra innings.

Only as Pierzynski began his walk to the dugout, he had an odd thought: He'd heard two sounds. That could only mean that he heard the ball hit the ground *before* it hit the catcher's mitt. You no doubt know the third-strike rule: If the catcher doesn't actually catch strike three, the batter is entitled to run to first base.

So A.J. Pierzynski ran to first base.

The Angels just watched him do it. Paul didn't even look back as he jogged to the dugout—probably because he knew that the whole thing was nonsense. There weren't two sounds, he'd cleanly caught the third strike. But the longer the ruse went on, the more the Angels started to worry. Then Pierzynski stepped on first base and Eddings, in a stunning move, ruled him safe.

All hell broke loose. Paul ran back on the field with his arms out in the universal "What in the heck are you talking about?" pose. Manager Mike Scioscia raced out screaming, "You already called him out!"

Eddings didn't have a great answer for that. But as an umpire, he was entitled to change his mind.

Then Fox began showing replays that clearly showed Paul had caught the ball. But there was no instant replay review in 2005 and Pierzynski was safe. Eddings had blown the call. The Angels had not reacted in time. Pablo Ozuna came in to pinch-run, he scored on a Joe Crede double, and the White Sox won the game and then won the next three to take the World Series.

THE IMPERFECT GAME (JUNE 2, 2010)

Armando Galarraga was a thinking man's pitcher. He didn't throw hard. He didn't have great breaking stuff. He didn't even have especially good control. He battled through games. Galarraga was always the underdog.

That's what made his greatest game so magnificent. It was a Wednesday night. Galarraga was the best version of himself. He struck out only three that day. He probably never broke 90 on his fastball. But he pitched to precise spots, kept hitters off balance, and kept getting outs.

That game just flew by—it ended up being 1 hour, 44 minutes, the shortest nine-inning baseball game played that year or, indeed, any of the next 15 years. Galarraga retired the first 24 batters he faced. Then in the ninth, Cleveland's Mark Grudzielanek led off with a fly ball to center field—probably the best-hit ball of the day for Cleveland—but Detroit center fielder Austin Jackson caught it over his shoulder for the first out. And Galarraga smiled.

Cleveland's Mike Redmond chopped a groundout to short. And Galarraga smiled again.

The last Cleveland batter was a rookie named Jason Donald, and he hit a squibber up the first-base line. First baseman Miguel Cabrera fielded it cleanly and flipped the ball to Galarraga in time for the out—and a perfect game.

Except first-base umpire Jim Joyce called Donald safe.

And he was dead wrong.

And somehow Galarraga still smiled.

As with the Pierzynski play, there was no instant replay review. Joyce's call was final. It still boggles the mind that Joyce, a very good umpire, could blow that call. It wasn't all that close; Galarraga beat Donald to the bag by a half step. But even more, you would think that with a perfect game on the line, Joyce would err on the side of out.

"Why is he safe?" Tigers' announcer Rod Allen kept saying as the heartbreaking replays played over and over again. "Why is he safe?"

The minute the game ended—Galarraga retired Trevor Crowe for the 28th out of the game—Joyce went over to umpire Darryl Cousins and asked for his brutal assessment.

"You kicked the call," Cousins told him.

Joyce's heart sank. He walked into the clubhouse and watched the replay just one time and knew: He'd cost that kid a perfect game. Joyce broke down in tears. On the way home, he called the commissioner's office to ask for his own call to be reversed. There was no answer.

This should be a sad story. Missed calls live forever; people in St. Louis will never forgive Don Denkinger for missing a call in Game 6 of the 1985 World Series. But our story isn't sad at all, and that's because of Armando Galarraga.

"Tell him no problem," Galarraga said to reporters when informed of how hard Joyce was taking his blown call. "I can go tell him. I should probably talk to him. It will be better."

He then went to talk to Joyce.

"I am so sorry in my heart," Joyce said to him.

"Nobody's perfect," Galarraga said.

Nobody's perfect. Is there anything quite as inspiring as someone gracefully handling a loss, a bad break, a missed call? The next day, the two men met at home plate before the game. Joyce was still in tears. Galarraga patted him on the shoulder.

"I am disappointed about this call," Galarraga would say. "Of course I am frustrated. But I cannot be angry. I am too happy to be angry."

ÁLEX GONZÁLEZ BOOTS THE BALL (OCTOBER 14, 2003)

Nobody, even now, calls it the González Game. No. Alas, people still call it the Bartman Game. And THAT is the blunder.

We go back to Game 6 of the 2003 National League Championship Series. The Cubs led the Marlins 3–0 in the eighth inning and were on the brink of reaching their first World Series since 1945. The champagne was chilling. Fox Sports was showing all sorts of fun Cubs facts.

Even when Florida's Juan Pierre then punched a double down the left-field line, nobody saw it as a harbinger of bad things. Chicago's Mark Prior was pitching brilliantly.

Then came the moment: Florida's Luis Castillo flared a foul ball to left field. Cubs' left fielder Moisés Alou thought he had a chance to leap and catch the ball before it got into the stands. Instead, several fans reached for the ball. It bounced off the hands of one of those fans, a young and devoted Cubs follower named Steve Bartman.

Alou lost his temper. He'd apologize for that later. But he threw his glove to the ground and screamed at the fans in general and Bartman specifically and a darkness took hold of the game. It would not be long before Bartman was escorted out of Wrigley Field for his own safety.

The Cubs collapsed from there—a walk by Prior, a single to Iván Rodríguez, and then Álex González botched an easy ground ball that was probably not going to be a double play, but we'll never know. After that, yes, everyone could hear the bells of doom. In the end, three different Cubs' pitchers gave up eight runs and the Cubs lost Game 7 and that was that.

Despite the Cubs burying themselves, Bartman was declared the villain. It was shameful and, even more to the point, just plain wrong. Illinois Governor Rod Blagojevich—who would have his own problems—said Bartman needed to go into witness protection. The *Chicago Tribune* ran a big color photo of Bartman dropping the ball with the headline "Uh Oh!"

All because he did what fans do: He reached for a ball hit to the stands.

MERKLE'S BONER (SEPTEMBER 23, 1908)

    "Censurable stupidity on the part of player Merkle in yesterday's game at the Polo Grounds between the Giants and Chicagos placed the New York team's chances of winning the pennant in jeopardy.**"**

—*THE NEW YORK TIMES*

Fred Merkle was a 19-year-old first baseman for the New York Giants in 1908. Manager John McGraw thought him a quick thinker, wise beyond his years. That's why McGraw started him at first base that Wednesday afternoon at the Polo Grounds. It was a big game between the Giants and Cubs. The winner would be alone in first place in the National League.

McGraw started his great pitcher Christy Mathewson, and Matty was typically good. He struck out nine and allowed just one run. But Cubs' starter Jack Pfiester matched him. The Giants came to bat in the bottom of the ninth with the score tied.

New York's Moose McCormick was hit by a pitch, and with two outs Merkle slashed a long single, moving McCormick to third. That brought up shortstop Al Bridwell, and he singled up the middle—"the greatest hit I ever saw because it was the most timely," McGraw would say—and that scored McCormick for what should have been the walk-off hit.

But Merkle made a fateful error. Instead of running to second, he headed for the dugout as fans swarmed the field.

Chicago's Johnny Evers caught the mistake. He was a crafty one, that

Johnny Evers. He knew that if he could force Merkle out at second base, the run wouldn't count.

He went looking for the baseball. But that turned out to be trickier than expected. During the celebration, Giants' pitcher Iron Man Joe McGinnity had thrown the ball into the crowd.* That ball was gone.

And then, suddenly, Evers had a baseball. Was it the same ball? Nobody knows for sure. One story has Cubs' pitcher Rube Kroh—who stood 6-foot-2—wrestling the ball away from a Giants fan and relaying it to Evers. Other versions (more likely in my view) have Evers grabbing a different baseball.

At this point, Merkle had caught on and he sprinted out to second base, perhaps even escorted by a panicky Christy Mathewson. But Evers got there first. The umpire was future Hall of Famer Hank O'Day, who, according to Mathewson "made a speedy departure under the grandstand and . . . finally, while somewhere near Coogan's Bluff, he called Merkle out."

That meant the game ended in a tie . . . and the Giants ended up losing the pennant by one game.

Merkle never lived it down. He had a fine 16-year big-league career and lived a modest but joyful life with his wife and three daughters. But he was immediately nicknamed Bonehead, and the nickname chased him for the rest of his life . . . and beyond.

"Fred Merkle, of Famous Boner Play, Dies," was the headline in the *Tampa Bay Times* and most other places on the day after his death in 1956. "He died in his bed of natural causes—and a broken heart," they wrote.

The *Baltimore Evening Sun* took a moment that day to write an editorial about him. It's worth reprinting a part:

---

* There are those who say that it was a fan who threw the ball into the crowd. Much of how the game ended has been in dispute for more than 100 years.

Fred Merkle is dead, the wire services reports from Florida say, and perhaps the clamor will now abate and his failure to touch second base for the Giants that day in 1908 will yield place in the minds of baseball people to some later boner.*

History contains bigger boners, better boners. Baseball itself is full of splendidly deplorable stuff—the World Series fly that Hack Wilson lost in the sun, the third strike dropped by Mickey Owen in a later series. Heinie Zimmerman chasing Eddie Collins across a home plate left unguarded by catcher and first baseman.

At that, Merkle was not so unlucky—the rest of his career, even in the International League, was ordinary, and he would have been long since forgotten but for that moment.

---

* As you will see—and have probably guessed—Merkle's Boner did yield way to a later one.

NO. 13:
BUCKNER

OCTOBER 25, 1986, SHEA STADIUM

★ ★ ★ ★ ★

Something occurred to me as I prepared to write about the most famous blunder in baseball history: We almost always tell the story from the side of the Red Sox. And more to the point, we almost always tell the story from the side of Bill Buckner.

Of course we do. The Red Sox were trying to win the World Series for the first time since 1918, that was the story. And Buckner—well, he had a fabulous two-decade career. He cracked 2,715 hits. He won a batting title. He twice led the league in doubles. And he was all but impossible to strike out. If we go back to 1969, the two toughest players to strike out have been Hall of Famer Tony Gwynn and, yes, Bill Buckner.

There's something terribly sad about reducing that full career to a ground ball that rolled between his legs.

But here's the thing: That ground ball was not just about Buckner and the Red Sox.

It was perhaps the greatest moment in New York Mets history.

That is the conundrum that runs throughout this book. Great moments are often terrible moments, terrible moments great, all depending on your point of view. If you grew up in, say, Wethersfield, Connecticut (as the famed botanist Charles Wright did!), you are, according to Google Maps, exactly 101.3 miles away from Citi Field, where the Mets play, and exactly 101.3 miles away from Fenway Park, where the Red Sox play.

So it all depends on perspective. If you lived in Wethersfield and looked southwest to the Mets, your heart was filled with joy when that ball went through Buckner.

And if you looked northeast to the Red Sox, the Buckner play breaks your heart into a million pieces.*

///

THE METS AND RED SOX CAME INTO THAT 1986 WORLD SERIES ON magic carpets. The Mets had beaten Houston in a wild six-game National League Championship Series. The Mets went into that Game 6 knowing that they absolutely had to win because, if not, the Astros would start Mike Scott, that year's Cy Young winner, in Game 7.

"We knew that we weren't going to beat Scott," the Mets' Keith Hernandez would say.

The Mets won Game 6 in 16 innings.

Boston played an even wilder seven-game series against the Angels. In Game 5, one of the most bananas games ever in the postseason, the Red Sox were down by a run with two outs in the ninth. Dave Henderson had two strikes. He hit a home run. The Red Sox won the game in 11 innings and then won both Games 6 and 7 to reach the World Series.

For the most part, the first five games of the Mets–Red Sox series were disappointingly bland. In Game 1, the winning run was scored on an error. Game 2 was a Boston blowout. Games 3 and 4 were controlled by New York. Boston's Bruce Hurst pitched brilliantly in Game 5, giving the Red Sox a 3–2 series lead and setting them up to finally win that World Series.

Game 6 was at Shea Stadium, a Saturday night.

Boston started fireballing superstar Roger Clemens. New York countered with the craftiness of left-hander Bobby Ojeda.† The Red Sox

---

* You could avoid both fates by simply tacking on 2.1 miles and choosing Yankee Stadium and the 27 World Championships that come with it.

† The 1980s was a wonderful decade for crafty lefties—Scott McGregor and Bob Knepper and Frank Tanana and Jerry Reuss and John Tudor and Mike Flanagan and Charlie

scored two runs in the first inning. The Mets chipped away against Clemens and tied things up. The Red Sox took the lead on a Dwight Evans groundout. The Mets tied it again on a Gary Carter sacrifice fly.

The night was soaked with tension. All New England was on edge—suffering being the plight of Boston Red Sox fans at that time in history—but it's easy to miss just how much this meant to New York fans. This Mets team was utterly beloved. The players on that team—Dwight Gooden, Darryl Strawberry, Mookie Wilson, Lenny Dykstra, Ron Darling, Keith Hernandez, Gary Carter, and so on—these were larger-than-life characters, superheroes even, and the idea that they could lose simply did not compute. The game went into extra innings.

And in the 10th inning, the Red Sox broke it open. They scored two runs—one on a home run by the irrepressible Dave Henderson. Relief pitcher Calvin Schiraldi then got two quick outs, and it seemed that yes, finally, 67 years after Boston owner and Broadway impresario Harry Frazee sold Babe Ruth to the Yankees, the Red Sox were going to win the World Series.

NBC was so sure the game was over that they had announcer Vin Scully name the player of the game, something you never do when the game is in doubt. "Tonight's Miller Lite player of the game is Marty Barrett," Scully said. "Marty had three singles and two walks and handled everything hit his way."

Then to add to the bad karma, they flashed this graphic on the screen:

Franchises that have gone the longest without winning:

Chicago Cubs (Last Won 1908)

Chicago White Sox (Last Won 1917)

Boston Red Sox (Last Won 1918)

Leibrandt and Tommy John and Shane Rawley and Bobby Ojeda. You didn't go anywhere in the 1980s without your Members Only Jacket, Van Halen cassette, and a crafty lefty.

Look, I don't believe in jinxes. But I also like to think: You would wait to run that graphic.

Gary Carter singled for the Mets. Kevin Mitchell was sent in as a pinch hitter and he also singled. Up came Ray Knight. Mets fans threw toilet paper on the field. Knight singled, too, scoring Carter, and pulling the Mets within a run.

Bob Stanley came in to pitch to Mookie Wilson.

Those nine words mean something different to you if you're a Red Sox fan or a Mets fan.

The Stanley/Mookie at-bat lasted ten pitches, but it felt like a hundred. It has to be one of the most grueling at-bats in postseason history, with Stanley throwing nasty stuff that was skidding and sliding all over the place and Wilson just fouling off pitches left and right in an effort to stay alive.

There were two pitches that changed the complexion of the game. With the count 2-2, Red Sox catcher Rich Gedman set up for an outside fastball. Stanley's pitch sailed inside. It wasn't as bad a pitch as it first appeared—Mookie Wilson acrobatically jumped out of the way, giving the illusion of the ball being way inside, which it was not—but it fooled Gedman. He reached for it but could not catch it or block it. The ball rolled back to the screen. Kevin Mitchell scored. The game was tied again.

"Five-five in a delirious tenth inning," Vin Scully said. "Can you believe this ball game at Shea? . . . So the winning run is at second base with two out, three and two to Mookie Wilson."

And what happened next . . . well, you can undoubtedly see it in your mind.

Wilson hit a slow roller down the first-base line. Buckner—who had a bad leg and was inexplicably still in the game rather than defensive replacement Dave Stapleton—awkwardly shuffled for it. "It was bouncing, bouncing . . . then it went under," he would later tell reporters. The ball rolled through. Ray Knight came around to score. Shea Stadium became a cloud of ecstasy and euphoria.

Here's what Michael Madden wrote in *The Boston Globe*: "The nightmare that every Red Sox fan has carried deep in his and her heart, the nightmare of despair could never rival this."

Here's what Mike Lupica wrote in the New York *Daily News*: "The Mets were two steps into next season but, in wee hours when the clocks got turned back, they turned back the clock. You ever see anything like it? In your life?"

It's all a matter of perspective.

NO. 12:
DIMAGGIO'S STREAK ALMOST ENDS

JUNE 17, 1941, BRONX

★ ★ ★ ★ ★

O K, so I'm going to share something with you now that, shamefully, I did not know until, like, five minutes ago.

The Yankees' Joe DiMaggio started a long hitting streak on May 15, 1941.

OK, that I knew.

The Red Sox's Ted Williams also started a long hitting streak on May 15, 1941.

And that I did not know.

That seems like something that as an obsessive baseball fan I should have known—that Joe DiMaggio cracked a single in a loss to the White Sox. He was in a slump when his streak began.

That Williams managed one infield single in a loss to Cleveland.

And that the two great hitters of their generation were off together.

Hitting streaks were not big a deal then. It took Joe DiMaggio to make them a big deal. If you think about it, why would you count the number of consecutive games that someone gets a hit? That seems such a random thing. Great hitters like DiMaggio and Williams should get a hit every game. I mean, look at it this way:

Joe DiMaggio in his career got 2,214 hits in 1,736 games.

Ted Williams in his career got 2,654 hits in 2,292 games.

So what's the big deal of getting a hit every day? Well, the big deal is that in baseball it really *is* every day, unlike just about every other sport. It is six or seven times a week, a different pitcher every day, fastballs some days, curveballs somedays, righties sometimes, lefties sometimes, it's a never-ending variety.

Take just a few of the early days of DiMaggio's hitting streak.

Day 2, DiMaggio tripled off Chicago's Thornton Lee, a 6-foot-3 lefthander with a blazing fastball that he had finally learned to control.

Day 4, DiMaggio went 3-for-3 off St. Louis Browns' starter Bob Harris, who didn't throw especially hard but was only the second big-league pitcher from the state of Wyoming.

Day 6, DiMaggio struggled against the Browns' Elden Auker, an awkward submarine-style sinkerball pitcher, but managed to get a hit in the eighth inning.

Day 9, DiMaggio faced four different Boston Red Sox pitchers and finally got his hit against the last of the four, Dick Newsome, a knuckleball pitcher, to keep the streak alive.

Day 13, DiMaggio tripled off Washington's Sid Hudson, a tall young right-hander with a great fastball. Hudson would stay in the game as a player and a coach for another fifty years.

Yes, every day something new. DiMaggio and Williams kept their hitting streaks going, side by side, and it wasn't until early June, when their streaks closed in on twenty games, that people started to notice. On June 7, DiMaggio got three hits to push his streak to 22 games. On the same day, Ted Williams got a hit and pushed his streak to 23 games.

The next day, Ted Williams dropped out. He failed to get a hit off Chicago's star pitcher Ted Lyons—it didn't help that Lyons walked him three times—and his hitting streak died there.

DiMaggio, as it turns out, was only getting started.

NO HITTING STREAK HAD EVER BEEN A NATIONAL STORY BEFORE. It took Joe DiMaggio's charisma to give the streak life and meaning. He gave you something special every day. That was his whole thing, his whole persona. He was the Yankee Clipper. He played a brilliant center field. He never threw to the wrong base. He hit baseballs into gaps and almost never struck out.

"I never saw him look bad," Ted Williams said of DiMaggio. "He made it look so easy."

A decade later, a breathless reporter asked Joltin' Joe: *Why do you play so hard every day?*

"Because," he said, "there's always some kid who may be seeing me for the first or last time. I owe him my best."

And so, when the consecutive games started to pile up—26, 27, 28!—people began to notice. They started to ask one another, "Did Joe get a hit today?" Reporters went back into the record books and found that the Yankees' consecutive-game-hitting-streak record belonged not to Babe Ruth or Lou Gehrig, but to their lesser-known teammate Earle Combs. They called him the Kentucky Colonel. He was, like DiMaggio, a Yankees' center fielder. Combs liked to hit everything up the middle or to the opposite field. He wouldn't pull the ball, and as such, he never hit 10 home runs in a season. But he had double-digit triples every year from 1925 to 1933, three times leading the league.

In 1931, Combs got hits in 29 consecutive games. Not one newspaper even mentioned it—heck, *The Brooklyn Daily Eagle* did a big story on Combs the day after he set the record and never mentioned it.

But that was the Yankees' record, and on June 16, 1941, DiMaggio tied it when he managed one hit in five at-bats against Cleveland. The next day was a Tuesday game between New York and Chicago at Yankee Stadium. Before the game, DiMaggio and Combs kibbitzed for the cameras.

The Chicago pitcher was Johnny Rigney, a hard-throwing righty. Rigney got DiMaggio to ground out to shortstop in the second inning.

In the fourth, DiMaggio hit the ball pretty hard, but he hit it right at right fielder Taffy Wright.

DiMaggio knew he was running out of time when he came up to bat in the seventh inning. And then he hit a routine ground ball to shortstop. It seemed like the streak might be coming to an end. White Sox shortstop Luke Appling stepped in front of the ball . . . and then the most ridiculous thing imaginable happened. The ball just jumped over Appling's head, like a grasshopper.

Appling walked over to the spot to find what the ball hit. A rock? A crevice? But, and this is the craziest thing, he couldn't find anything. It's like that ball had a mind all its own.

When DiMaggio got to first, he could not hide what the Brooklyn paper would call "a foolish grin." It was his only hit of the day, but he needed only one. That pushed his streak to a Yankees' record 30 games. And that, he always said, was his luckiest day.

His streak would go on for another month. George Sisler had the previous modern record at 41 games, and DiMaggio just sailed by him. Dutiful researchers found that Wee Willie Keeler had hit in 44 straight games over two seasons, 1896 and 1897, and nobody knew if that should count, but DiMaggio raced by Keeler, too.

He kept going until July 16, in Cleveland, when he got three hits. That was No. 56. The streak ended the next evening in front of 67,568 fans in Cleveland, when third baseman Ken Keltner made a couple of dazzling defensive plays. DiMaggio, frankly, was ready to be done with it.

"I'm tickled to death it's over," he said. "I'm sure proud of the record, but I might as well admit it now, it was quite a strain."

Baseball is very much a counting game. We count everything. We count strikeouts and home runs and stolen bases and runs batted in, sure, but we also count broken bats and errors and putouts and foul balls. We obsessively count, like children counting cracks in a sidewalk, because every now and again we find something extraordinary in the numbers.

Nobody will ever hit in 56 straight games again.

NO. 11:
DON LARSEN'S PERFECT GAME

OCTOBER 8, 1956, BRONX

★ ★ ★ ★ ★

Mickey Mantle called Don Larsen the greatest drinker he'd ever known. That's really something. The Mick knew a lot of drinkers in his day, from Billy Martin to Frank Sinatra. It gives you a pretty good idea of just how wild Larsen could be.

Don Larsen was a big ol' mess of gifts, flaws, and hangovers. He was a terrific high school basketball player, good enough to get several college scholarships. He turned them all down; as he later told biographer Lew Paper, "I was never much with studies."

Instead, he signed with the St. Louis Browns for $850 and was sent to Aberdeen, South Dakota, to start his baseball life.* He was just 17 years old, and he could throw about as hard as anybody. And he was utterly fearless. Nobody quite knew where that came from, but when Don Larsen stepped to the mound, he just knew that hitters didn't stand a chance.

As Baltimore's manager Jimmy Dykes would later say: "The only thing Don fears is sleep."

Larsen's results, however, did not always match his certainty. In 1954, he went 3-21 for the Baltimore Orioles. But he had excellent timing—two of those three wins were complete-game victories over Casey Stengel's New York Yankees. Stengel liked the kid, liked his panache, liked his flamboyance, and didn't mind his late-night carousing. Stengel did a little of that himself. He arranged for Larsen to be

---

* When Larsen got to Aberdeen, nobody was expecting him, and nobody had ever heard of him. He had to buy a ticket to get into the ballpark for his first professional game.

included in a whirlwind 18-player trade between the Yankees and Orioles.

Larsen remained an enigma with the Yankees. He pitched well in a limited role in 1955, well enough that Stengel started Larsen in Game 4 of the World Series against Brooklyn. Larsen got rocked, giving up long home runs to Roy Campanella and Gil Hodges.

"I thought Don pitched very well," Stengel said after the game, "until those guys got those long hits."

During spring training of 1956, Larsen fell asleep while driving and ran his car into a telegraph pole. The newspaper reports suggested this wasn't unexpected. There was some pressure on Stengel to dump him. But Stengel stood by Larsen then and kept standing by him even as Larsen pitched poorly early in the season.

"Don't worry about my man," Stengel promised, and sure enough, as the weather warmed up, Larsen did, too. After June 22, Larsen started some games, pitched relief in others, and posted a 2.26 ERA. Stengel beamed. He had personally worked with Larsen on a special no-windup pitching style* and was thrilled with the results. He started Larsen in Game 2 of the 1956 World Series against Brooklyn.

And once again, Larsen was terrible. He walked two in the first and barely got out of it when Jackie Robinson hit into a double play. In the second inning, he walked two more and gave up a hit and the Yankees committed an error. Stengel pulled him even though the Yankees led 6–1 at the time. The Yankees eventually lost 13–8.

"I have nothing to say," Larsen barked at reporters. "Not a thing."

Nobody expected Larsen to pitch again in the series. But when Game 5 came around, Stengel felt stuck. The series was tied at two games apiece, this was clearly the pivotal game, and he trusted only one

---

* Stengel himself had learned the no-windup style from one of the great Negro Leagues pitchers, Bullet Rogan. Stengel later called Rogan the best all-around player in the world (Rogan was both a hitter and outfielder) and one of the best pitchers who ever lived.

pitcher, his ace Whitey Ford, who had already pitched twice. Everybody else was a wild card.

As he looked around at his options, Stengel kept thinking about going back one more time to his man Don Larsen.

ONE OF THE GREAT AND STILL UNSETTLED QUESTIONS ABOUT the day that Don Larsen threw his World Series perfect game is this: Did he even know he was going to pitch that day?

Larsen always insisted he did not. He always told the story the same way: that when he got to the ballpark, he did not know who was starting Game 5. Then he looked in his locker and saw that coach Frank Crosetti had put a baseball in one of his shoes. That was the sign that Stengel had chosen Larsen to pitch.

In Larsen's memory, he was utterly and completely stunned.

"You had a look of shock and disbelief on your face," he quoted his teammate Hank Bauer saying. "And you took a big gulp. It was like you had an apple stuck in your throat."

It's a marvelous story, and the only trouble with it is that it clashes with various other equally marvelous stories about that day.

For example, we know that Casey Stengel had decided to go with Larsen the day before because he told all the reporters (adding that he wouldn't hesitate to go to Bob Turley in the bullpen). It was all over the newspapers the morning of the game that Larsen would be facing Brooklyn's Sal Maglie.

Larsen deflected this by saying that Stengel and the coaches had never told *him* he was starting, and he had not seen the papers.

"They were probably concerned I would get nervous, worry too much, and not get a good night's sleep," he later wrote.

Possible. But that would still counter the best story leading up to the game.

Larsen went out on the town before Game 5. Obviously. He and his friend Arthur Richman, a famed New York sportswriter, went to Bill Taylor's Restaurant across town and definitely had at least a couple of beers. Then while they were taking a cab back to the Bronx, according to Richman, they had this conversation:

> **LARSEN:** Artie, I got one of those crazy feelings that I'm gonna pitch a no-hitter tomorrow.
>
> **RICHMAN:** A four-hitter will be good enough.
>
> **LARSEN:** Nope. It's gonna be a no-hitter.

And then Larsen gave Richman a dollar coin and said, "Give that to your mother to donate to the synagogue. For luck, you know."

What's the truth? Who knows? As great stories go, though, I prefer Richman's memory.

THE DODGERS CAME INTO THE GAME WITH A SIMPLE PLAN: BE patient and let Larsen blow himself up. They knew that even if he started well, he'd eventually crack. It was his nature.

For his part, Larsen was surprised how passively the Dodgers began the game. Leadoff hitter Junior Gilliam looked at strike three. Pee Wee Reese did the same. Larsen felt amazing. He was putting the ball just where he wanted. He got Duke Snider to fly to right to end the inning. The perfect game was on.

The Dodgers would come close to a hit four times.

In the second inning, Jackie Robinson lined a shot to the hole between third and short. Third baseman Andy Carey made a stab for it but was only able to deflect the ball toward shortstop Gil McDougald, who picked up the ball and fired it across the diamond. "I threw that ball so hard," McDougald would say, "I could feel the muscles pull right down to my toes."

The throw beat Jackie Robinson by six inches.

"We would never have gotten Robinson out if the game had been played two or three years earlier when he still had his speed," Carey said.

In the fifth inning, Larsen threw a hanging slider to Gil Hodges—"his one bad pitch," catcher Yogi Berra would say—and Hodges blasted a long fly ball to left center. It would have gone out of most stadiums. But left center field was a canyon at Yankee Stadium, and Mickey Mantle chased it down and made a terrific running catch.

The very next batter, Sandy Amorós, blasted a ball into the right-field stands. Umpire Ed Runge was standing deep down the line, and he called it foul.

By how much?

"That much," Runge said, and he held his thumb and index finger four inches part.

And finally, in the eighth inning, Hodges at the plate again, he checked his swing and cracked a low line drive that hit Carey's glove and jumped a few inches in the air. Carey brought the ball back in for the out.

Everything else was pretty routine. Larsen was in complete control of his pitches and his emotions.

"I never saw him pitch like that before," Berra said. "He never shook off one sign. He hit the glove wherever I put it."

Larsen ended the perfect game just as he started it; he threw a fastball that Brooklyn's Dale Mitchell watched go by for strike three. It was as if, to the very end, the Dodgers could not quite believe what was happening. Yogi Berra leaped in the air and raced toward the mound and jumped into Larsen's arms.

Don Larsen never grew tired of talking about it and never minded being a symbol. Why would he? "How many people get to be remembered for throwing a perfect game?" he asked, but it was more than just that. Don Larsen understood that he represented this deeply hopeful notion that any of us, no matter how flawed, can wake up one morning, find the baseball in our shoe, and just go out there and be perfect.

OK, I'M GOING TO ADD ONE MORE STORY, EVEN THOUGH IT MIGHT not interest anyone but me. When the game ended, the New York *Daily News*'s Joe Trimble found himself unable to find words for such an enormous moment. He was literally shaking with anxiety when, as the story goes, his *Daily News* colleague Dick Young walked over to Trimble's typewriter and typed the seven-word lede that might be the most famous in the history of baseball writing:

"The imperfect man pitched a perfect game."

So great. But when you go back to look at the *Daily News* archives, you find an odd twist. That was not the first lede that Joe Trimble wrote.

No, originally, he wrote: "The unperfect man pitched a perfect game yesterday. Don Larsen, a free soul who loves the gay life, retired all 27 Dodgers in the classic pitching performance of all time . . ."

And only later did someone change it to "The imperfect man pitched . . ."

Who changed it? Trimble? Young? An editor? I fear we'll never know. Imperfect is grammatically correct. But, for me, unperfect is better.

FIVE

DUELS

Baseball was not supposed to be a battle between pitcher and hitter. No, in the early days of the game, the pitcher was just a trigger to start the action. That's why they're called *pitchers*. They were supposed to *pitch* the ball, underhand, the way people pitch horseshoes or slow-pitch softballs. The real duel in those early days was between the hitter and all the fielders.

Pitchers had no interest being used that way. They began to skirt the rules and put speed and spin on the ball. In time, the rules were changed to let pitchers throw however they wanted.

And that's when baseball duels really began.

BUGS BUNNY VS. THE GAS-HOUSE GORILLAS (1946, SHORT *BASEBALL BUGS*)

The scheduled game at the Famous Polo Grounds that day was between the Gas-House Gorillas and the Tea Totallers. However, that part was not especially competitive; the Gorillas were leading 95–0 after just three and a half innings.* That's when the players overheard Bugs Bunny shouting that he could beat the Gorillas all by himself.

---

* Trivia: The scoreboard had the Gorillas scoring 10 runs in the first inning, 28 in the second, 16 in the third, and 42 in the fourth. That's 96 runs. We can only assume that one

"All right, big shot," the Gorillas' pitcher said while blowing cigar smoke in Bugs Bunny's face. "So you think you can beat us all by yourself? Well, you got yourself a game!"

Bugs realized that a comeback of that magnitude takes patience; you can't just score 96 runs with one swing of the bat. First, he needed to slow down the Gas-House offense. He did this by mixing speeds, at first throwing the ball right by hitters with his heater (and then catching them himself). Then he started perplexing them with his slow ball; in one inning, he struck out the entire side on one particularly slow pitch.

Bugs then began scoring runs in a variety of ways, once by distracting the catcher with a poster of a pretty woman, another time by tricking the umpire (who was one of the Gorillas in disguise) into calling him safe. He also scored a bunch of runs by hitting a ball so hard it bounced off all the Gorillas' fielders like a pinball machine.

In the top of the ninth, Bugs Bunny led 96–95, but the Gorillas put a man on and sent their best hitter to the plate, and he had a fully grown tree for a bat. This is when, for the first time, Bugs lost focus. He looked to the crowd and said arrogantly: "Ehh, watch me paste this pathetic palooka with a powerful, paralyzing, perfect, pachydermous, percussion pitch."

The Gorillas batter crushed the pitch. Bugs Bunny had to take a cab and a bus and then climb to the top of the Umpire State Building to chase it down. Then he threw his glove in the air and caught the ball, and the umpire—apparently having not read Rule 5.06(a), which says that a fair ball that passes over a fence at a distance from home base of 250 feet or more shall be ruled a home run—ruled the batter out to end the game.

---

of those runs was disallowed by the umpire, perhaps because one of the Gorillas players passed another on the bases during the run-scoring conga line in the fourth inning.

REGGIE JACKSON VS. BOB WELCH
(OCTOBER 11, 1978)

One of the baseball moments that towers over my childhood happened in Game 2 of the 1978 World Series. The Dodgers led the New York Yankees by a run with two outs in the ninth inning. Two runners were on.

The Dodgers' hard-throwing rookie Bob Welch was on the mound.

It was pure spectacle and NBC played it up beautifully, like a boxing match.

"You couldn't ask for a more dramatic moment," Tom Seaver said up in the booth.

Welch's first pitch was a fastball as hard as he could throw it. And Reggie swung so hard that he fell to one knee and almost fell over entirely. The crowd at Dodger Stadium was electrified. "Listen to 'em," Joe Garagiola shouted.

Welch's second pitch was high and tight. Jackson hit the deck to avoid it.

The third pitch was up, and again Jackson swung with everything he had and fouled it back. Fourth pitch the same. Fifth pitch, the same. They had never seen each other before, but already there were no secrets between Welch and Jackson. It was eternal. One would throw a rock as hard as he could. The other would swing a stick as hard as he could.

"Look at that face," Garagiola said as the camera closed in on Welch.

Pitch 6 was way up, out of the strike zone, overthrown a bit.

"You're getting it all here," Garagiola said. "The kid against the veteran. The fastball pitcher against the fastball hitter."

Pitch 7 was perhaps the hardest one yet; again Jackson fouled it back.

Pitch 8 was high and outside, and now the count was full.

Jackson dug his cleats hard into the dirt and adjusted his helmet. Welch looked in and took the sign; there really was no question what pitch he would throw.

He threw the fastball right past a swinging Jackson for strike three.

"It worked out just the way it does in your dreams," Jim Murray wrote the next morning in the *Los Angeles Times*. "You just go out there and bust that fastball in—and 55,982 fans scream your name, and it goes down in baseball lore as the night Mr. Schoolboy struck out Mr. October with two outs on in the ninth, and the good guys won for the home nine, and it turned out the way it always does for me in my sleep. Except that if Bob Welch wakes up and pinches himself, he won't feel a thing. Because his dream is not something he ate, it happened."*

CHET BREWER VS. SMOKEY JOE WILLIAMS (AUGUST 2, 1930)

The first night game played in the American or National League was in 1935 at Crosley Field in Cincinnati. Most hard-core baseball fans know that.

What many people did not know, at least until recently, was that by 1935, they had been playing night baseball in the Negro Leagues for five years.

The key innovator was a man named J. L. Wilkinson, who also happened to be the only white owner in the Negro Leagues. Wilkie, as he was called, mortgaged everything he had in 1930 to get portable lights that his Kansas City Monarchs could travel with. With the Depression going on, night games saved the franchise.

Make no mistake, though: It was pretty hellish playing under those lights. For one thing, they made an ungodly racket. "You couldn't even hear the crack of the bat," Kansas City catcher Frank Duncan once said. But even more to the point, the lights were dim and low. When

---

* Six days later, Jackson faced Welch again. The situation had none of the drama—the Yankees were leading by three runs and were close to wrapping up the World Series—but it meant something to Jackson. He wanted his revenge. And on the first pitch, he crushed a home run into the right-field seats.

pop-ups went above the lights, as Buck O'Neil said, "You were on your own."

Lights set up one of the most incredible pitchers duels ever, a Saturday-night game played between the Kansas City Monarchs and Pittsburgh's Homestead Grays. It's one of the first night games, and it so happened to feature two of the best pitchers in the Negro Leagues. Pittsburgh started Hall of Famer Smokey Joe Williams, who had an astonishing fastball. That's why they called him Smokey.

"If you have ever witnessed the speed of a pebble in a storm," Negro Leagues owner Frank Leland said, "you have not even then seen the equal of his speed."

Kansas City countered with Chet Brewer, who didn't throw nearly as hard as Smokey Joe, but he made up for it with his nearly unhittable emery ball. Brewer would scuff and cut the ball with an emery board— the Negro Leagues in those days were lax when it came to emery ball enforcement—and he could then make the baseball do all sorts of circus tricks.

And, the lights were particularly faint that day.

For 11 innings, the game was scoreless. Williams was already 44 years old, but he could still throw a fastball by anybody. He allowed one hit and struck out 27 batters.

"The Monarchs might as well have remained on the bench with their trainer," *The Kansas City Star* reported.

Brewer was almost as good. He struck out 19. "The emery ball in daylight," *The Star* wrote, "is very elusive but at night it is about as easy to see as an insect in the dark."

But in the 12th, Brewer lost the game after giving up what the game report called "a fluke double." My guess is that it was a fly ball that went above the lights.

AMOS RUSIE VS. KID NICHOLS (MAY 12, 1890)

This is widely believed to be the first great pitchers' duel in baseball history. The Giants' Amos Rusie was the hardest thrower of his day; many believe he was the motivating force to move the mound from 50 feet to today's measurement of 60 feet, 6 inches. Boston's Kid Nichols was a thinking man's pitcher who threw an optical-illusion pitch that seemed to jump up just as it approached the plate.

They are both in the Baseball Hall of Fame now.

For 12 innings, Rusie and Nichols held the opposing teams scoreless. Great defense played a big role. This was at a time when few players wore gloves, and the fans were treated to a spectacular display of defense from men called Pebbly Jack Glasscock, Foghorn Tommy Tucker, Pop Smith, and, particularly, the original Flying Dutchman, Herman Long.

"Wonderful indeed was the playing of Herman Long," *The Boston Globe* wrote. "Such pickups and throws fairly bewildered the spectators, and no less than three times did he save the game for Boston."

In the bottom of the 13th, with the game still scoreless, the Giants sent Silent Mike Tiernan to the plate. Tiernan, as you can guess, was a taciturn man. On Nichols's third pitch, Silent Mike hit the ball over the center-field wall for the game-winning home run.

"It was," *The New York Times* would write, "the finest contest ever played by two professional teams and will go down on record as such."

The *Boston Globe* headline captured the moment even more vividly.

TIERNAN WAS TIRED

Thirteen Innings Were All He Wanted

So He Put the Ball Over the Fence and Won the Game

JUAN MARICHAL VS. WARREN SPAHN (JULY 2, 1963)

On a cold and windy Tuesday night at Candlestick Park in San Francisco, two of the best pitchers ever, Juan Marichal and Warren Spahn, matched brilliance for more than four hours. They were men at different stages of their lives. Spahn was 42 and needed to use all the guile and cunning he'd gained over his 18-year career.

Marichal was 25 and just beginning. He kicked his leg high—"that foot's up in your face," Henry Aaron would say of him—and threw from whatever arm angle felt right in the moment and threw fastballs and sliders that buzzed.

Put another way: Marichal was seven when Spahn fought in the Battle of the Bulge.

They rolled through the early innings. The famous Candlestick Park wind* was blowing in, which made hitting a home run all but impossible. In the fourth inning, Milwaukee's Henry Aaron got a hold of one against Marichal. Aaron would later say he hit it about as hard as any of the 755 home runs he hit. This one, though, just died in the wind.

The Braves did miss a great chance of scoring in the seventh. Del Crandall led off with a single. He was then caught stealing. Had he stayed at first, he probably would have scored on Warren Spahn's double off the top of the right-field fence. Then again, Spahn's shot probably also would have been a home run had it not been for the wind. It wasn't a day for scoring.

Marichal was throwing mostly fastballs, and he grew stronger as the game went along. Spahn mostly threw screwballs, and the Giants' hitters could not square them up. And the scoreless game went on into the 11th inning, the 12th, the 13th, the 14th . . .

---

* In the 1961 All-Star game, it was blowing so hard at Candlestick Park that it actually blew pitcher Stu Miller off the mound. After the game, outfielders Rocky Colavito and Roger Maris said they would quit baseball before having to play regularly at Candlestick.

Both pitchers were exhausted and yet both refused to be taken out of the game. Spahn always refused to come out of games; he led the league in complete games every year from 1957 to 1963.

And as for Marichal—well, Giants' manager Alvin Dark was one of the early proponents of counting pitches. And when Marichal crossed 200 pitches thrown, Dark went out to the mound to see if Marichal could keep on going.

"You see that man over on the other side?" Marichal said. "He's 42 and I'm 25. You can't take me out until that man's not pitching."

Then Marichal threw a scoreless 16th inning and knew that he was done. He'd thrown 227 pitches. He had nothing left to give. He saw Willie Mays standing in the on-deck circle.

"Hey, Willie," Marichal called out. "It's time for you to hit one now."

Mays went up to the plate looking for a screwball. Spahn had thrown 201 pitches. His 202nd pitch was indeed a screwball, but as Spahn would say, "It didn't do a thing." Mays turned on it, and even though it was into the teeth of the wind, it had enough to get over the fence. The Giants had won. But really, everybody had won.

"Oh, my back," Marichal joked. "But tonight was beautiful."

Across the way, Warren Spahn walked into the clubhouse. Everybody stood and applauded.

NO. 10:
SATCH VS. JOSH

SEPTEMBER 10, 1942, PITTSBURGH

★ ★ ★ ★ ★

You may have heard this line from the movie *The Man Who Shot Liberty Valance*: "When the legend becomes fact, print the legend."

That is what we are doing with Satch and Josh.

We are printing the legend.

There has been a remarkable and admirable effort in recent years to find out more about the Negro Leagues. Researchers have dug into the archives and uncovered innumerable facts, detailed statistics, and incredible stories. Just one example: A network of investigators, led by a determined Uber driver named Peter Dorton, have uncovered 413 verifiable wins for a once-forgotten Negro Leagues pitcher named John Donaldson. It's wonderful. Donaldson, I believe, will soon be elected to the Hall of Fame because of Dorton's research.

But—and I think most people agree on this—in our pursuit of facts we should not lose the legends.

The fact is that researchers have determined that Cool Papa Bell stole 285 bases in elite Negro League competition. The legend is that Cool Papa Bell could turn out the lights and be in bed before the room got dark. You tell me what's more fun.

The fact (at this point) is that Josh Gibson hit 165 home runs in elite Negro Leagues competition (and led the league in homers seven years in a row). The legend is that Josh Gibson once hit a home run in Pittsburgh so high that it didn't come down. The next day, while he was playing in Philadelphia, a ball came flying in and was caught.

"Gibson," the umpire said, "you're out. Yesterday. In Pittsburgh."

You tell me which is better.

But it isn't just that the Gibson and Cool Papa stories are better, it is that those sorts of stories kept the memories of the Negro Leagues alive through many forgotten years. Buck O'Neil, whom I will turn to in a moment, spent more than a half century telling those stories, and much of that time, people did not want to listen. But they did listen because the stories were so good and painted such a vivid picture of a time and place and collection of players who were denied their chance to play in the American or National League. Still, they played.

The Satch and Josh story was Buck's favorite. I heard him tell it dozens of times. He was playing first base for the Monarchs that day. Buck O'Neil was a fine player in the Negro Leagues, a pennant-winning manager, the first African American coach in the National League, a brilliant scout, and the game's most passionate and inspirational spokesperson. But I think of him most as my friend. He died in 2006, but there isn't a week that goes by that I don't think of him.

Facts about the day when Satchel Paige faced Josh Gibson are hard to come by. Details are patchy. Heck, Satchel Paige himself told the story three or four different ways. Here's what we know: Satchel toyed with Josh that day. The bases were loaded. This was in the papers. Some details Buck will relate do not match up with surviving facts and may, in fact, be borrowed from another time.

But we're printing the legend.

Now, I'm going to go back through my notes and memory and let Buck O'Neil tell you the way he remembered it—it's Game 2 of the 1942 Negro Leagues World Series between Paige's Kansas City Monarchs and Gibson's Homestead Grays. The Monarchs led by two runs.

Tell it, Buck . . .

///

What you have to understand is that Satchel and Josh used to go kid each other about which one was better. But it wasn't just a joke. Satch told me that one day, when they were both part of the Pittsburgh Crawfords, they had a conversation.

Satch said: "Everybody says you're the greatest hitter in the world."

And Josh went, "Uh-huh, that's right."

Then Satch said: "Well, I know I'm the greatest pitcher in the world. And there's gonna come a day when you and I are going to find out once and for all which one's better."

And all Josh said was: "I'll be there."

So now it's the 1942 World Series, Satchel Paige and our Kansas City Monarchs, Josh Gibson and his Homestead Grays. We won the first game in Washington, 8–0. The Grays committed a bunch of errors, Josh didn't get a hit, but he did hit one a long way to center field, would have been out of most parks. You couldn't hardly hit a ball out in Washington, though you know Josh actually hit one out of the stadium there.

Anyway, we go to Game 2 in Pittsburgh,* and we were leading 2–0 going into the seventh. Satchel had come in to relieve Hilton Smith.

First batter for the Grays was a speedy little hitter named Jerry Benjamin; he hits a ball down the third base line, it's a standup triple.†

After that, Satchel motions me over to talk to him. He says to me: "Nancy,‡ you know what I'm fixin' to do?"

I say, "Yeah, you're fixin' to get these other guys out."

He said, "No! I'm gonna walk the next two guys. And then I'm gonna pitch to Josh."

I said, "Stop, don't be facetious."

---

* The Homestead Grays split time between Washington and Pittsburgh.
† Benjamin was often called the second-fastest player in the Negro Leagues, behind only Cool Papa Bell.
‡ The amazing story of how Satchel Paige nicknamed Buck O'Neil "Nancy" is too long to tell here, but it's been told many times, including in *The Baseball 100*, starting on page 709.

He said, "You can call it what you want, but that's what I'm gonna do."

I couldn't believe it. This was the World Series! So I said, 'Time," and I call out our manager Frank Duncan, and I tell him, "I want you to hear what this fool is saying."

Satchel told him. Now, Frank was a smart guy. He knew that Satchel was going to do what he wanted to do—there was no way to stop him. So Frank turned to me and said, "Buck, you see all these people here? Why do you think they're here? They're here to see Satchel pitch to Josh. You let him do what he wants to do."

Then he walked back to the dugout. I think he wanted to see it, too.

Satchel walked the next batter. And the batter after that.

And here comes Josh, man, looking bigger than he ever looked before.

Satch, he knew how to play up a moment, now. Before Josh could get into the batter's box, he called for the trainer, who brought a big ol' glass of soda. Satch drank it down. Then he let out this giant burp that you could hear all over the park. The crowd went wild.

Then he shouted out: "OK, Josh, I'm ready. Let's find out who's best. First thing I'm going to do is throw you a fastball."

First pitch, Satchel wound back and threw a fastball harder than I'd seen him throw it in years. Josh didn't even move his bat. Boom! Strike one!

Satch says, "OK, I'm gonna throw you another fastball just about the same place, only this time it will be a little faster than that one."

Josh goes: "Stop talking and throw the ball, Satchel."

Boom! 100-mph fastball. Strike two!

Now Satch says, "Josh, I got you oh-and-two, and in this league, I'm supposed to knock you down and move you off the plate. But I'm not gonna throw smoke at yo' yolk. I'm gonna throw a pea at yo' knee.'"

Boom! 105-mph fastball. Strike three. Right down the middle. Josh doesn't even move the bat.

And as Satchel walked off the mound—you know, he's 6-foot-4—he looks 7 feet tall. He smiles and he says, "Nancy, you know something? Nobody hits Satchel's fastball."

NO. 9:
MAZEROSKI

★ ★ ★ ★ ★

As the fiftieth anniversary of Bill Mazeroski's famous home run approached, Bob Costas got the oddest call. It was from an archivist at Bing Crosby's estate. It seems the man was looking through the Crosby wine cellar for old movies he could use to put together a Bing Crosby Christmas special. There, as expected, he saw some of Crosby's old movies—*Road to Rio*, *Going My Way*, *The Bells of St. Mary's*, and so on—but he saw something else that he did not expect at all.

It was a film can labeled "1960 World Series."

"What can I do with this?" the archivist asked Costas.

The archivist had no idea that he had just uncovered baseball gold. See, Crosby was a part owner of the Pittsburgh Pirates.* He was in Paris during the World Series between his Pirates and the New York Yankees. He listened to the games on Armed Forces radio. When the World Series went to Game 7, he felt too nervous to fly back and attend.

Instead, he called up one of his assistants and told him to somehow record the game. The only way to do that in 1960 was to put a camera in front of the television set and create a kinescope. That's what the assistant did. The film inside that can was, as far as anybody knows, the only film of Game 7 of the 1960 World Series.

"What you have to understand," Costas says, "is that NOBODY has seen this. Nobody. None of the players have seen it. None of the fans have seen it."

---

* Crosby's friend and frequent movie costar Bob Hope was a part owner of the Cleveland Indians.

Finding that kinescope was like finding yesterday. Costas and the MLB Network rented a beautiful theater in Pittsburgh, and they invited the Pirates who played in that series along with any number of other Pittsburgh luminaries. MLB Network set up cameras all around the theater.

And then, together, 50 years later, they all watched Game 7 of the 1960 World Series.

"It is," Costas says, "one of the greatest things I've ever been a part of."

///

THAT WAS A BIZARRE WORLD SERIES. THE YANKEES HAD TO BE there; they had been in the World Series ten times in the previous 13 seasons. But the Pirates? That made no sense at all. The Pirates had been a baseball laughingstock for the better part of a quarter century.

And the series itself seemed to reflect the absurdity of it all.

The Pirates squeaked by in Game 1.

The Yankees won the next two games 16–3 and 10–0.

The Pirates squeaked by in Games 4 and 5.

The Yankees angrily responded by winning the next game 12–0.

And then it was time for Game 7, even though the Yankees had outscored the Pirates 46–17. It's no wonder Bing Crosby was so nervous.

What Costas remembers most about watching that kinescope was the faces of awe and wonder he saw everywhere. "This was the first time Vern Law had ever seen himself pitch in the prime of his youth," he says. "All of these men, they're old men by now, and they're seeing themselves as they never have before."

The player who emerged most joyfully from the screen was Pittsburgh's breathtaking right fielder Roberto Clemente. "He didn't do much in the game," Costas says. "He actually fumbled a single and allowed Roger Maris to take second. But it didn't matter. Every time he came on-camera, people spontaneously cheered."

NOW, LET ME TELL YOU ABOUT *MY* FAVORITE THING ABOUT THE Bing Crosby reprise: Hal Smith finally got his moment.

Sure, everybody knows how that game ended. The score was tied, Bill Mazeroski led off the bottom of the ninth against Ralph Terry. It was 3:36 P.M. Maz hit a long fly ball to left field; the Yankees' Yogi Berra chased it back to the wall, then sadly looked up; the ball sailed over the fence; Mazeroski ran around the bases while waving his cap; and the crowd raced onto the field to celebrate with him. It's as iconic a moment as any in baseball's colorful history. The scene is forever.

And it always makes me think about Hal Smith.

It's the plainest of names. If you google it, you will probably get pointed to the actor Hal Smith, best known for being the voice of Owl in *Winnie the Pooh* and playing the town drunk Otis Campbell on *The Andy Griffith Show*.

Our Hal Smith was not even the best catcher named Hal Smith. There was another, who played for Pittsburgh and made three All-Star teams. Our Hal did not make any.

That's not to say our Hal Smith was a slouch; no, he was a good hitter. But his defense was suspect, and he bounced from New York to Baltimore to Kansas City to Houston and finally to Pittsburgh.

Hal Smith had come up with two outs in the bottom of the eighth inning and the Yankees up by a run. There were two runners on.

In the theater in Pittsburgh, fifty years later, there was a nervous hush. "People were watching the game like it was happening live," Costas would say. Presumably everyone in there knew how the game would end, but they didn't know other details. Hal Smith himself sat in the theater quietly. He wore a brown suit that looked roughly four sizes too big. Few noticed him.

Hal Smith on the screen faced a 2-2 count against the Yankees' Jim Coates.

Then came the pitch, and Hal Smith turned on it. He hit it almost *exactly* to the same spot where Bill Mazeroski would hit it just moments later. If you watched it and didn't know, you would assume that it WAS the Mazeroski home run; that's how identical they are.

"I really didn't even know what happened until I rounded second base," Hal Smith said that day, 50 years later. "When I went around second base and I looked up and the people in the stands were on the dugout, I thought, *What have I done?*"

In the Pittsburgh theater, everybody leapt to their feet to cheer wildly. "They really went nuts, like it had just happened," Costas said.

That home run should have made Hal Smith famous. He had given the Pirates the lead against the New York Yankees in Game 7 of the World Series; how can you hit a bigger home run than that? Instead, the Yankees tied the game up in the ninth, setting the stage for someone else.

Still, in that theater that day, the cheers flowed for Hal Smith.

"You know what I thought?" Hal Smith told the crowd as he tried to hold back tears. "I thought, *No matter what happens, I really helped in the World Series*. And that had been my lifelong dream."

NO. 8:
CAL RIPKEN PASSES GEHRIG

SEPTEMBER 6, 1995, BALTIMORE

★ ★ ★ ★ ★

Lou Gehrig did not want to speak on that Independence Day in 1939. In truth, he didn't want to be there at all. Only two months had passed since he'd played his last game, but they had been a hard two months, a painful two months. He felt himself withering. He didn't want people seeing him like that.

But the New York writers had lobbied Yankees' president Ed Barrow to have a Lou Gehrig appreciation day. More than 61,000 fans attended. He had to be there.

Still, he did not want to speak. He accepted the many gifts. He listened to the heartfelt words of friends and teammates. He cried too many times to count. And when they asked him to say a few words, he shook his head.

"Ladies and gentlemen," the master of ceremonies said, "Lou asked me to thank you all for him. He is too moved to speak."

The crowd needed to hear him. They began to chant, "We want Lou! We want Lou!" Then the Yankees' Joe McCarthy, Gehrig's friend and mentor, leaned in and whispered something in Gehrig's ear. Gehrig nodded. He stepped to the microphone.

"For the past two weeks, you've been reading about a bad break," he began. And then he uttered the words that ring through the years.

"Today," he said, "I consider myself the luckiest man on the face of the earth."

Less than two years later, Gehrig would be gone, killed by the terrible disease that would carry his name. He was just 37 years old. He left behind those stunning words, a legacy of grace on and off the field, and a consecutive streak of 2,130 games that nobody thought would ever be broken.

//

IF YOU HAD TO PICK THE PLAYER LEAST LIKELY TO BREAK GEHRIG'S consecutive game, you might have started with Cal Ripken Jr. He played shortstop, probably the most grueling defensive position on the field behind catcher.

Before Ripken, the longest consecutive game streak for a shortstop was Ernie Banks at 717—not even a third of the way to Gehrig.

Ripken stood 6-foot-4 and weighed 200 pounds. There had never been an everyday shortstop in the big leagues that big. People thought Orioles' manager Earl Weaver was nuts to even try Ripken at short for one game. The idea that he would play 2,217 consecutive games at shortstop (and then a few hundred more at third base) was, in the truest sense of the word, unimaginable.

As remarkable as Ripken's consecutive game streak is, his consecutive innings streak might top it. Cal Ripken Jr. played 8,264 consecutive innings at shortstop. How mind-boggling is that? Nobody since the end of World War II has had a streak even half as long.

Think about this consecutive innings streak for a minute: For more than five years, Ripken never came out for a pinch runner, a pinch hitter, a defensive replacement—nothing. During that innings streak, the Orioles played two 16-inning games, a 15-inning game, a 14-inning game, four 13-inning games, nine 12-inning games, and twenty-one 11-inning games.

He played through all of them.

People first began taking notice of Ripken's superhuman durability and fortitude in 1986, when he was only about 750 or so games into the streak. "I've been lucky to stay healthy," he said. "But to tell you the truth, the streak is no big deal."

That would remain his stance throughout. *It's no big deal.* But it was a big deal to fans, who loved Ripken and saw the streak as a perfect representation of Ripken's persistence and dedication to baseball. And it was also a big deal to Ripken's critics, who saw every 0-for-4 game, every misplay, and every double-play groundout as a consequence of the man's never taking a day off.

"I just don't think a day off does much good," Ripken said. "It's an easy excuse that everyone uses. I dislike it because that's all it is—an excuse. It seems like everyone hops on the bandwagon as soon as I'm not hitting. The first thing out of their mouth is: 'He's tired, he needs a day off.' I wonder what excuse they would use if I did take a day off and still was in a slump."

From 1987 to 1990, Ripken's production at the plate unquestionably tumbled. On the day he played in his 1,308th consecutive game—passing Everett Scott into second place on the all-time list behind Gehrig—he went 0-for-4, his season average dropped to .213, and some fans even booed him.

That hurt. Ripken was a baseball lifer, the son of a baseball man, the brother of a baseball man. He knew that he couldn't get a hit every time up, knew that he wouldn't make every play, knew that slumps were an inevitable part of the game. But playing every day—that was the best of him. He always gave his all, no matter how tired, no matter how hurt, no matter how bad the team was, no matter how few people were in the stands.

How could people boo the best of him?

"Everyone is going to have an opinion," he said sadly. "I've just got to worry about how I approach it and keep in mind what it means to me."

In 1991, rather suddenly, Ripken played as if reborn. He hit .323, with career highs in home runs and RBIs. He even stole six bases, that too a career high. He won the MVP award even though the Orioles were terrible. And suddenly nobody was complaining about the streak.

By then, Gehrig was clearly in his sights. He would always say that passing Gehrig was not his motivation, and while that probably was true, Ripken was now too close to 2,130 to stop. He played every game in 1992 and 1993. In 1994, he played in the Orioles' first 112 games and then the season was canceled because of the players' strike.

He finished the 1994 season with 2,009 consecutive games. He was just 121 games shy of Gehrig's record. If he could stay healthy—and the owners and players could come to some agreement—he would break the record in 1995.

And he did: Ripken broke the record on a Wednesday night in early September. It would have been a big deal in any year, but in 1995, after the cancellation of the World Series, Ripken's streak and indeed Ripken himself came to represent something more.

He was there every single day.

The Orioles played the California Angels that day. President Bill Clinton was in the crowd with his daughter, Chelsea. Rock icon and Orioles fan Joan Jett sang the national anthem.*

Ripken slept late after taking his daughter to her first day of school, but he still got to the ballpark early. He warmed up, like always, and signed some autographs, like always. When he led the team on the field, his teammates stayed back so that the cheers would be his alone.

The cheers would follow him all night. The second-biggest cheers came when, on a 3-0 count, he hit a home run off Angels' pitcher Shawn Boskie. And the biggest followed 12 minutes later, when the game was official. Fireworks went off. A cannon was shot. A flag with the number 2,131 on it was unfurled. Ripken took a lap around the field, high-fiving fans and sharing the moment.

"I know that if Lou Gehrig is looking down on tonight's activities," he

---

* Joan Jett told the story of how she became a huge Orioles fan, and it's a good one. Her father took Joan to numerous Orioles games, but the first was August 13, 1969, when she was 10 years old. I've said this often: Baseball is never as good as it is when you're 10 years old. In that first game, Jim Palmer pitched for the Orioles . . . and he threw a no-hitter. "How can you not be an Orioles' freak after seeing that for the first game?" she asked.

said to the crowd after the game ended, "he isn't concerned about someone playing one more consecutive game than he did. Instead, he's viewing tonight as just another example of what is good and right about the great American game."

Ripken did not rest until September 1998, after 2,632 games.

"I think the time is right," he said.

Then he added: "Now that I know what it feels like, I don't want to sit and watch a game anymore." He played every game for the rest of the season.

NO. 7:
ROBERTS STEALS SECOND
(AND OTHERS)

OCTOBER 17, 2004, BOSTON

★ ★ ★ ★ ★

Michael Schur is the creator and writer of some of the most beloved television shows of our time—*Parks and Recreation, Brooklyn Nine-Nine*, and *The Good Place*, among others. He's also my podcast partner and one of my best friends.

He's also the world's biggest Boston Red Sox fan.

He will tell you that I asked him to write this chapter.

All I remember is that I told him I was going to write about the greatest moment in Red Sox history—the Dave Roberts steal, of course—and next thing I knew the room went dark and when I woke up there was a 400,000-word dissertation on the subject.

///

Recently my friend Joe Posnanski told me he was writing a book and asked if I'd like to help by choosing (and subsequently writing about) the greatest moment in Red Sox history. I was stunned for two reasons. First, because I had no idea Joe writes books. And second: Would I like to write about the greatest moment in Red Sox history? Of goddamn course I would. The problem here would be if Joe *had not* asked me to write about the greatest moment in Red Sox history. That would have been tantamount to treason and would have ended our friendship.*

---

* Which is saying something. After I wrote a book in 2021, Joe came with me to Kansas City and quietly sat with me for 18 hours over two days as I signed more than 2,000 copies of that book in a dark basement, and also I gave him COVID, and that somehow didn't end our friendship.

But: Which moment? This team has been playing baseball since William McKinley was shot. They still play in a stadium that opened the week the *Titanic* sank. When a franchise has this much history, this much tragedy and success and drama and notoriety, there are bound to be dozens and dozens of moments one might call its "greatest."

Fortunately, Red Sox history can be broken roughly into three chunks:

1. We're Great, but Who Cares? It Was a Hundred Years Ago! (1910–1918)

2. We Are Sometimes Terrible and Occasionally Great, but Even When We're Great, We Fail Dramatically at the Worst Possible Times Because of Terrible Luck and Institutionalized Racism and Mismanagement, and These Failures Are So Embarrassing and Constant That Sportswriters Theorize That the Team Is, Like, Actually Cursed, Like, by a Ghost (1919–2003)

3. We're Great Again! (2004–present)

This makes things easier. The moment won't come from the first era. I mean, come on. The ball was dead, the league was segregated, the players were all, like, plumbers and dentists in the off-season to make extra cash. And, spoiler alert, the moment also will not come from the number two chunk, even though it is the era of Ted Williams and Yaz and Fisk and Rice and Nomar and Boggs. I would hope Joe put some of those moments elsewhere in the book.

No, let's be realistic. The Greatest Moment comes from the We're Great Again! era.

After much wrestling and wrangling and rending of garments, I managed to narrow it down to three potential moments:

1. Dave Roberts Steals Second Base

2. Pedro Martínez Strikes Out 17 at the Stadium

3. That Time David Ortiz Cursed on Live TV

My temptation is to write about all of them. But that wouldn't be professional. Joe asked for one moment. And that's what I'll do. One moment. Here goes:

The greatest moment in Red Sox history is Pedro's 17-strikeout game at Yankee Stadium.

Now, I know what you're thinking: Uh, didn't Joe write about that game already?

Apparently, yeah, he did. And I'm furious. I was *at that game*, in the upper-deck bleachers with my friend Eben, and it was the second-greatest live baseball experience of my life. I wrote a 1,200-word essay on that game.* You're telling me Joe just deleted that? I think it's his revenge for me giving him COVID.

Anyway, Joe's insolence aside, Pedro's game is the greatest moment in Red Sox history.

Except, of course, it's not.

The greatest moment in Red Sox history is when Dave Roberts stole second base.

Actually, I'm glad you already read about the Pedro game, because that was the promise, the flicker of hope.

Dave Roberts stealing second was the moment when the hero, bloodied and left for dead, got up off the mat and began to fight.

You probably know at least some of the details by now. One year earlier, in 2003, the Red Sox had a historically great offensive team. They closed the regular season on a crazy heater, and they stormed into the American League Championship Series against the Yankees.

There was this most unfamiliar and uneasy feeling for Red Sox fans: optimism. These Red Sox were newly owned by a billionaire who actually cared about advanced metrics (he even hired BILL JAMES, the guru of such things). Their general manager was a 20-something wunderkind adorably named Theo, and he was a local boy, Ivy League educated and quietly confident, the dream husband/boyfriend/best friend/brother/son of

---

* Joe note: Mike's not joking; he did write a super-long essay on the Pedro game. Maybe it will be in included in *Why We Love Baseball: The Director's Cut.*

every Red Sox fan from Presque Isle, Maine, to Waterbury, Connecticut.

Plus, those Red Sox had swagger—Pedro, Johnny Damon, David Ortiz, Kevin Millar. The Yankees seemed vulnerable. We really thought: Hey, we can win this. The series went all the way into extra innings in Game 7 in New York. Then manager Grady Little hung an exhausted Pedro out to dry and Aaron Boone did something I still can't talk about without flying into a blackout rage, and the Red Sox ended up where the Red Sox always ended up: at home watching the Yankees play in the World Series.

Then it was 2004. Theo had replaced Grady Little with Terry Francona. He scooped up Curt Schilling from the Diamondbacks. He signed a brilliant closer named Keith Foulke, who, despite vocally preferring hockey to baseball, promised to lock down games. The season ended well; the unfamiliar optimism reappeared.

And then . . . misery again.

For three games, the Yankees annihilated the Red Sox. Chased them down, snapped their necks, devoured their flesh, and left their bones for the vultures to pick clean. Schilling was lit up in Game 1, largely because a freak injury to his ankle made it impossible for him to push off as he threw, a mildly important aspect of pitching.

Game 2 was a typical Yankee strangulation affair, where some dumb pitcher you barely know (Jon Lieber?) three-hits you, some dumb role player takes Pedro Martínez deep (John Olerud, are you kidding me? He's a thousand years old!), and then Mariano Rivera puts a pillow over your face in the ninth inning and shushes you as the air drains from your lungs.

Back in Boston for Game 3, desperate for a momentum swing, the Red Sox got their collective ass handed to them, 19–8. My friend Seth attended the game and sent me a text that read, and I quote, "I would rather be inside Satan's butthole than here."

No baseball team had come back down 3–0 in a seven-game playoff series. Not once. Not ever.

And in Game 4, the Yankees entered the ninth inning up a run.

There was Mariano Rivera again, armed with his suffocation pillow. When Kevin Millar stepped to the plate to lead off the ninth inning, the battery powering Red Sox Nation was at roughly 0.001 percent.* We were about to die again. Again, we were about to die.

Then the craziest thing happened: Mariano Rivera walked Kevin Millar. I don't know how; Rivera never walked anyone. Millar looked as surprised as anyone. Then another crazy thing happened: Rivera angrily snapped his glove when he got the ball back. Rivera never showed emotion. Millar jogged down to first.

Dave Roberts came in as a pinch runner.

Theo Epstein had picked up Roberts when no one was looking. He made so many front-page moves that year: He got Schilling and Foulke, and biggest of all, he traded Nomar Garciaparra to the Cubs. That sent shock waves through New England.†

Everyone was so worked up about Nomah being gone that most didn't even notice the trade for Roberts, a diminutive gentleman who played good defense, could slap a single the other way, and most important, ran very quickly. He was the kind of marginal upgrade you make to your roster in the hope that he might, on the right day, do one thing that gets you 1 percent closer to winning.

This was that day. Everyone knew Roberts was going to try and steal second. The announcers knew. Rivera knew—he threw over to first three times, the last of the three close enough to make Roberts's mouth form a perfect O as he exhaled with relief. Catcher Jorge Posada knew. I knew.

On the first pitch, he went. He slid headfirst. The throw was nearly perfect.

---

* If you rewatch those games, as I do on an embarrassingly frequent basis, you'll notice shots of fans in the crowd waving signs that say, like, "We Believe!" or "The Comeback Starts Now!" or whatever, and honestly, props to those fans, because literally zero percent of me believed.

† It is a law of Boston-metro physics that the more Rs a player has in his name, the more Boston fans love the player, due to how fun it is to say the player's name in a Boston accent. Nomah Gahciahpahrah is still the best-sounding athlete in Boston accent sports history. Before 2004 it also traditionally helped if you were white, but that's a whole other chapter in a whole other book.

Roberts made it.

Most of the other moments in this book, I can only assume, are endings. I don't know that; Joe hasn't let me read the book.* But I assume most are endings.

Roberts's steal was a beginning. The first brick in a wall. In and of itself, it didn't *do anything*. If the Red Sox followed up that steal by making three straight outs . . . if the Red Sox lose Game 5 or 6 or even 7 . . . then my Greatest Moment in Red Sox History would have just been the latest in an 86-year run of almosts, nearlys, and not-quites.

But not this time. Bill Mueller singled and Roberts scored the tying run. David Ortiz walked it off in the 12th. The Red Sox won Game 5 in 14 innings (another Ortiz walk-off) and won Game 6 in New York, when Schilling was masterful thanks to an experimental ankle surgery first tested on a cadaver.† Impossibly, Boston won Game 7 in a laugher. Then they blitzed the St. Louis Cardinals in four World Series games, never trailing in a single inning.

I loved that World Series so much. We'd had enough drama. We needed peace.

Here's what I believe about the Dave Roberts steal: It was a beginning and an ending. It began a new era. And it ended the 85-year fog when every big game the Red Sox played was plagued by something going wrong.

Suddenly, after Dave Roberts, stuff went right. The umpires (pre-replay, mind you) overturned two key calls in the Red Sox favor: Mark Bellhorn's Game 6 home run (initially called a double) and Alex Rodriguez's cheap and illegal swipe of Bronson

---

* When Joe told me he was writing a book about the 50 moments explaining why we really love baseball, I told him that if No. 1 was not the ball hitting José Canseco's head and bouncing over the fence for a home run, the entire project was invalid.

† Not kidding about Schilling and the cadaver. The doctors were like, "I guess we could try to secure his tendon so it doesn't cause discomfort . . . so, OK, someone get us a dead body so we can practice."

Arroyo's arm (initially called an error). Those calls were reversed! In Yankee Stadium!

Would that have happened before the Roberts steal?

No way. Not a chance. For eight decades, the Red Sox rolled snake eyes. After Roberts, it was nothing but sevens.

For that reason, Roberts's stolen base is definitely the greatest moment in Red Sox history.

Except, of course, it's not.

The greatest moment in Red Sox history was when David Ortiz cursed on live TV.

[Joe note: Hey, Mike, we kind of need to wrap this up. Plus are you really going to swear more? I mean, you know, I'd like kids to buy this book.]

Just one curse. Sorry, kids, but it's an important curse. And I'm almost done, just another four to five thousand words. This is on you for asking me to write about the Red Sox.

Look, you have to understand the whole journey. Before Pedro, the franchise was desperate. Before Roberts's steal, the franchise was inevitably doomed.

Now—and only now that the past no longer haunts us—we look to the present and hopefully the future. Which leads us to David Ortiz.

On April 15, 2013, two terrorists detonated a bomb at the finish line of the Boston Marathon, killing three people and injuring hundreds more. Patriots' Day in Boston is holy. Everyone is up early, in a good mood. The Red Sox play at eleven A.M. because Fenway sits at the 25-mile mark, and when the game ends, people pour out of the stands and cheer on the finishers. The attack wasn't just an act of terrorism, it was an assault on the spiritual core of a city.

In the aftermath, we asked all the questions we always ask: Why did this happen? What kind of world are we living in? Should we be scared to go out? How do we go back to normal? Can we? Should we? What happens now?

Five days later, the Red Sox returned to Fenway. There was a pregame ceremony, featuring police and politicians and first responders and the sorts of folks who show up in moments like this to try to cry out that we are unbroken and unbowed. People clapped and cheered. And then someone made the brilliant decision to give David Ortiz a microphone.

All right. All right, Boston.

Apparently, Ortiz didn't know he'd be saying anything until right before game time. He was still rehabbing an Achilles injury that had ended his 2012 season early. He started talking:

This jersey that we wear today doesn't say Red Sox. It says Boston.

What do you say in such moments? Platitudes, mostly. I worked at *Saturday Night Live* from 1998 to 2004, and in the first show after 9/11, Lorne Michaels invited Mayor Giuliani, dignitaries, and dozens of first responders to open the show by telling the world that New York would go on and that comedy was necessary for healing. It was moving and tear-inducing and wonderful . . . and I don't remember a single thing that was said. Because the words weren't the point. The point was simply to be reassuring.

We want to thank you, Mayor Menino, Governor Patrick, the whole Police Department for the great job that they did this past week.

Right. That's what these boilerplate speeches are. Thank you, Mayor, thank you, police, we see you and we're grateful to you for working so hard to keep us safe. Everybody applauded appropriately. And then David Ortiz said this:

This is our fucking city. And nobody's gonna dictate our freedom. Stay strong.

. . . Welp. That certainly isn't boilerplate.

Go back and watch it. Listen to the way people clap after each of the previous lines. Nice, right? Now listen to what happens when a 6-foot-3, 240-pound charisma monster drops an f-bomb on live television. The cheers become real. They lurch out of people. They rip through the skin and leap from the throat. These were yelps and yawps that come from love and joy and hope and relief.

This is what catharsis sounds like.

It had to be David Ortiz. No one else. In an oral history of the moment done by Bleacher Report, longtime broadcaster Dave O'Brien remembered it this way: "I remember the broadcaster for the Kansas City Royals came racing into our booth and said, 'Are you allowed to say that?' I said, 'David is.'"

Who are Boston's greatest sports heroes? If you asked this question twenty years ago, everybody would have said Ted Williams, Larry Bird, Bobby Orr, Bill Russell, and maybe the ascendant Tom Brady. There would have been those chiming in with Carl Yastrzemski, Bob Cousy, or John Havlicek. Except for Russell, yes, every single one of those guys is white. That's Boston, too. The Red Sox are the city's great shame in this regard; they didn't have a black player until 1959, twelve years after Jackie Robinson broke in with the Dodgers.* Just spitballing here, but that—and not some vague curse—might have been a big part of the Red Sox constant failures.

That's why it mattered that it was Ortiz standing on that field, wearing that uniform, saying those words. The guy saying "We are Boston, and this is our bleeping city" was dark-skinned and Dominican and the unquestioned leader of the team. He was the present and the future, and both of those things looked a whole lot better because of him.

If I didn't have Joe just standing there with a giant hook, I could argue that Ortiz's grand slam in the 2013 American League Championship Series was the greatest moment in Red Sox history. Detroit was about to go up 2–0 in that series. That magical season, borne of tragedy, was about to end sadly. And then Ortiz hits a freaking grand slam to tie the freaking game? Are you kidding me?

---

* And 14 years after the Red Sox gave Jackie Robinson a sham tryout at Fenway Park—they could have signed him!

Franchises maybe get three moments that incredible every hundred years. If they're lucky. David Ortiz gave us fifty of them in a decade and a half.

The Red Sox beat Detroit that day, and then they won the series, and then they won the World Series because David Ortiz went supernova. He went 11-for-16 (you read that correctly) with two homers, two doubles, and eight walks. He picked up the whole city and put them on his back. Again.

There will be a statue of David Ortiz outside Fenway Park very soon. It could be Ortiz in any of 50 in-game poses—any of his many heroic swings full of smooth violence that saved so many afternoons and evenings and games and series. But my guess is that it will instead depict a still-injured David Ortiz standing on the Fenway infield speaking from his enormous heart and giving not only Boston but the whole country something it desperately needed: one perfectly delivered and remarkably reassuring curse word.

Yes, that is, without question, the greatest moment in Red Sox history.

Except, of course, it's not.

The greatest moment in Red Sox history is Mookie Betts robbing that home run in Rich Hill's f—

TRANSMISSION TERMINATED BY PUBLISHER

NO. 6:
BABE'S CALLED SHOT(S)

OCTOBER 1, 1932, CHICAGO

★ ★ ★ ★ ★

Here's the question: What is a called shot?

In May 1918, when Babe Ruth was still pitching for the Boston Red Sox, he faced the New York Yankees at the Polo Grounds. Even though he was still a pitcher, he was also the most prolific home run hitter in baseball. And in the seventh inning he smashed a long fly ball to right field off Yankees' pitcher Allen Russell.

"Foul!" boomed first-base umpire Billy Evans.

"Foul?" Ruth asked.

"Yes, foul!"

"Well, that's all right," Ruth said. "I'll just hit the next one a little bit to the left."

On the next pitch, Ruth crushed the ball to almost the same spot . . . but as he had promised, a little bit to the left so that it was fair and a home run.

Isn't that a called shot?

IN THE EARLY FALL OF 1926, A BOY NAMED JOHNNY SYLVESTER fell off a horse and was then kicked in the head. He was rushed to the hospital where, for a time, it seemed like he would not make it. His father, John, a vice-president of the National City Bank in New York City, sent a variety of telegrams on behalf of his son to their favorite baseball player, Babe Ruth.

The Babe was playing in the 1926 World Series, but he found time to send a package to Johnny with two baseballs, one signed by the entire Cardinals team, the other signed by the entire Yankees team.

On the Yankees ball, under his own name, he wrote: "I'll knock a homer for you Wednesday."

Wednesday was Game 4 of the World Series. The Yankees trailed in the Series two games to one. Ruth came up in the first inning against St. Louis's Flint Rhem and homered to deep right field. He came up again in the third inning and homered to deep right center field. And in the sixth, he came up against relief pitcher Herman Bell and, yes, homered one more time, this time to straightaway center.

"Boy," he said, "that was a darling!"

There were many newspaper reports—and later a movie reference— to those home runs saving Johnny Sylvester's life. Obviously, that's ridiculous. But Johnny did live on. And as *The New York Times* wrote in their obituary of Sylvester 64 years later, in 1990: "If the three homers Ruth hit against the Cardinals in St. Louis on October 6 did not bring about an instant cure, they most certainly did no harm."

Isn't that a called shot?

BEFORE GAME 2 OF THE 1918 WORLD SERIES, WHILE STILL WITH Boston, Babe Ruth was taking batting practice at Comiskey Park in Chicago. A few Cubs fans were giving him an earful. Ruth wheeled around, looked at the offending fans, and smiled.

"Watch this one," he said.

On the next pitch, he crashed a gigantic blast into the right-field bleachers.

"Told you so," Ruth said.

Once more: Isn't that a called shot?

MAYBE THOSE ARE ALL CALLED SHOTS, BUT NONE OF THEM IS *THE*
Called Shot, the one that has been argued about and debunked and
reconsidered and investigated for almost a century.

The difference, I guess, is the point.

It was Game 3 of the 1932 World Series. The Yankees had easily
won the first two games—the Cubs couldn't get Lou Gehrig out—and
things were getting pretty heated between the teams. When Ruth came
up in the first inning against Charlie Root, Cubs' players and fans vi-
ciously taunted him. People threw lemons on the field. It was pretty
ugly.

Root's first two pitches to Ruth were balls. This infuriated Ruth even
more, and he pointed angrily at the plate as if to say: "Hey, how about
throwing one of those pitches over this thing?"

Root obliged with his next pitch, and Ruth hammered it to right center, a long home run. The boos for Ruth as he rounded the bases were
loud and even ominous. Ruth luxuriated in them.

That's not the Called Shot. Not yet.

The score was tied in the fifth. New York governor Franklin Delano
Roosevelt—a month away from being elected to the presidency—sat
on the first-base side. Commissioner Kenesaw Mountain Landis was on
the third-base side. Eleven future Hall of Famers played that day, and
another four, including Chicago pitcher Burleigh Grimes, sat in the
dugouts.

I mention Grimes specifically because he was shouting the obscenest
insults imaginable as Ruth stepped to the plate. All the Cubs' players
were doing it, but it seems Grimes's abuse was particularly foul. Ruth
glared at them all, particularly Grimes and Guy Bush, and began waving
his arms and screaming back.

Root threw a strike. Ruth didn't even take the bat off his shoulders.
He simply held up one finger as if to say, "OK, that's strike one."

A couple of pitches later, Root threw another strike. Again, Ruth let it pass.

And this time he held up two fingers for all to see. Strike two.

Then ... well, then it gets a little murkier. Ruth definitely made a motion with his arm. What was that motion? Did he point at the Cubs' players? Did he point to the outfield? Did he just wave his arm in disgust? Everybody had an opinion.

Nobody disputes what happened next: Ruth hit a towering home run to center field, beyond the flag pole, the longest home run anyone had ever seen at Wrigley Field. As Ruth ran around the bases, he made several gestures toward the Cubs bench. The crowd was quite a bit quieter this time; awe will do that to you.

Meanwhile, FDR was laughing in his seat and saying, again and again, "You lucky bum!"

BABE RUTH SAID HE POINTED TO THE SPOT WHERE HE HIT THE home run. "I point," he would say, "and I say, 'I'm going to hit the next pitched ball right past the flagpole.'"

Cubs' manager Charlie Grimm and Yankees' catcher Bill Dickey swore that he pointed at the mound, not the outfield. Future Supreme Court Justice John Paul Stevens was 12 years old and in the crowd that day; he said Ruth most definitely pointed to center field. Cubs' catcher Gabby Hartnett never could quite make up his mind. He's on record saying Ruth most definitely *did* and most definitely *did not* point to outfield.

In the late 1990s, a home movie of the game taken by a businessman named Harold Warp* emerged, and while it is not quite a smoking gun, *The New York Times* reported that it offers "telling evidence that Ruth's gestures were directed at the Cubs dugout, not to the outfield."

---

* Warp invented Flex-O-Glass, a plastic window material that made him millions.

In 2022, though, a Lou Gehrig interview was uncovered. Gehrig was standing in the on-deck circle when Ruth hit the Called Shot, and this interview was given five days later to NBC radio. Gehrig had only just gotten back from a fishing trip he and Ruth had taken together.

Here's what Gehrig said about that home run: "I've played a lot of baseball. But I've never seen such a display of nerve before. Babe had two strikes on him. There were 50,000 Cub fans giving him the ol' Bronx cheer. And the Cub players were riding him from the field.

"What does he do? He stands up there and told the world that he was going to sock that next one . . . and not only that, but he tells the world right where he's going to sock it, into the center-field stands. A few seconds later the ball was just where he pointed, the center-field stands. He called his shot and then made it. I ask you: What can you do with a guy like that?"

FOR OUR FINAL PIECE OF EVIDENCE, WE TURN TO JAMES BARK. James was in the Marines during the Vietnam War and he worked as a loading dock worker, but his lifelong passion has always been baseball. When he was 16 years old, he became fascinated by the question: Did the Babe call his shot? So he wrote to the man who would know, the pitcher that day, Charlie Root.

"Did he really call his shot?" James asked Charlie in the letter. "I would appreciate an answer to this letter very much."

And Charlie Root wrote back.

"Babe Ruth did not call his shot!" Charlie wrote. "If he had pointed as they say, he would have been knocked on his fanny!"

Many years later, James wrote another letter, this one to Charlie's daughter Della Arnold Root. Della was 90 at the time—she passed away three years later—but her memory was strong.

"On Oct 1, 1932, I went to the World Series with my mother and we sat in her box—58, tier 12—which was about 60 feet from home plate.

My dad, Charlie Root, had thrown two strikes to Babe Ruth, and Babe held up two fingers. . . . Catcher Gabby Hartnett said the pitch was about seven inches off the ground, and Ruth golfed it a country mile. But, he did not point!!"

Two exclamation points. That seems to me the final word.

FIVE
CATCHES

AL GIONFRIDDO (OCTOBER 6, 1947)

I f you are a fan of baseball history, you have probably seen the catch by Dodgers' left fielder Al Gionfriddo of a Joe DiMaggio fly ball in Game 6 of the 1947 World Series . . . or at least you think that you have. It's one of the most famous baseball scenes ever filmed for one very specific reason: After Gionfriddo stumbled back toward the wall to make the catch, DiMaggio kicked the dirt in frustration.

DiMaggio *never* showed emotion on the field; that was the point.

That catch was so great that it broke even the Great DiMaggio.

Many years later, Brooklyn Dodgers fan Philip Roth in his novel *Portnoy's Complaint* would call Gionfriddo "a baseball player who once did a great thing."

But here's a funny thing: On film, the catch doesn't look all that great.

In fact, the catch doesn't look very much like the *description* of the catch in the newspapers. The writers wrote of Lil' Al, as reporters called the 5-foot-6 Gionfriddo,* reaching up and catching the ball as he crashed into the fence. But on film—and you can pop over to YouTube

---

* Joe Trimble of the New York *Daily News* called Gionfriddo "the hydrant-high lefty outfielder."

anytime you like, to confirm—Gionfriddo catches the ball well before he got to the fence and, in fact, never even touches the fence.

How do you explain it?

Well, it's like this and it might blow your mind.

That film is not of the actual catch Gionfriddo made.

Well, hey, it blew my mind. I always thought that was the real catch. But what you see on film is a *re-creation*. See, the newsreels didn't get the actual catch because they didn't have a camera trained on deep center field. The next day, as newspapers reported, "they had Gionfriddo reenact his catch of DiMaggio's 'homer' time after time as the bleacher fans roared their approval each time."

So now when you look at it, watch for the reaction behind him. You'll see one fan leap to his feet in celebration. You'll also see a guy in a suit who stands around for a moment, then begins clapping without much emotion, like he was at the State of the Union Address. Another woman halfheartedly claps only after remembering to do so.

"Did he look silly," one reporter wrote of Gionfriddo re-creating the catch.

We will assume that DiMaggio kicking the dirt is actual footage. I can't imagine they could have convinced him to re-create that.

RON SWOBODA (OCTOBER 15, 1969)

In May 1965, in a game in St. Louis, Ron Swoboda dropped a routine fly ball in a game. Lost it in the sun. He was so angry about it that later, in the dugout, he put his batting helmet on the ground and stomped on it with the full intention of smashing it to pieces. Instead, it stuck on to his cleats, and he rather absurdly tried to shake it off while the crowd watched in awe.

"If he lays down on the ground," Mets' manager Casey Stengel said, "fly balls will have less a chance of hitting him."

No, catching fly balls was not Swoboda's thing. He was a pure slugger,

6-foot-2, 200 pounds. The Mets had signed him for $35,000 to blast home runs. "Finally I got someone who can hit the ball against the wind," Stengel crowed. And sure enough, Swoboda led the Mets with 19 home runs as a rookie.

Then again, those Mets were atrocious, the most ridiculous team in baseball. And Swoboda's comical defense was a big part of the show.

Then in 1969, suddenly, inexplicably, the Miracle Mets emerged. It wasn't *actually* inexplicable; their great young pitchers Tom Seaver, Jerry Koosman, Gary Gentry, and a spot starter named Nolan Ryan all came into their own at the same time. The Mets reached the World Series against Baltimore and continued to surprise everybody by taking a 2-games-to-1 lead.

Then came Game 4. The Mets led 1–0 in in the ninth, but Baltimore had runners on first and third. Brooks Robinson ripped a line drive to right field. Swoboda was playing out there, and he charged the ball and then made what sportswriter Jim Murray would call "one of the greatest catches and dumbest decisions in Series history." Swoboda dived for the ball, meaning that if he had not come up with it, two runs would have scored, at least.

"If it had gone to the wall," Murray continued, "the home plate ump would have got dizzy from all the runs going by him."

But it did not go to the wall. Swoboda made a spectacular catch, the Mets went on to win the World Series, and forever Ron Swoboda is remembered for his defense.

MASAFUMI YAMAMORI (SEPTEMBER 11, 1981)

My favorite television show as a kid was *This Week in Baseball*. If I hear just a few notes from its theme song "Gathering Crowds," I'm 40 years younger, sitting in front of our fuzzy 18-inch television, watching the plays with my jaw dropped open.

It was the defensive plays I wanted to see most. Toward the end of the show, *TWIB* would show the greatest plays from the previous week while announcer Mel Allen was guaranteed to say his catchphrase "How about that!" several times.

The play on *TWIB* I remember most wasn't an American play.

No, it happened in Japan. Before I even started writing this book, I promised myself that I would find that play. It wasn't easy. I didn't remember the outfielder's name. I didn't remember the year it happened. I didn't know what to do except type "ridiculous catch by Japanese outfielder" into various search engines.

But I did eventually find it. The reason the play was so hard to find is because it was made by a man named Masafumi Yamamori. He was not a star in Japan. To the contrary, he spent pretty much all of his 14-year career as a defensive replacement. He hit just .239 and seemed to specialize in bunting over runners.

But on one day, he was immortal. It happened on a Friday in Hankyu Nishinomiya Stadium.* There's no record I can find of attendance that day, but the stadium's capacity was 35,000, and there was literally nothing but empty seats behind him. He was playing left field for the Hankyu Braves against the Lotte Orions.

Lotte's Sumio Hirota pulled a ball to left field. It seemed a sure home run.

Yamamori raced back to the wall anyway. He put his right foot on the wall and pulled himself up, like he was climbing into an attic. Then he put his left foot on top of the wall. Then he reached out with his glove and backhanded the ball when it was probably three feet above the fence.

When I was 14 years old, it was literally the most thing amazing I had ever seen.

Now, many years later, it's still right up there.

In 2006, Ichiro Suzuki made a similar catch on a long fly ball hit by

---

* Nishinomiya is the hometown of Daisuke Inoue, whose name you might not know, but there's a pretty good chance he has impacted your life: He invented the karaoke machine.

the Angels' Garret Anderson. He raced back to the wall, pulled himself up the wall, and reached up for the catch. It was not quite a carbon copy of the Yamamori catch, but it was close. And that's no coincidence. Ichiro said he had been practicing it ever since he was young, ever since he saw Yamamori do it.

GARY MATTHEWS JR. (JULY 1, 2006)

Sometimes for fun I'll watch this catch and then I'll immediately watch the next catch on the list, the Jim Edmonds catch, and I'll try to determine which one is better.

I've decided, in the end, it's impossible to pick between them.

They're both amazing catches. But they're like different species.

The Matthews catch is more eye-popping. There's something about it, something about the way Matthews pulls in the ball, that eludes the senses, something that just doesn't make sense.

Texas was playing Houston, and the hitter for the Rangers was Mike Lamb. It might not add anything to the catch itself, but Lamb was having one of his greatest days at the plate—he'd already hit a double, a triple, and a home run. This time he smashed the ball to center field.

Back went Matthews. He would say that when the ball first came off the bat, he thought it would be a routine play. But the ball was hit better than he thought, and it kept carrying and he had a new thought: *Forget it, that ball's gone.* Then finally he decided to at least try for the ball. When he got to the wall, the ball was already over his head. There was no time to backhand the ball, which is what he would have normally done.

So he did the only thing he could think to do—put his right foot on the wall, jumped as high as he could, and reached forward with his glove.

And he pulled it in.

"That," Astros' manager Phil Garner said after the game, "was disgusting."

JIM EDMONDS (JUNE 10, 1997)

Jim Edmonds's catch is more classic. He was playing for the Angels in Kansas City on a near-meaningless Tuesday night. David Howard stepped to the plate for the Royals. He was no slugger, so Edmonds came way in, as he loved to do. He was practically a fifth infielder.

Then Howard hit a shot to center field. It wasn't exactly a blast—the ball would not have reached the warning track—but Howard hit it on a low trajectory, and as I mentioned, Edmonds was playing super shallow. Edmonds turned his back to home plate and sprinted as hard as he could to a spot in center field. He wasn't even looking at the ball. He would figure out the timing later.

"I looked up," he would say, "and saw the ball over the bill of my cap. I figured the game was on the line, so I figured I might as well lay out for this."

He dived as far as he could, and the ball hit his glove. It popped out for an instant when he hit the ground but dropped right back in.

"That," umpire Dave Phillips said, "makes Willie Mays's play look routine."

Well, no, not quite that. But it was some kind of catch.

NO. 5:
THE CATCH

SEPTEMBER 29, 1954, NEW YORK

★ ★ ★ ★ ★

I'm no mathematician, that goes without saying, but I do like inventing silly mathematical formulas. For instance, I came up with an idea for what makes a great baseball moment. It looks like this:

$(I + D + E) \times A$ = Great Moment Score!

I is Importance. How important is the play? For example, the Jim Edmonds catch I just wrote about was important in the context of the game (the Royals were rallying) but not important in the grand scheme of things (the Royals stunk).

D is Distinctiveness. How distinguishable was the play? Does it stay in your memory? Does it stand out among the millions of other baseball moments?

E is Emotion. Did the play bring you out of your seat? Did the play crush your spirit? Did it make you laugh or cry or scream out?

Finally, you multiply all that by A, which is Awesomeness, no definition necessary.

We are now down to the final five, and so it goes without saying that each of these moments score brilliantly. We start with Willie Mays's catch in the 1954 World Series. Was it the greatest catch in baseball history? Maybe not. Even Mays said it wasn't his own best.

But . . . it's the catch that matters most.

WHEN THE 1954 WORLD SERIES BEGAN, CLEVELAND WAS PLAYING for something larger than a championship. They were playing for a place in history. They had won 111 games, an American League record, something even the mighty Yankees had never done. They had what many were already calling the best pitching staff in history, led by three future Hall of Famers: Bob Feller, Bob Lemon, and Early Wynn.*

Yes, that team was not only going for a championship. They were going for best ever.

"The odds don't mean a damn thing to me," Giants' manager Leo Durocher said. "You win them on the field, not with bets."

Durocher, an inveterate gambler, knew something about that.

Game 1 was at the Polo Grounds and the score was tied in the eighth when Cleveland's Vic Wertz stepped up, with runners on first and second. Wertz was 3-for-3 with a triple. Don Liddle had just been brought in to pitch for the Giants. I'll tell you a great story about him in a minute.

Liddle threw a fastball down the middle and Wertz caught all of it, driving the ball to deep, deep center field.

And the Polo Grounds center field was indeed very deep. It was an unusually shaped ballpark, to say the least; from above it looked a little bit like Homer Simpson's head. The deepest part of center field in 1954 was 483 feet from home plate. That's where Wertz hit the ball. There was no chance of his hitting the ball out, but it sure looked like he hit the ball over the center-fielder's head. Alvin Dark, the Giants' shortstop, was among many who thought so.

Only he didn't.

The center fielder, you see, was Willie Mays.

Mays was 23 years old then and just beginning to fully harness his baseball powers. He led the league in hitting, in triples, in slugging, and OPS that year—he would win the MVP—but it was his defense that had people wonderstruck. "Imagine," actor and baseball fan Cary Grant would say of Mays's fielding genius, "knowing when a fellow is going

---

* And Cleveland fans will tell you their best pitcher that year was none of them but instead a modest son of a Mexican immigrant named Mike Garcia.

to hit the ball and how far and where and at what instant it will come down at a given point and being there when it does."

Mays knew he would catch it. His big concern—even as he was running after the ball—was not catching the ball but getting it back to the infield in time to prevent the speedy Larry Doby from tagging up and scoring from second base.

If you want to understand the genius of Willie Mays, consider that *this* is what he was thinking with the ball still in the air and ask yourself what the rest of us would be thinking.*

When Mays got to the ball, he simply stopped—there is no human way to just stop like that, but he was no human; he was Willie Mays—and he whirled and threw "like some olden statue of a Greek javelin hurler," the novelist Arnold Hano would write. Doby stopped at third. Cleveland did not score. The Giants won the game in extra innings.

Then the Giants won the Series in a four-game sweep.

Now rank the catch on my formula. Important? As important as it gets. Distinctiveness? Nobody will ever forget that play. Emotion? Giants fans broke down in tears.

Multiply all that by awesomeness. That's why it's *the* Catch.

///

DON LIDDLE WAS A SMALLISH LEFT-HANDED PITCHER WHO DIDN'T make it to the big leagues until he was twenty-seven. He lasted in the majors about four years. But he enjoyed his baseball life. He even started and won a game in that 1954 World Series.

But he's most famous for that pitch he threw to Vic Wertz, the one that sent Willie Mays racing backward. After Mays caught the ball,

---

* Roughly: "AARRGH! GLAH! GOTTA [huffing] RUN FASTER [huffing]. HOW BIG IS THIS OUTFIELD ANYWAY? HELP! HEY WHERE'S THE BALL? IS IT GOING TO HIT ME IN THE HEAD?"

Liddle was immediately replaced by another relief pitcher, Marv Grissom. It was his only out of the game.

When the game ended, Durocher came over to Liddle to shake his hand.

Liddle grabbed it and, with a glint in his eye, said, "Well, I got my man."

NO. 4:
"I DON'T BELIEVE WHAT I JUST SAW!"

OCTOBER 15, 1988, LOS ANGELES

★ ★ ★ ★ ★

Here's how Dennis Eckersley remembers the postgame. He sat in the visitors' locker room at Dodger Stadium, and he was surrounded by reporters, and he just kept saying the words *backdoor slider* over and over and over again.

"How did it feel?" they asked him.

"What were you thinking?" they asked him.

"What was it like?" they asked him.

"Backdoor slider," he remembers answering. "Backdoor slider, backdoor slider, backdoor slider."

He was still in shock. He was still trying to make sense of things. Twenty minutes earlier he was on the mound and about to close out an Oakland Athletics' World Series Game 1 victory. Oakland was beating Los Angeles by a run. Eck was born in Oakland. He had grown up a few miles away, in Fremont. He had dreamed this scene a hundred times, a thousand times, more.

Yes, just 20 minutes earlier, Eck was on the mound, and the Dodgers' Kirk Gibson was at the plate, and Gibson could hardly stand up because of intense pain in both of his legs. The man could barely even swing the bat.

Gibson wasn't supposed to be out there. He had told Dodgers' manager Tommy Lasorda before the game that he couldn't play. So why was he playing? Well, that's easy: He was Kirk Gibson. He was a stubborn son of a gun.

You know what happened the first day of spring training? Gibson

showed up at Dodgers camp after years of playing for the Detroit Tigers. The guys figured they would give him a silly welcome, you know,
the way ballplayers do. Dodgers' reliever Jesse Orosco lined his cap
with eye-black so that Gibson would have a black line on his forehead
after he took it off. Hilarious!

Gibson took his cap off and then stormed out of camp.

"I don't want to be part of their fun and comedy act," Gibson told the
Los Angeles Times after returning to a flood of apologies. "I like to have
a good time, but a good time to me is winning."

"Let's just say I won't be doing it again," Orosco said. "That's because
I don't want to read my name in the obituaries."

Fast-forward to the World Series: Gibson was sitting in the trainer's
room watching the game on television, getting angrier and angrier
about missing it, when he heard announcer Vin Scully say, "I don't see
Gibson in the dugout. I guess that's a pretty good sign he's done for the
night." Gibson swore at the television. Then he swore again. Then he
asked the bat boy to get him a tee so he could take some swings. Then
he sent the bat boy up to get Tommy Lasorda.

"What do you want?" Lasorda shouted.

Gibson just gave him the look. Lasorda told him to get ready to
pinch-hit.

Gibson limped to the plate—"It took about a half an hour for him to
get from the dugout into the batter's box," Eckersley tells me—and
then he stepped into the box.

"*Just throw him the gas,*" Eckersley remembered thinking. "He can't
catch up with the gas. . . . I had all the respect in the world for him. But
he was half a guy up there."

Eck was right; Gibson couldn't handle fastballs. He barely fouled
off pitches. He looked terrible. He only just stayed alive in the
at-bat.

Then the count was full, and Eckersley made the fateful decision to
throw something other than his fastball. He threw, yes, the backdoor
slider.

"He flips the bat," Eckersley says. "Almost one-hands a ball about 420 feet and . . ."

He'd just hit the wildest home run in baseball history.

///

SO LET'S TALK ABOUT THE TWO ANNOUNCER CALLS.

They were made by two of the true giants in baseball broadcasting history, Jack Buck and Vin Scully.

They were different men, Buck and Scully, with different broadcasting styles. Sinatra used to say that his instrument was not his voice, it was the microphone. Scully's instrument was the microphone, too. He made games sing. And he was one hell of a guy.

Jack Buck—well, he was your favorite uncle, the one who told the best stories and told the best jokes and made you feel a little bit more alive. He was a World War II veteran, wounded during the Battle of Remagen, and he was the guy hosting every charity event in St. Louis. He, too, was one hell of a guy.

And their calls of the Kirk Gibson home run could not more perfectly represent their Hall of Fame styles.

I heard Buck's call live on the radio. I was driving through South Carolina after a Clemson football game. I was approaching the huge peach-shaped water tower in Gaffney, South Carolina.

"We have a big three-two pitch coming here from Eckersley," Buck said. "Gibson swings and a fly ball to deep right field. This is gonna be a home run! Unbelievable! A home run for Gibson! And the Dodgers have won the game 5–4 . . ."

Then he made the call only Jack Buck could make: "I don't believe what I just saw! I don't believe what I just saw!"

The first time he said it, Buck put the emphasis on the word *saw*.

The second time, Buck put the emphasis on the second syllable of *believe*.

I remember being so overcome by emotion that I pulled off to the side of the road, got out of the car, and walked around in the dark.

In the television booth, at that exact same time, Vin Scully said a little prayer for Gibson as he came up to the plate.

"Not for him to hit a home run," Scully would say. "My prayer was that he worked so hard and he has meant so much to them, and now he can't even walk—let him hit a fly ball. Let him ground out. But don't have him strike out, not now, because he has been so important, and he has worked his tail off to get the team where it was."

When Gibson hit the home run, this was all Vin Scully said:

"High fly ball into right field . . . she is GONE!"

Then there was silence. Scully did love to let the crowd tell the story. Vin stood up and walked around the booth as I walked around by that giant peach. Then he returned to the microphone and finished the call the way only Vin Scully could:

"In a year that has been so improbable, the impossible has happened!"

"How did those words come out?" I asked Vin.

"I really think God had a hand in it," he said.

DENNIS ECKERSLEY HAD A CAREER LIKE NOBODY ELSE. HE WAS A fantastic young starting pitcher; back then he could throw the ball by anybody. As the years went along, his stuff faded, and his career looked to be over. That's when Oakland's manager Tony La Russa invented a new role for him. Eck became baseball's first great one-inning closer. In that role, he'd save 390 games and win an MVP award and eventually get elected to the Baseball Hall of Fame.

When asked about the Gibson homer again, he can only smile.

"Incredible moment," he says. "Incredible moment for the game. It really was."

He pauses.

"But not for me."

NO. 3:
THE RAIN DELAY SPEECH

NOVEMBER 2, 2016, CLEVELAND

★ ★ ★ ★ ★

The goat's name was Murphy. I tend to forget that.* Elizabeth never does. Elizabeth is our older daughter. She has spent a challenging lifetime being a sportswriter's daughter who, with few exceptions, doesn't care at all about sports.

The only sportsy things she cares about, best I can tell, are:

- Going to baseball games for the nachos. She insists, correctly in my view, that they don't taste as good anywhere else.

- Anything to do with Chiefs quarterback Patrick Mahomes.

- Murphy, the goat.

"If you need help on the Murphy chapter," she said, "I will do the research."

She never says stuff like that. But this is the story of Murphy.

Murphy the goat belonged to Sam Sianis, owner of Chicago's Billy Goat Tavern and man about town. Yes, Sianis was a Chicago original; John Belushi celebrated him in the *Saturday Night Live* "Cheeseburger-Cheeseburger" skit.

Sianis would do anything to drum up interest. And one of the things he would do was bring his pet goat Murphy with him to various events around Chicago. In 1945, he brought Murphy with him to the fourth

---

* I shouldn't forget the name. In the 2015 National League Championship Series, the New York Mets beat the Cubs and New York's big star was a typically fine hitter who for that series became Babe Ruth. He hit .529 with four home runs and was named the series MVP. His name was Murphy—Daniel Murphy.

game of the World Series between the Cubs and Tigers. The Cubs were regulars to the World Series in those days; they had been to five in the previous 16 years. They had lost all five, yes, but they were still an elite team.

When Billy and Murphy settled in, there was a ruckus. The people sitting around demanded that Murphy be removed from the stadium. Why? There are different versions—some say it was the smell, some say it was because Murphy was eating people's food—but it's not hard to guess reasons why people wouldn't want to watch the World Series with a goat.

The Cubs asked Billy and Murphy to leave.

Sam Sianis—or Murphy himself—placed a curse that there never would be another World Series game at Wrigley Field.

That's the Billy Goat Curse.

"A goat?" comedian and fanatical Cubs fan Jeff Garlin told me. "OK, let's get something straight. It's not a curse to not want a goat at a baseball game, all right? That is not a curse. Nobody wants live-stock at baseball games! You sell Babe Ruth, yeah, OK, maybe that's a curse. But kicking a guy and his goat out of a baseball game, that is *not a curse*."

Maybe not. But immediately the Cubs started losing.

Sure, you could argue that the reason the Cubs started losing was because their owner, Philip K. Wrigley, was opposed to the minor leagues. It was an honest and principled stand*—he thought every city and town in America should have its own team that was not beholden to the whims of the major leagues—but it put the Cubs behind every other team in baseball when it came to developing players.

---

* Wrigley was peculiar, to say the least, but he did fight for tradition. In addition to his minor league stand, he also believed baseball should be a day game and vowed to never allow lights at Wrigley Field. He never did. He died in 1977 and his son sold the team to the Tribune Company, which put up lights in 1988.

What did the Cubs do? It's obvious what they did: Wrigley wrote a letter to Murphy.

"Please extend to Murphy my most sincere and abject apologies," Wrigley wrote in 1950. "And please ask him to remove the hex."

Sianis read the letter to Murphy. He felt sure that his pet goat would be forgiving.

Alas, the Cubs just kept on losing. By the early 1960s, they did have some good players—Ernie Banks, Lou Brock, Billy Williams, and Ron Santo would all go to the Hall of Fame—but they still did loony things. One year, Wrigley hired a hypnotist to travel with the team and put whammies on opponents. In 1962, they instituted a "college of coaches" system where the coaches alternated as manager. The team had three managers that season; each of them finished with a losing record.

Over the next 50 years, the Cubs alternated between lovable losers, hard-luck losers, and contented losers. In 1969, they were in first place for most of the season, and then in September they played a game against the hard-charging Mets. In the first inning, a black cat started prancing around the Cubs' dugout. The Mets ran away with the game, and the next day the Cubs fell out of first place for good.

The Cubs in the 1970s more or less stopped even trying to win; they started marketing the idea that, hey, win or lose, what could be better than a day at Wrigley Field? They were not entirely wrong: An afternoon at Wrigley Field was wonderful. But Cubs fans would not have minded a winning team every now and again.

And they did have a few winning teams in the 1980s and 1990s and 2000s. They had a lot of good players—Ryne Sandberg and Andre Dawson, Greg Maddux and Kerry Wood. Sammy Sosa hit home runs and blew kisses to the sky. They almost made the World Series a couple of times.

But what is *almost* to a Chicago Cubs fan? The Cubbies became a symbol of "never." They became one of America's idioms of improbability:

When hell freezes over. When pigs fly. When the Cubs win the World Series.*

Then: Theo Epstein took over at team president.

There's nobody like Theo Epstein. Someday they might create a whole new wing at the Baseball Hall of Fame just for him. He achieved baseball immortality by the time he was 30 years old by being Boston's general manager when the Red Sox finally won the World Series. And that was the team he grew up cheering. If he never did anything else, he would be a forever hero in baseball.

Then in October 2011—after the Red Sox took an ugly turn—Epstein did the unthinkable: He became president of the Chicago Cubs. Think about the chutzpah that took. He had led the most haunted team in the American League to glory. Now he was going to try to do the same for the National League's most haunted team?

Chicago was rapturous. The *Chicago Tribune* was filled with all sorts of over-the-top exhilaration and wild optimism, including a marvelous Drew Litton cartoon of Murphy the goat sitting in a bar crying and drinking away his sorrows as he looks at a television report showing that Epstein was coming to the Cubs.

"I've been there, kid . . . you had a good run," Babe Ruth tells Murphy.†

Yes, people were ready to line up for World Series tickets the day Theo got to town. Unfortunately, the Cubs were in bad shape. They were tied down to some bad contracts. Their minor league system was in

---

* Wikipedia has an international list of idioms of improbability that is just delightful. The Portuguese say, "When chicken have teeth." In Spain, they will say, "When frogs grow hair." In Turkey, it's "When the fish climbs the poplar tree." But I do think "When the Cubs win the World Series" is particularly charming.

† My absolute favorite part of the *Trib*'s coverage was under the headline "Theo Epstein: Hot or Not?" Reporter Tracy Swartz decided that he was hot. Fellow reporter Ernest Wilkins countered that he wasn't. "I swear to you," Wilkins wrote, "if Epstein was just some guy sitting in a River North bar, he wouldn't get a second glance from most girls."

shambles. Epstein made a calculated—and he will now admit, fairly cynical—decision: The Cubs had to fully collapse before they could rise.

"If there was a better path, we would have chosen it," he later told NBC Sports Chicago. "But given what was here, I felt like it was clearly the best move."

The Cubs did not try to win for the next three seasons. They lost 101 games in 2012. They lost 96 the following year. They were a little better in 2014, but not enough for most to notice. Some Cubs fans were beginning to have their doubts about the savior.

But behind the scenes, exciting things were happening. Thrilling young players like Javier Báez, Kris Bryant, and Kyle Schwarber were coming on even faster than Epstein had expected. A couple of minor pitching trades for Kyle Hendricks and Jake Arrieta turned into gold. By 2015, Epstein thought the team was ready to compete. He hired celebrated manager Joe Maddon and signed big-money free-agent pitcher Jon Lester.

And the Cubs were sensational. They won 97 games, which tied for the most they had won since Murphy cursed the team in 1945. True, they did lose to the (Daniel) Murphy–led Mets in the National League Championship Series, but they were so young, so talented, so exciting, yes, you could sense that the Billy Goat curse was about to be broken.

And sure enough, everything came up aces for the Cubs in 2016. Until Game 7.

THE CUBS WON THE FIRST GAME OF THE 2016 SEASON 9–0 AND one of the most drama-free seasons in baseball history began. The Cubs moved into first place on April 11 and stayed there the rest of the season. They had the best pitching staff in the league. They scored the second-most runs. Kris Bryant won the league MVP. They clinched the division with two weeks left in the season.

"This is just the first step," Maddon assured everyone. "I mean, we have much larger baseball fish to fry in our skillet."

While that may be a tortured analogy and it's unclear what a baseball fish even is, the Cubs rolled through the playoffs, beating the Dodgers in the National League Championship Series and making it to their first World Series since Murphy was ejected from Wrigley Field.

And that World Series was a classic. The Cubs played another haunted team, the Cleveland Indians, and it was Cleveland that won 3 of the first 4 games. But the Cubs fought back to force a Game 7 in Cleveland, and that turned out to be one of the greatest games ever.

Our moment is Jason Heyward's rain delay speech, but so much happened before then. The Cubs' Dexter Fowler led off the game with a home run. Cleveland tied it up. The Cubs scored four and carried a three-run lead into the bottom of the eighth inning. That's when Cleveland's Rajai Davis hit a game-tying home run off the hardest thrower in baseball, Aroldis Chapman. If things had turned out differently, that home run would have been remembered forever.

In Cleveland, even how things turned out, it will be remembered forever anyway.

The game went into extra innings. And just as it did, a hard rain started to fall. The game was delayed for 17 minutes.

And during those 17 minutes Cubs' outfielder Jason Heyward called his teammates into the weight room.

And he gave a speech.

And it must have been one helluva speech.

When the rain delay ended, the Cubs came out looking fresh and hungry. Schwarber raced out to the plate and lashed a single to start things off. The Cubs scored two runs. Cleveland tried to fight back one more time, but this time the comeback fell short. Mike Montgomery was on the mound for Chicago. Michael Martínez was the batter. He chopped a ground ball to third base. "Tough play," Joe Buck said on television, but third baseman Kris Bryant had no doubts, and he grabbed the ball and threw it across the infield.

As he threw, he smiled. That's the part every Cubs fan remembers. The smile.

Martínez was out, the Cubs were champions, and 108 years of sadness, heartbreak, and absurdity came down crashing.

And I've always wondered: What the heck did Jason Heyward say?

OK, SO NOW I'M GOING TO TELL YOU WHAT JASON HEYWARD said. I'm not saying it went *exactly* like this—I obviously was not there—but I feel certain that I have the gist of it.

My original idea was to have this speech reimagined by my dear friend, the wonderful actor, hilarious comedian, and skilled woodworker Nick Offerman. He is an enormous Cubs fan, as I imagine all good Minookans are,* and he graciously agreed to try. He watched Game 7 all over again. He exchanged texts and ideas with Theo Epstein. He made some notes.

And . . . in the end he just couldn't do it.

It wasn't a fair request. That speech is holy to Nick Offerman, as it is to all Cubs fans, even though none of us outside that room know exactly what was said.

"The moment," he said, "is of too great of magnitude. It unmanned me. It disarmed me, certainly. . . . It's the most important speech in the history of Major League Baseball, I think everyone can agree on that. And I thought, 'Who am I to even try.'"

I totally get it. I'll take a crack at it anyway.

Scene: We're in the very small visitors' weight room in Cleveland. Players are practically on top of one another. Aroldis Chapman is

---

* Nick is from Minooka, Illinois. I can only assume they're called Minookans. And if they aren't, they should be.

despondent; he believes he cost the Cubs the game. Javy
Baéz, the thrilling Cubs' infielder, bounces around, a bundle of
energy and nerves—you get the sense he sleeps standing up.
Kyle Schwarber is gripping the bat so tightly sawdust is falling
beneath him. Schwarbs would have been one heck of a football
player.

Up steps Jason Heyward. J-Hey. He's the one who called
everyone into the room. He's 6-foot-5, 240 pounds, all muscle.
The Cubs had signed him for $184 million during the off-season,
and he fell into a batting slump that he never escaped. But
it was OK; Theo and the guys wanted Heyward for more
than his bat. He was a defensive marvel. He ran the bases
beautifully.

And he was a leader.

Theo didn't know it then. But he had signed Heyward for this exact
moment.

And this, I believe, is what Jason Heyward said:

Once more unto the breach, dear friends, once more;
Javy, eyes up here, buddy, I'm talking
We shall win this game
We shall win it for Ernie Banks and Steve Bartman
We shall win it for Lakeview and Lincoln Square and Wrigleyville
For Fergie and Santo and Ryne and Sweet Swingin' Billy Williams
For Royko and Garlin and Vedder and Murray
We shall . . . hey, Schwarbs, you can't go out yet, it's still raining
We shall end this blasted goat's curse
We few, we happy few, we band of brothers
And Cubs from time immemorial
Shall think themselves accursed they were not here
For today, at last, the Cubs shall be the last team standing

And bells will ring from Minooka to Thailand

As it was foretold on this *Parks and Recreation* episode I saw*

I'm pretty sure that's how it went. It's also possible that Heyward just stood up in front of everyone and said, "We're the best $*@&# team! Let's #@^$ go out there and #*&!@ prove it!" That would have worked, too.

"In the end, I would argue," Nick says, "the speech is best left to the imagination."

---

* It is surprising that Heyward would reference the *Parks and Rec* prediction to end his speech I imagined, yes, but he was exactly right—in a 2014 episode that took place in the year 2017, some of the characters are walking around Chicago and one says, "And obviously everyone's in a really good mood now because of the Cubs winning the Series." Mike Schur, who wrote the episode, calls it his greatest baseball-related accomplishment.

NO. 2:
JACKIE AND LARRY AND . . .

APRIL 15, 1947

JULY 5, 1947

JULY 19, 1947

JULY 8, 1949

APRIL 18, 1950

MAY 1, 1951

ETC.

★ ★ ★ ★ ★

What is the most important moment in baseball history?

Obviously, it's Jackie Robinson taking the field.

Except . . . wait. I would argue that it's wrong to reduce that to one moment. That was a hundred moments. It was a thousand moments. It was the first day that Major League Baseball could justly begin to call itself the "national pastime," but the journey to that ideal would last for another 30 years. In many ways, the journey that Jackie Robinson started still goes on.

For a brief time, in the late nineteenth century, there was a small number of Black players playing on white teams in organized baseball. Moses Fleetwood Walker played for Toledo in the American Association when that league was considered major league in 1884. He would be the last African American to play in the white major leagues for more than a half century.

Jackie Robinson broke through on April 15, 1947, in Brooklyn. He played first base for the Dodgers, and he batted second. His play was mostly unmemorable that day. He went 0-for-3, and he hit into a double play ("I must not have been hustling," he said after the game, admonishing himself). He did reach base when his sacrifice bunt was thrown away by Boston pitcher Johnny Sain. He came around to score on Pete Reiser's double.

"I wasn't at all excited or scared," Robinson said. "I was as loose as could be."

April 15 is now Jackie Robinson Day across baseball every year. The No. 42 he wore on his jersey is now retired across baseball. The Rookie of the Year Award, which he won in 1947, is now named for him. There have been so many Jackie Robinson books, movies, documentaries, songs, paintings . . .

As it should be for the man who, more than any other, through his brilliance and determination and strength of character, truly made baseball *America*'s pastime.

But I can't help but think that in some ways, focusing all the attention and applause and admiration on him diminishes his achievement. The story does not end with Jackie Robinson. It begins with Jackie Robinson.

In 2022, for the first time in more than 70 years, there was not a single African American player in the World Series. How do we think Robinson would feel about that?

"Honoring Jackie Robinson," Major League Baseball Players Association executive director Tony Clark says, "is a never-ending job."

---

66 When Larry Doby joins the Cleveland Indians today, he will be facing a tougher assignment than confronted Jackie Robinson. 99

—JOE GOOTTER, *PATERSON EVENING NEWS*, JULY 5, 1947

LARRY DOBY DID NOT HAVE A MOMENT TO THINK ABOUT WHAT was happening. On Independence Day, he played for the Newark Eagles in the Negro Leagues. He homered in his last at-bat.

The very next day he was in Chicago and in a Cleveland uniform.

Everybody knows what Jackie Robinson went through as he broke through baseball's color barrier. Now consider this: Robinson was famous before he ever joined the Dodgers. He was a superstar football and basketball player at UCLA. He was also a renowned track star.* He was an Army veteran who made international news by refusing to go to the back of the bus; his court-martial case sparked headlines everywhere (Robinson was acquitted).

Almost nobody outside the Negro Leagues knew Larry Doby.

Robinson was 27 years old, experienced, outspoken, and fierce.

Doby was just 23, and he was introverted and, he would admit, somewhat sheltered.

Robinson spent a full year in the minor leagues in Montreal, a year he would call pivotal to his development.

Doby was not even given a game to acclimate himself. He was used as a pinch hitter on his very first day.

And there was this: Robinson played in the National League. And while it's true that he had to overcome racism at every turn, things were quite possibly worse in Doby's American League. The league's most prominent teams, the Yankees and Red Sox, were adamantly opposed to African American players and would not sign any for years. While Robinson, in short order, found allies among teammates and the press, Doby felt alone for a long time.

Still, he endured.

"I hope Doby won't try so hard that he'll tighten up and lose some of his effectiveness at the plate," Robinson said. "The signing of Doby by Cleveland is a good thing for everybody. It's good for baseball. It's good for Negro baseball. And it's even good for me. . . . I'm no longer in there by myself."

In truth, Doby did feel the tension that first year. "He carries a heavy load," the *Akron Beacon Journal* reported. He hit just .156 in 29 games.

---

* Though not as renowned as his brother, Mack Robinson, who had won the silver medal in the 200-meters behind Jesse Owens at the 1936 Summer Olympics in Berlin.

But the following year, he would become one of the game's stars and play a pivotal part of Cleveland's World Series championship.

Here's one more Larry Doby story: He came to Cleveland as a second baseman, but the Tribe already had a great one in Joe Gordon. Lou Boudreau asked Doby to play the outfield.

Well, it wasn't an easy transition. Cleveland owner Bill Veeck brought in a defensive tutor, a guy regarded then as the best defensive center fielder of them all, Tris Speaker.

But there was something else about Speaker: He was a bigot. He was unabashed about it. He was at one time a member of the Ku Klux Klan. He was openly anti-Catholic. He was known to spend much of his free time talking about the Civil War, which he called "The War of Northern Aggression."

But you know what? He would call the hours he spent working with Doby among the happiest of his post-playing career.

"I've never seen a young ballplayer with such high potential," he said.

"He taught me everything about being an outfielder," Doby would say many years later. "I can't know what was in his heart, but I know how he treated me like a son."

AUGUST 13, 1947

IN JULY, WILLARD BROWN AND HANK THOMPSON—BOTH STARS of the Negro Leagues' Kansas City Monarchs—joined the St. Louis Browns. The Browns were a farce then, the worst team in the American League, and the signing was little more than a publicity stunt.

But on this day, Willard Brown did become the first African American to homer in an American League game. It was an inside-the-park home run against the Chicago White Sox. The story goes that he borrowed teammate Jeff Heath's bat when he hit the homer—and Heath broke the bat afterward.

Brown and Thompson were both sent back to the Monarchs four days later.

AUGUST 26, 1947

DAN BANKHEAD BECAME THE FIRST AFRICAN AMERICAN PITCHER in MLB history when he pitched for Brooklyn against Pittsburgh. Bankhead was a star in the Negro Leagues, but as his son Dan Bankhead Jr. told me, he could not tolerate the unabashed hatred that came with being a pioneer. He was endlessly terrified of what might happen if he hit a white player with a pitch. Dan Jr. said his father was once throwing a no-hitter against a white team, and then he threw an easy pitch right down the middle so that they would get a hit.

"Nothing against Jackie Robinson, who was a great man," Dan Jr. said, "but it was harder to be a Black pitcher in those days. People would say, 'OK, maybe Black guys can hit or run, but they can't pitch.' People *still* stay that kind of stuff."

JULY 8, 1949

HANK THOMPSON RETURNED TO THE MAJOR LEAGUES ALONG with fellow Negro Leaguer Monte Irvin. They became the first Black players for the New York Giants. Irvin had been a Negro Leagues superstar, and even though his skills were diminished, he was a fantastic player for the Giants and key figure in their 1951 and 1954 pennants. In 1951, he finished third in the MVP balloting behind the Dodgers' Roy Campanella.* "Monte was the best all-around player I have ever

---

* Campanella was the first Black catcher in the National League. He was also the first Black American athlete on a Wheaties cereal box in 1952.

seen," Campy said. "As great as he was in 1951, he was twice that good ten years earlier."

///

MAY 1, 1951

MINNIE MIÑOSO BECAME THE FIRST BLACK PLAYER FOR THE Chicago White Sox . . . and the first dark-skinned Latino player ever in the white major leagues. He became a star for the White Sox. He paved the way for so many great Latino players over the next decade, including Roberto Clemente.

"He was," Orlando Cepeda would say, "our Jackie Robinson."

///

APRIL 14, 1955

ELSTON HOWARD BECAME THE FIRST AFRICAN AMERICAN TO play for the New York Yankees—almost exactly *eight years* after Jackie Robinson played his first game.

The Yankees had been claiming for years that they would be happy to sign the right African American player. Here was *New York Times* columnist Arthur Daley:

> The charge has been leveled against the New York Yankees that they've been prejudiced against Negroes. This tourist has never believed a word of it. . . . The men in the Yankee front office have stubbornly refused to be panicked into hiring a Negro just because he was a Negro. They've waited for one to come along who answers the description for "the Yankee type."

The Yankee type. In the end, Elston Howard was so overqualified— he had starred in the Negro Leagues, then starred in the Yankees minor league system (he was the International League MVP in 1953), and he was universally beloved and admired—that the Yankees simply could not overlook him. In all, Howard would play in twelve All-Star Games and win two Gold Gloves and an MVP award for New York.

More than four years later, the Red Sox became the last team to play a Black player when they put Pumpsie Green in as a pinch runner in their game against the White Sox.

MAY 30, 1962

THE CHICAGO CUBS HIRED BUCK O'NEIL AS THE FIRST AFRICAN American coach in MLB history. But they never put him on the field. That was the year the Cubs were alternating different coaches as the teams' manager; they made absolutely sure to let everyone know that O'Neil would not be part of the rotation.

"He primarily is an instructor," Cubs' vice-president John Holland said, "and cannot be considered a potential head coach or manager."

It was around this time that Jackie Robinson began loudly asking the hard question: When would Major League Baseball have a Black manager?

APRIL 8, 1975

FRANK ROBINSON BECAME THE FIRST AFRICAN AMERICAN manager in MLB history. This fulfilled Jackie Robinson's last wish. He did not live to see the day—Robinson died in October 1972—but his widow, Rachel, was there.

"It has taken too long to get here," she said. "But I feel it very definitely has historic significance. For me, having started on the road with Jackie in '46, this feels like the culmination of a dream."

IN THE EARLY 1940S, A YOUNG MAN NAMED HENRY AARON READ about the exploits of a great pilot and announced to his father, Herbert, that he too would be a pilot when he grew up.

"Ain't no colored pilots," Herbert said plainly.

This set young Henry back. He thought about it for a moment and then came up with a new plan.

"Well then," he said, "I'll be a ballplayer."

"Ain't no colored ballplayers, either," Herbert said.

A few years later, Jackie Robinson joined the Brooklyn Dodgers. Henry Aaron was 13. The world opened. "He gave us our dreams," Aaron would say.

More than a quarter century later, Henry Aaron stood at home plate in Atlanta. He was tired and downhearted and disillusioned, yes, but he would go on. He had to go on.

"There were times, yes, I was so angry and tired and sick of it all that I wished I could get on a plane and not get off until I was someplace they had never heard of Babe Ruth," he would say. "But damn it all . . . I had to do it for Jackie."

A MOMENT FOR EVERY TEAM

In May 1935, a few weeks before the third All-Star Game was to be played in Cleveland, baseball commissioner Kenesaw Mountain Landis made an announcement: Going forward, he said, every big-league team would have at least one representative in the All-Star Game.

Landis's new rule was in response to complaints about the 1934 All-Star Game at the Polo Grounds, which did not feature any players from the Cincinnati Reds or Philadelphia Phillies. True, the Reds and Phillies were both atrocious teams without any obvious All-Star candidates. But, Landis reasoned, if the All-Star Game is meant to be a celebration of baseball, it should be a celebration for all fans in every big-league town across America.

That rule is still in place—at least one player from all 30 teams is chosen for the All-Star Game—and it gets argued about every year. There are those who, quite reasonably, wonder why you would pass over more deserving All-Stars just so that you could include players from going-nowhere teams.

Personally, I think the "every team gets represented" rule is great. It's very much a reason why I love baseball. My childhood was spent rooting for going-nowhere Cleveland teams, and one of the few brilliant moments of summer was seeing one of my heroes—say, a Jim Kern* or Sid Monge or Andre Thornton—lining up with the greatest players.

---

* Jim Kern was a big and hard-throwing relief pitcher and also the first baseball autograph I ever got. Unfortunately, I had him sign that autograph in pencil and later

In that spirit, I put together an online survey and asked baseball fans to vote for the greatest moment in their team's history. At last check, more than 4,000 people have voted.

Inspired by those responses—and Kenesaw Mountain Landis's decree from long ago—I am including a reason to love baseball for every team in baseball:

Los Angeles Angels: The Angels have had their share of moments—four Nolan Ryan no-hitters, a Mike Witt perfect game, Jim Edmonds's otherworldly catch, various miracles performance by Mike Trout and Shohei Ohtani, the creation of the rally monkey—but the team has won just one World Series. And the top vote-getter among fans was the titanic two-run double hit by Troy Glaus in the eighth inning of Game 6 of that 2002 World Series. That double completed an absurd comeback from a five-run deficit. Second place among the voters was Scott Spiezio's three-run home run from the same game.

Houston Astros: Some teams, as you will see, have one obvious moment that towers above all the rest. The Astros, though, have a half-dozen moments that fans love equally. They love Nolan Ryan's fifth no-hitter. They love Yordan Alvarez's massive home run against Seattle in the 2022 playoffs. They love Alex Bregman's walk-off single to win Game 5 of the 2017 World Series. They love Mike Scott's division-title-clinching no-hitter in 1986.

The last of these is my favorite, because Scott rather suddenly and unexpectedly became the best pitcher on earth that year. He had perfected what was then a new pitch, a split-fingered fastball, and batters just swung over it time and again. He won the Cy Young Award that year and was unhittable in the playoffs, but the highlight came when he clinched the division title by throwing a no-hitter against the San

---

could not find it among my scraps of paper. I told that story many times, and years later, it must have gotten back to Kern, because he sent me an autographed baseball inscribed with the words *Quit whining!*

Francisco Giants. The Giants' manager Roger Craig just so happened to be the guy who taught Scott the split-fingered fastball.

"I thought there was no harm," Craig said after the game.

Oakland Athletics: The Athletics have won four World Series titles since moving to Oakland, but as I write these words it has been 33 years since their last championship. I think that's the reason why most fans passed on such wonderful moments as Catfish Hunter's perfect game, Reggie Jackson's over-the-roof home run during the 1971 All-Star Game, Gene Tenace's four home runs during the 1972 World Series . . . they happened too long ago. Instead, the top vote-getter was the 20-game winning streak put together by the 2002 Athletics. That winning streak was featured in the movie *Moneyball*.

Toronto Blue Jays: Joe Carter's World Series home run was the runaway choice of fans, as it should be, but I'd like to make special mention of the no-hitter Dave Stieb threw against Cleveland in 1990. That one's special because two years earlier, in one remarkable week, Stieb had no-hitters broken up with two outs in the ninth inning *twice*. The first of those was September 24, 1988, against Cleveland, and Julio Franco singled with two outs in the bottom of the ninth. Six days later, Stieb's no-hitter was again busted with two outs in the ninth, this time by Baltimore's Jim Traber.

"Maybe it just isn't meant to be," Stieb said. But less than two years later, he finally completed a no-hitter.

Atlanta Braves: Henry Aaron's 715th home run is the fans' choice, obviously, but there have been many magical moments in Atlanta Braves history (and in this book). One I think about is the 84-pitch shutout that Atlanta's Greg Maddux threw against New York at Yankee Stadium in 1997. It has to be one of the most artistic and graceful games ever pitched—Maddux had the Yankees swinging at shadows that day—but, more to the point, it inspired baseball writer Jason Lukehart to come up with the Maddux. Maybe you've heard of it. Anytime a pitcher throws a complete game shutout on fewer than 100 pitches, it is called a Maddux. Unsurprisingly, Greg Maddux has pitched the most Madduxes with 14.

Milwaukee Brewers: The Brewers, alas, are one of only six teams in the major leagues to have never won a World Series. And they are the oldest of the six teams. As such, they do not have one moment that towers over all the rest. They have had several nice moments. Cecil Cooper cracked a bases-loaded single to lead Milwaukee to a victory over the Angels in the 1982 American League Championship Series. In 2011, Nyjer Morgan came up with an extra-inning walkoff hit against Arizona in the National League Division Series. Henry Aaron hit his 755th and final home run while playing for the Brewers. Paul Molitor put together a 39-game hitting streak, the longest in the American League since Joe DiMaggio.

But the fans' choice was Robin Yount's 3,000th hit, which came on September 9, 1992, at Milwaukee County Stadium. "You've got a whole generation of people who grew up with Robin Yount," the Brewers' president, a guy named Bud Selig, said that day. "That's the beautiful part of the story."

St. Louis Cardinals: The Cardinals have won 11 World Series and 12 more pennants, so there are surely too many moments to choose only one. The fans' choice was Bob Gibson striking out 17 Tigers in Game 1 of the 1978 World Series. I do want to make special mention of Ozzie Smith's famous home run off the Dodgers' Tom Niedenfuer in Game 5 of the 1985 National League Championship Series. Many years later, I joined director Jonathan Hock in making the film *Generations of the Game*, which they show several times a day at the Baseball Hall of Fame. For the movie, I went to St. Louis to talk with Smith about that home run.

And do you know what he did?

He, word for word, recited Jack Buck's call on that home run.

"Smith corks one into right down the line! It may go! Go crazy, folks, go crazy! It's a home run, and the Cardinals have won the game by the score of 3–2 on a home run by the Wizard!"

"People think I hit 500 home runs because of that call," Ozzie told me.

Chicago Cubs: The Cubs have won three World Series in their history—but there is nobody in the world old enough to remember the first two. The final out of the 2016 World Series was not just the fans' top choice. It received about 82 percent of the vote, the highest percentage for any team moment. Other fans' nominees included Gabby Hartnett's "Homer in the Gloamin'" from 1938; the 1984 Sandberg Game, when Ryne Sandberg hit game-tying home runs in both the ninth and 10th innings; and every time Harry Caray sang "Take Me Out to the Ball Game" during the seventh-inning stretch.

Arizona Diamondbacks: The Diamondbacks have only been in existence since 1998, but in that short history, Randy Johnson threw a perfect game against Atlanta, J. D. Martinez hit four home runs in a game against the Tigers, and Luis Gonzalez hit a broken-bat single off the Yankees to clinch Game 7 of the 2001 World Series. It was the last of these that received far and away the most votes, but I'd like to throw one more moment in there.

In 1999, the Diamondbacks' second season, a woman named Gylene Hoyle won a radio contest. She was given free tickets to the game and asked to select one player on the team and a specific inning—if that player happened to hit a grand slam in that inning, she would win $1 million. Hoyle was not an especially big baseball fan, but she and her husband, Clayton, picked Jay Bell because they liked him, and they chose the sixth inning randomly.

And sure enough, in the sixth inning, Jay Bell came up with the bases loaded.

He homered and the Hoyles won $1 million.

"My career highlight," Bell told *The Arizona Republic*.

Los Angeles Dodgers: Jackie Robinson breaking the color barrier would be the top moment in Dodgers history, but it happened before the team moved to Los Angeles. The top Los Angeles Dodgers moment by the fan vote is the Kirk Gibson home run in the 1988 World Series.

But let's be honest, there are countless others to choose from. Heck, there are ten Sandy Koufax moments alone.

San Francisco Giants: Two of the greatest moments in baseball history—Willie Mays's catch in the 1954 World Series and Bobby Thomson's Shot Heard Round the World—are both Giants' moments, but they both happened before the team moved to San Francisco in 1958. For pure San Francisco Giants' moments, fans nominated Barry Bonds's 756th career home run and Bonds's 73rd home run in 2001, Matt Cain's perfect game, and Will Clark's otherworldly performance in the 1989 National League Championship Series.

But they chose Madison Bumgarner's Game 7 performance against Kansas City in the 2014 World Series. He came into the game in the bottom of the fifth inning to protect a one-run lead. He was pitching on two days' rest. He threw five shutout innings to clinch the championship.

Cleveland Guardians/Indians: Cleveland has not won a World Series since 1948; this is now the longest drought for any team in baseball. Fans did go back to 1948 to nominate Lou Boudreau's critical two-run homer in the playoff game against Boston. Others nominated Frank Robinson's debut as the first Black manager in baseball in 1975. The winner was Bob Feller's opening day no-hitter in 1940. Feller knew his own stats and achievement better than anyone, and often said that game remains the only time in baseball history that every player on a team had exactly the same batting average after the game as they did before: They were all hitting .000.

Clevelanders my age do not have many grand moments to remember—but we do have the perfect game that Large Lenny Barker threw on May 15, 1981.*

---

* I originally intended to include this moment in the book, so in my files I have a long essay on the game, another thing to perhaps include in *Why We Love Baseball: The Director's Cut.*

Seattle Mariners: The Mariners have had so many incredible players through the years—Ken Griffey Jr., Ichiro Suzuki, Randy Johnson, Alex Rodriguez, and so on—and each of those players had many unforgettable moments. But as historian Mike Duncan talked about at length earlier in the book, the Edgar Martinez Double is far and away the biggest moment in team history.

Miami Marlins: The fans voted convincingly for Édgar Rentería's walk-off single against Cleveland's Charles Nagy in the 1997 World Series. Also receiving votes; Josh Beckett's final out in the 2003 World Series, Dee Strange-Gordon's home run for his fallen teammate José Fernández, and Giancarlo Stanton's 59-home-run season in 2017.

New York Mets: The top moment is obvious: You can still hear Vin Scully saying, "Little roller up along first . . . behind the bag! It gets through Buckner!" But the Mets have had plenty of other fantastic moments, including Ron Swoboda's catch in the 1969 World Series; Bartolo Colón's only home run, Dwight Gooden's emergence, and Johan Santana finally throwing the team's first no-hitter in 2012.

Washington Nationals: The Nationals have been in Washington only since 2005, but this has been a franchise rich with amazing moments. Max Scherzer struck out 20 in a game and also threw two no-hitters in 2015. Bryce Harper won a fabulous Home Run Derby. Stephen Strasburg had one of the most hyped debuts for any pitcher in baseball history. Ryan Zimmerman hit a walk-off home run in the team's first game in Washington.

But the runaway choice of fans was Howie Kendrick's go-ahead home run in Game 7 of the 2019 World Series.

Baltimore Orioles: As you might expect, Cal Ripken playing in his 2,131st consecutive game won the fan vote, but I want to make special mention of Brooks Robinson's remarkable 1970 World Series. My father adored Brooks Robinson. His greatest wish (and mine) was that I would become the next Brooksie.

And I feel sure that wish was formed during that World Series. My father had immigrated to America only six years earlier, and he came knowing absolutely nothing about baseball. He learned the game watching Brooks Robinson, the "Human Vacuum Cleaner," play defense. Robinson made a dozen or so remarkable plays in that Series, the most famous when he backhanded a Lee May ground ball, and while deep in foul ground and falling away, made an impossible throw across the diamond to get May by a half step.

"Brooks Robinson," Pete Rose said after that series, "belongs in a higher league."

San Diego Padres: The Padres have not yet won a World Series—they were drubbed by the Tigers in the 1984 World Series and swept by the Yankees in 1998—but they have had some very cool moments just the same. The San Diego Chicken was not the first mascot in Major League Baseball,* but he was a pioneer of the genre. Hall of Fame relief pitcher Trevor Hoffman used to come out of the bullpen to the ringing bells at the beginning of AC/DC's song "Hells Bells," and it inspired goose bumps every time. Padres' announcer Jerry Coleman was a wonderful and beloved baseball announcer famous for his malapropisms, particularly this one:

"Dave Winfield goes back to the wall, he hits his head on the wall . . . and it rolls off! It's rolling all the way back to second base! This is a terrible thing for the Padres!"

Most of all, there was Mr. Padre, Tony Gwynn, one of the purest hitters in the history of the sport. Fans chose his 3,000th hit—off Montreal's Dan Smith on August 6, 1999—as the team's top moment.

Philadelphia Phillies: Fans nominated a bunch of moments—Bryce Harper's massive home run in the 2022 National League Championship Series, Roy Halladay's postseason no-hitter against the Reds, Brad Lidge closing out the 2008 World Series, Mike Schmidt's

---

* The first mascot was Mr. Met, who first appeared at a Mets game in 1964.

500th home run—but they ended up choosing Tug McGraw's strikeout of Kansas City's Willie Wilson to clinch the 1980 World Series.

Pittsburgh Pirates: Bill Mazeroski's walk-off home run in the 1960 World Series was the runaway winner in the fan vote. There should be special mention, though, of Willie Stargell's two-run home run in Game 7 of the 1978 World Series. Pops, as Stargell was called, was 39 years old that season, but he had a renaissance season and he led and willed the Pirates all the way to the World Series, and in the biggest moment he came through with what turned out to be the game-winning home run.

I always have loved this Willie Stargell quote: "They give you a round bat, and they throw you a round ball, and they tell you to hit it square." Few ever did it better.

Texas Rangers: The Rangers have never won a World Series and are sometimes labeled as the least interesting team in recent baseball history. But they've had their moments. Nolan Ryan threw his seventh no-hitter while with the Rangers. Texas's Josh Hamilton had one of the most remarkable single performances during the 2008 Home Run Derby. Those two moments basically split the fan vote. But there have been other Rangers' moments, such as David Clyde's professional debut right out of high school, Kenny Rogers's perfect game, and Adrian Beltré's 3,000th hit.

Tampa Bay Rays: For a franchise that hasn't been around very long, the Rays have had some great times. There was Randy Arozarena's hitting 10 home runs during an incredible 2020 postseason. Brett Phillips had a walk-off hit in Game 5 of that 2020 World Series against the Dodgers. Wade Boggs got his 3,000th hit while with the Rays. But the fan vote went to Evan Longoria's home run that beat the Yankees in the final day of the wild 2011 season.

Boston Red Sox: The Red Sox moment was well covered in Michael Schur's very long Boston Red Sox chapter. The fans chose Carlton's Fisk's wave-it-fair home run in the 1975 World Series; I think there are a number of younger fans who believe that home run won that World Series. It did not. That was only Game 6.

Cincinnati Reds: It was the Reds who won Game 7 of that 1975 World Series, and the fans' choice for the team's greatest moment was Joe Morgan's game-winning hit from that game. There were plenty of other options—Pete Rose's 4,192nd hit, Johnny Vander Meer's back-to-back no-hitters, Tom Browning's perfect game, the first night game in MLB, and the Reds becoming the first openly professional team in 1869.

Colorado Rockies: The Rockies do not have a wealth of magical moments just yet, but in 2007 they had a magnificent end to the season. They won 14 of their last 15 games to wipe out the gap between them and the San Diego Padres. The last of those victories was in a classic one-game playoff, which the Rockies won when Matt Holliday tripled in the 13th inning and scored on Jamey Carroll's sacrifice fly. This was the fan's chosen moment. Numerous Padres fans will point out that Holliday did not actually touch home plate on the slide. But home plate umpire Tim McClelland called Holliday safe, and the Rockies went to the playoffs.

Kansas City Royals: The fans selected George Brett's pine tar home run off Goose Gossage in 1983 as the team's greatest moment. But I imagine hard-core Royals fans prefer Brett's home run off Gossage in the 1980 American League Championship Series, the one that sent Kansas City to its first World Series. Other great Royals moments include Eric Hosmer's mad dash to the plate in the 2015 World Series against the Mets, Salvador Pérez's walkoff hit to beat Oakland in their remarkable 2014 wild-card game, and the famous double that George Brett hit in 1980 that put his batting average over .400 in August 1980.

I don't know if Royals fans will appreciate this, but I have a long list of favorite Royals moments that I love; these come from my time as a columnist at *The Kansas City Star*. The team was hilariously terrible every year, and I began to keep a mental list of the remarkably silly and self-destructive things they did. The best of these happened in 2006 when they were playing the White Sox when, with two outs in the fourth inning, Juan Uribe lifted a lazy fly ball to left center.

Left fielder Terrence Long and center fielder Chip Ambres closed in on the ball. As it fell, they looked at each other knowingly and seemed to nod. Then they both ran into the dugout, contented with a job well done.

Only thing is they had forgotten to catch the ball, which plopped on the grass behind them.

Detroit Tigers: Many people remember the 1968 World Series for Bob Gibson's overpowering Game 1 performance when he struck out 17 batters—you can look back and see why Cardinals fans chose that as the team's greatest moment.

But the 1968 World Series belonged to another pitcher, one too often forgotten: Mickey Lolich. He did not necessarily look like an elite athlete—he described himself as the "beer-drinker's idol"—but he threw very hard,* and he pitched and won three games in the '68 Series, including Game 7, when he outdueled Gibson himself. This was the fans' choice.

I have a special fondness for the emergence of the Tigers' 21-year-old pitcher Mark Fidrych in 1976. I was 9 years old, the perfect age to fall in love with the Bird, as he was called. He was something else. He would talk to baseballs. He would smooth out the dirt on the mound with his hand and do a little dance around the mound every time he got an out. It was wonderful and he was briefly a national sensation. Unfortunately, he had to deal with injuries after his rookie year, and he was never the same.

Minnesota Twins: The fans' top three moments in Twins' history

---

* Lolich pitched left-handed, but he was actually a natural righty. When he was very young, a motorcycle tipped over and fell on his left arm. While rehabilitating, he found that he preferred throwing left-handed.

happened on back-to-back days in October of 1991. Two of those moments happened in Game 6 of the 1991 World Series—Kirby Puckett's leaping catch against the wall and, later, his walk-off home run, which forced Game 7. And the top moment was Jack Morris's 10-inning shutout in Game 7.

I'll throw in another moment involving one of the coolest players in Twins' history, local hero Joe Mauer. He was catching in a game against Washington—this was in 2013—and the Nationals' Denard Span fouled the ball straight back. The ball hit the backstop behind home plate and ricocheted back toward the field. Without even looking, Mauer reached behind his back and snagged the ball. It was just so cool and so smooth and so Joe Mauer.

Chicago White Sox: The White Sox, like the Cubs, have won three World Series, but just one in the last century. In truth, the White Sox are probably more famous for a World Series they lost—in 1919, when players took money from gamblers to throw the Series—than any of the Series they did win. Still, the fans' choice for greatest moment came from Game 2 of the 2005 World Series, when light-hitting Scott Podsednik hit the unlikeliest of home runs.

I very much like a play White Sox pitcher Mark Buehrle made on opening day in 2010 against Cleveland. Lou Marson slapped a ball up the middle that hit Buehrle's left foot and deflected into foul ground on the first-base side. Buehrle raced over, picked up the ball with his glove, and flipped it through his legs to Paul Konerko in time to get the out.

"I was as surprised as everyone else," Buehrle told reporters after the game.

New York Yankees: I don't know how well I've hidden my personal Yankees' antipathy in this book; I've tried, but I've hated the Yankees all my life, as any self-respecting Clevelander will. There are too many magical Yankees moments to even list as contenders. I could write a Yankees-only version of *Why We Love Baseball*. I assure you, I will not. Anyway, Lou Gehrig's speech won the fan vote.

NO. 1:

A NEW HOME RUN CHAMPION OF ALL TIME

"There's a new home run champion of all time, and it's Henry Aaron!"

—MILO HAMILTON, APRIL 8, 1974

Of all the wonderful broadcasting calls in baseball history, I've always had a special place in my heart for Milo Hamilton's because—and I say this with all the love in my heart—it's so uninspired. He obviously just wanted to let the moment ring. He just blurted out words.

And though it is simple, I consider it one of the great calls ever.

Here's why: When Henry Aaron hit his 715th home run—after months and months of steeling himself against death threats and hateful letters and the worst of America—Hamilton didn't have some pat call that he had worked on for hours and hours. He did not reach deep into himself the way, say, Al Michaels had at the end of the 1980s U.S.–Soviet Union Olympic hockey game when he shouted, "Do you believe in miracles? Yes!"

No, when Aaron hit the home run—fourth inning off the Dodgers' Al Downing at Fulton County Stadium in Atlanta—Hamilton's words were plain and direct and spoken loudly enough on the broadcast to be heard over the enormous roar from the crowd of 53,775.

There's a drive into left center field.

That ball is gonna be . . .

Outta here! It's gone! It's 715!

There's a new home run champion of all time!

And it's Henry Aaron.

I love that last part in particular. *"And it's Henry Aaron."* I love it for a million reasons, but the big one is that few called him Henry Aaron. People called him "Hank." He was Hank Aaron on just about all his baseball cards. He was Hank Aaron in newspaper stories. He was introduced everywhere as Hank Aaron.

Aaron himself preferred his childhood name of Henry.

See, friends called him Henry.

And that's what Milo Hamilton called him in the biggest moment of them all. The ball is out of here. There's a new home run champion of all time.

And it's Henry Aaron.

IF YOU'VE WATCHED AARON'S 715TH, YOU HAVE SEEN THE TWO high school kids who stormed the field and ran briefly around the bases with him. I tracked them down almost 30 years ago. I got the sense from their shock that I was one of the first reporters to do so. One was named Cliff Courtenay, the other Britt Gaston.

When I caught up with them, Cliff was an optometrist in Valdosta, Georgia, and Britt was a businessman in Isle of Palms, South Carolina. Time has passed. Cliff is retired now. Britt, alas, died at 55 after an extended fight with cancer.

I can't tell you exactly why I was so interested in finding them; I think I wanted to know how they turned out. They were an odd part of this magical thing; even now it's jolting to see these two white guys, dressed very much in 1970s garb, running alongside the elegant Henry Aaron as he rounds the bases. It is like watching footage of the moon landing and just suddenly seeing one of the *Soul Train* dancers walking beside Neil Armstrong.

Turns out, they were not intending to cause trouble. They were mischievous kids; they did goofy things to get attention. Before the game, Gaston kept telling their friend Wimpy Gibson, "I know Hank Aaron."

"Prove it," Wimpy said—or words to that effect.

At 8:07 P.M. EST, Aaron connected with Downing's pitch. Courtenay and Gaston were seated by the railing. They looked at each other. They had not exactly planned it. But at the same time, they both thought the same thing: Go! They hopped over the railing and raced onto the field and closed in on Aaron. They got so close to him that both patted him on the back in triumph.

Even now, it's stunning considering all the death threats made against Aaron that they would both get so close, and even more stunning that Aaron seemed untroubled by their presence.

"I just knew they weren't any danger," Aaron would tell me. "I don't know why. There was just something about the way they approached me, I guess."

Aaron's bodyguard did consider shooting them. That really could have happened. But instead, the police caught Courtenay before he could make it back into the stands and caught Gaston about ten rows up. They were both hauled off to jail. Their memories of the night differed in so many ways, but they both remembered sharing a jail cell with a 6-foot-7 behemoth who kept muttering, "I'm going to kill somebody."

Eventually the charges were dropped. Courtenay and Gaston lost touch after a while. They would reunite now and again when there was some special anniversary of the home run. Neither one, as I recall, was especially proud of that moment, but neither one was ashamed of it, either. "We were kids, man," Courtenay said. "And kids do dumb things."

When Henry Aaron died in early in 2021, Courtenay wrote a post on Facebook.

"It's no small irony that your passing occurs at this troubled time when so many could benefit from examining your life," he wrote. "The negativity, hypocrisy, dishonesty, and petty divisiveness that exist today stand in stark contrast to your example of personal integrity and quiet dignity . . . you walked the walk.

"Thank you for being nice to me, Hank . . . no, Mr. Aaron."

FOR MANY YEARS, HENRY AARON REFUSED TO TALK ABOUT
breaking the home run record. It was too painful. The scars still bled.

I've always said that "Home Run King" is a terribly inappropriate
name for Henry Aaron. If you want to call Pete Rose "The Hit King,"
sure, that fits, as his life was all about collecting hits, and he collected
more than anyone, at least in the United States.

But Henry Aaron? He was never about home runs. He was about supernatural consistency, excellent defense, fine baserunning, high batting averages. He still holds the record for driving in more RBIs than
anyone. He still has more total bases than anyone. Home runs were, for
Aaron, happy accidents that came with hitting baseballs hard every day
of every season.

Aaron thought that a sportswriter got it right when he called his
homers "doubles that happened to go over the wall."

"I was never out to break Babe Ruth's record," he said. "I wasn't even
thinking about Babe Ruth's record. I didn't want them to forget Babe
Ruth. But I also didn't want them to forget Hank Aaron."

As he approached Babe Ruth's home run record, though, he knew: He
had to go for it. He couldn't even put words to it, he just knew it was
about something more than the record, more than baseball, more than
anything.

"I don't want to sound immodest," he said. "But I think the Good
Lord had his hands on me."

In other words: It was his cross to bear. And he did have to bear the
weight. In 1974, he set a *Guinness Book* world record that he never
wanted: most pieces of fan mail received by one person. Some of it was
lovely. But much of it was poisonous, venomous, toxic. Death threats
poured in. People threatened to kidnap his children.

All his life, he kept those letters in shoeboxes, every last one of them,
as a reminder of what he had to overcome. "It was terrible," he said. "It

was bad. I couldn't leave the ballpark without an escort. I had to eat most of my dinners in the hotel room. My kids, who were in school, had to be escorted. It was probably one of the saddest moments for me.

"I'd look at myself and say, 'What are you doing wrong? What are you doing here except bringing a little enjoyment to people around the country so they could say, 'Hey, did he hit a home run today? No? Well, I'll bet he will hit one tomorrow!' Was that such a terrible thing?"

Henry Aaron's 715th home run is the most magical moment in baseball history, a moment at the heart of why we love baseball, because Aaron did overcome, because he refused to yield, because he picked up Jackie Robinson's dream, because he announced to the world—in his own words—"on this field, it doesn't matter what color you are or where you're from. All that matters is if you can play."

I think by the end of his life, Aaron was able to look back at the home run with perhaps something more than anger and pain. It was never easy. He loathed being reduced to one moment. He could never quite look back at the home run without thinking back to the ugly part of America that came with it.

But he did understand what it meant for a modest Black man from Alabama to pass Babe Ruth and break what was surely the most cherished record in American sports. And he did understand how much joy it brought to so many people.

"It could have been Willie Mays who broke the record," he said. "It could have been someone else. It didn't have to be me. But I was the one called. There were times I didn't know if I could go on. But I always did. . . . When I hit the home run, all I felt was relief."

"What do you feel now?" I asked him.

"Pride," he said. "I did it."

EPILOGUE

I think now of a baseball story.

It will probably not surprise you that it involves Ichiro Suzuki. Has there ever been a more joyous player than Ichiro? Everything he did— from the way he stretched in the batter's box to the way he began running before he'd even connected with the ball to just the cool way he jogged on and off the field—was breathtaking and beautiful and fun.

I mean: Take the *Star Wars* Throw. That was in 2001. It was only his eighth game in the major leagues after a short but legendary career in Japan. Nobody quite knew what to make of Ichiro yet. Seattle was playing Oakland, and the A's had Terrence Long on first, and Ramón Ramírez grounded a single to right field.

Ichiro rushed in and, in one seamless motion, scooped up the ball and fired a throw to third base that never seemed to be more than five feet off the ground. Long was out.

"I'm here to tell you," Seattle's marvelous broadcaster Dave Niehaus shouted, "that Ichiro threw something out of *Star Wars* down there at third base."

But this is a different Ichiro story. And it involves a young woman named Iris Skinner.

She was 17 years old in the summer of 2010. She was at the beach when her friend Mackenzie asked if she wanted to go the Mariners game. Iris figured: Why not? It was a beautiful day. Mackenzie's parents had great seats. And Iris loved the Mariners. She was not an obsessive fan who could recite stats, but she knew all the players, especially Ichiro.

Iris and Mackenzie took the ferry over to the game and sat in right field, front row, just by the foul line. In the first inning, the Yankees' first baseman Mark Teixeira hit a high foul ball their way. Ichiro started running toward it.

"I couldn't see it," Iris says, "so I was kind of leaning away to my right."

Then suddenly Iris felt something hit her in the face. She was dazed for a moment.

Then she looked up into the sun and saw a silhouette of a baseball player.

"Are you OK?" a voice asked.

She knew that voice instantly.

She had been struck, right in the face, by the arms of a running Ichiro Suzuki.

Even now, she cannot explain the fireworks explosion that went off in her head. Ichiro. She had just touched Ichiro. And he had talked to her. He wanted to be sure she was OK! And slowly, very slowly, as she came to realize what it meant, her jaw dropped, and her legs began to shake, and she couldn't stop smiling, couldn't stop laughing.

"Oh my god! Oh my god! Oh my god!" she repeated. Then she pulled out her phone to text every person she knew.

All of this was captured on-camera.

"She is freaking out!" an announcer said on the broadcast. "This is hysterical."

It was hysterical. And wonderful. The video was white-hot happiness, and when it got to social media, naturally it went viral. People all over the world could not stop watching it.

Iris had become Ichiro Girl.

"Why do you think people loved it so much?" I ask Iris.

"I don't know," she says. "I mean, it's really funny seeing me lose my mind like that. But I mean, that's me, you know? I'm just a bubbly gal."

In 2022, the Mariners asked Iris to come back to the ballpark to throw out the first pitch.

"Will Ichiro be there?" she asked. They told her they weren't sure.

Still, she agreed. She practiced throwing a baseball, and then she went out to the stadium. It turned out this was the day that the Mariners were inducting Ichiro in to the team Hall of Fame. And as Iris walked to the mound to throw her pitch, the announcer's voice boomed: "And to Iris's surprise, here's Ichiro!"

And out came Ichiro Suzuki to catch her first pitch, and he said, "It's so great to see you," and Iris Skinner lost her mind again, and the whole thing made people everywhere laugh and feel good all over again.

"You know what it is?" Iris asks. "I think people liked seeing how happy I was. It's infectious, I think. You see somebody who is that happy, and maybe you feel happier also. I think that's why I love going out to games so much. I mean: Isn't that the point of baseball?"

ACKNOWLEDGMENTS

I still remember the first time I talked to pitcher Zack Greinke; he was just 20 then, and I asked him if he was nervous before a game. "No, *nervous* isn't the word," he said.

"What word would you use?"

"Like, I'm feeling something. But it isn't nervous."

"Excitement?"

"No," he said, "not excitement, either."

We went back and forth for a while trying to find the emotion he was feeling. We never did find the word. I suspect there is no word for what he was feeling. But I have spent many, many years searching for it anyway.

What a lucky life I've been able to live: I have spent so much of it writing about baseball. If I was able to thank every person who helped me write this book, I would thank every ballplayer, every manager, every scout, every analyst, and every fan who ever spent time talking baseball with me. All of you are in here somewhere.

Since I can't thank everybody, I'll keep my gratitude list short. Of course, I thank every person in this book, particularly Chelsea Baker and Iris Skinner, who trusted me to tell their story even though they had no reason to do so.

Thank you to the good folks at the Baseball Hall of Fame—Josh Rawitch, Tom Shieber, Jon Shestakofsky, and Cassidy Lent especially—who helped with research and inspired me to love baseball even more.

Thank you to Mike Schur, Gary and Helen Schwab, Jodie Valade, Tom Haberstroh, Tommy Tomlinson, Alix Felsing, David Hale, Dan and Debby McGinn, Brandon McCarthy, Nick Offerman, Brian Hay, Jim Banks, Ellen Adair, Eric Gilde, Alexis Gay, Bob Kendrick, Mike Vaccaro, Sloan Harris, Alan Sepinwall, and Jonathan Abrams for directly helping with some book editing and indirectly offering a whole lot of moral support.

A big thank-you to the legendary Bill Chuck for doing some fantastic research.

Thank you to my family, to my in-laws, Cecil and Judy; my parents, Steven and Frances; my brothers, David and Tony.

And finally, thank you to those people from my dedication page; my wife, Margo, who read versions of this book at every stage and offered plenty of thoughts; my daughters, Elizabeth and Katie, who won't read this book but will look to see if they're mentioned in the acknowledgments; and Buck O'Neil, who I miss every day.

And thank you to our poodle, Westley, who chewed up the autographed baseball that Jim Kern sent me years ago.

INDEX

ABOUT THE AUTHOR

Joe Posnanski is the number one *New York Times* bestselling author of six books, including *The Baseball 100*, *Paterno*, and *The Secret of Golf*, and has been named National Sportswriter of the Year by five different organizations. He writes at JoePosnanski.com and currently lives in Charlotte, North Carolina, with his family.